LIBRARY RECORDS

Library Records

A RETENTION AND CONFIDENTIALITY GUIDE

Shirley A. Wiegand

THE GREENWOOD LIBRARY MANAGEMENT COLLECTION
Gerard B. McCabe, Series Adviser

Greenwood Press
WESTPORT, CONNECTICUT • LONDON

Library of Congress Cataloging-in-Publication Data

Wiegand, Shirley A.
    Library records : a retention and confidentiality guide / Shirley
A. Wiegand.
        p.   cm. — (The Greenwood library management collection, ISSN
0894–2986)
    Includes bibliographical references and index.
    ISBN 0–313–28408–3 (alk. paper)
    1. Library records—United States—Management. 2. Government
paperwork—United States. 3. Confidential communications—Library
records—United States. 4. Public libraries—United States—Records
and correspondence.   I. Title.   II. Series.
Z678.82.W54   1994
025.6—dc20   93–14465

British Library Cataloguing in Publication Data is available.

Library of Congress Catalog Card Number: 93–14465
ISBN: 0–313–28408–3
ISSN: 0894–2986

First published in 1994

Greenwood Press, 88 Post Road West, Westport, CT 06881
An imprint of Greenwood Publishing Group, Inc.

Printed in the United States of America

The paper used in this book complies with the
Permanent Paper Standard issued by the National
Information Standards Organization (Z39.48–1984).

10 9 8 7 6 5 4 3 2 1

Contents

Acknowledgments

I have many people to thank for their assistance on this project. On a very practical level, I thank my dean, David Swank, for providing me with summer research grants and for his willingness to relieve me of committee work when I needed the time to write. I am also grateful to the law faculty secretarial staff (Robin Mize, Eugenia Sams, Lee Townsend, and Jacquelyn Wilkins), and particularly to Eugenia Sams and Jacquelyn Wilkins, who retyped the manuscript over and over, and suggested a number of ways to make it more presentable, all more quickly than I had a right to expect. My research assistant, Sara Farr, was of great help in researching the hundreds of statutes relevant to this work.

I am grateful to Arthur Curley, director of the Boston Public Library; to James Nelson, state librarian for the Kentucky Department for Libraries and Archives; and to Richard N. Belding, Kentucky state archivist and records administrator; who endorsed the questionnaire and allowed me to use their names in my letters to state officials all around the country. Thanks also must be extended to Mary Jo Lynch, director, Office for Research and Statistics, American Library Association, for her helpful advice concerning the questionnaire.

I must also extend my gratitude to more than one hundred public officials who responded to my questionnaire in late 1991 and early 1992 and to those who took the time to send me even more information than I requested. All are busy professionals who took time from their schedules to answer questions from someone they had never met (and probably never heard of). Their comments were invaluable.

Most of all, I thank my husband, Wayne, who first brought the problem of library record destruction to my attention and who convinced me that I would find it interesting. He was right. His faith in my abilities, his wise counsel, and his twenty-eight years of patience have provided me with the strong rudder that usually keeps me on course. I am grateful.

Introduction

This book discusses two major issues that apply to public library records. The first has to do with "lawbreaking" and refers to the library profession's disregard or unawareness of state public record retention laws, which often results in violation of the laws. The second has to do with "lawmaking" and refers to the success and failure of the library profession to enact tough library confidentiality laws.

The laws discussed herein apply to public records generally, unless they are written specifically for library records, as in the case of a number of library record confidentiality laws. Because library records are by definition "public," laws that deal with the retention, destruction, and disclosure of public records also apply to library records, unless library records are specifically exempted.

In analyzing these laws, I have attempted to demonstrate the unique problems that arise when laws are not drafted specifically for libraries. I have also attempted to demonstrate that the generality of public record laws often results in the library profession assuming that such laws do not apply to the records they keep. Given the wide array of state laws, it is no wonder that the profession is not fully informed of the variations. I have attempted to draw the variations to its attention.

My goal is not to dictate to the profession how it can best handle these complex problems, even assuming that I could do so with such a huge, complex, diverse community. My goal instead is to draw attention to problems that have arisen and to suggest that more can be done to prevent them from occurring in the future. My goal is also to stimulate debate about the problems so that the profession will continue to address them thoughtfully, purposefully, and wisely. If, after due consideration, the profession decides to go in one direction rather than another, it will do so with its organizational eyes wide open.

The book is divided into two parts. Part I deals with library record retention and destruction laws, a misnomer itself, since such laws have not been drafted with libraries specifically in mind. Instead, they have been drafted to apply to records of traditionally recognized state, county, and local government agencies. But, in most states, they also apply to library records.

The library profession, like other professions, has long expended much of its time and energy on record keeping. Like other professionals, the library professional creates records involving library employees, budgets, expenditures, and other administrative responsibilities. But unlike such professionals as private attorneys and physicians, the records the public librarian keeps are created on public time by public employees. As such, they are "public records," governed by public records laws.

Public records laws have been enacted in all fifty states and the District of Columbia. In many cases they require that governmental entities (state, county, or local) establish record retention schedules. Such schedules are designed to provide for the systematic disposal of various types or categories of records—termed "record series." A record series may consist of all budget records or all personnel records; in many cases these broad categories are further subdivided. The categorization's primary purpose is to determine the "value" of each category—that is, do the records serve a particular administrative or fiscal or legal need? Once that determination is made, it can be determined how long each category should be retained.

Both federal and state laws influence these determinations. For example, if federal tax laws include a five-year statute of limitations, after which no action may be brought against the public agency, it may make sense to destroy fiscal records affected by federal tax laws after five years, assuming the records have no other value. If, however, state laws carry a seven-year statute of limitations, then fiscal records will need to be kept an additional two years. The retention schedule may also be affected by laws relating to unemployment and workers' compensation and other employment issues.

This book does not provide detailed guidance in setting up record retention schedules; it is not a "how-to" book. Others have provided such assistance, however, and librarians may find their work helpful.[1] This book instead examines record retention laws generally and discusses their applicability to library records. Because the laws vary significantly, I discuss them one at a time, state by state.

Part II addresses the confidentiality of library registration and circulation records. It does not address other records that may be protected by the state's confidentiality laws. For example, many states protect personnel files, which would include the files of library personnel. This book addresses issues relating solely to library patron privacy.

Most states have laws protecting the privacy of library patrons, but they operate with varying success. Because the laws are similar in many respects, I do not discuss them one at a time, state-by-state. Rather I discuss their general features in the text and provide a state-by-state listing in Appendix D.

Part II bears a close relationship to Part I. Librarians need to know not only how long they are obligated by law to retain library records, but also what can be done with the records while they are retained. The modern trend is to destroy circulation records as soon as library materials are returned, ignoring the many state laws that forbid the destruction of such records. This course of action demonstrates the profession's commitment to library patron privacy at the expense of other competing values and, in some states, in violation of state law. It is my goal to focus attention on these competing values and suggest options from which the library profession may choose, in order to best satisfy its commitment to its patrons, to the public in general, and to the profession.

NOTE

1. See, for example, Bruce W. Dearstyne, The Management of Local Government Records: A Guide for Local Officials (1988) and H. G. Jones, Local Government Records: An Introduction to Their Management, Preservation, and Use (1980). These authors provide practical, step-by-step advice on how to set up retention schedules for local government records. See also John M. Fedders & Lauryn H. Guttenplan, *Document Retention and Destruction: Practical, Legal and Ethical Considerations*, The Notre Dame Lawyer, Oct. 1980, at 5. This work deals with the destruction of business records to avoid legal liability, focusing on private corporate records, thus making it less helpful than Dearstyne's and Jones' books.

The best known works in this field are those of Donald Skupsky. His works include: Recordkeeping Requirements (The First Practical Guide to Help You Control Your Records . . . What You Need to Keep and What You Can Safely Destroy!) (2d ed. 1989); Legal Requirements for Business Records: Guide to Records Retention and Recordkeeping Requirements: Federal Requirements (1990 & annual updates); Legal Requirements for Business Records: Guide to Records Retention and Recordkeeping Requirements: State Requirements (1990 & annual updates). These works are very helpful in setting up record retention schedules, giving close attention to such things as state and federal tax laws, statutes of limitation, employment records, and such. The works are geared toward private business records, so state retention statutes pertaining to public records are not discussed. For example, Skupsky's work on "state requirements" is organized by business organization, employment, evidence, limitation of actions, and tax. The book lists state statutes that mandate the retention of specific private business records, such as corporate and partnership, unemployment and workers' compensation, statutes of limitation for products liability and contracts, and so on.

PART I

Library Record Retention and Destruction

1

Introduction to Record Retention and Destruction Issues

WHY SAVE LIBRARY RECORDS?

A library historian first brought the issue of library record destruction to my attention.[1] He had been planning to write a book that examined the history of several small public libraries in this country. He was particularly interested in comparing their holdings at various points in their history and in learning how often the materials were used. He also hoped to examine circulation records to determine the gender, race, socioeconomic class, and other identifiers of the library patrons during various historical periods. In contacting a number of libraries, he was dismayed to learn that many of them "cleaned house" from time to time, dumping boxes of records indiscriminately into the local garbage bins. He lamented the loss of records that uniquely provide a microscope into a society's cultural history. They are lost forever.

This discussion led to further speculation. A public library, like other governmental institutions, belongs to the public. The public fisc pays for the librarian, the employees, the materials, and the time and energy expended in the creation of library records. Would the public stand idly by while the White House staff "cleans house," simply dumping records once a president leaves office?[2] Or while local or state agencies decide they no longer wish to store old records? If members of the public decide they want to check an old title on a piece of real estate or look up an old court case, don't they assume such records will be available? In response to a Freedom of Information Act request to a government agency, would anyone accept the explanation that the agency decided to discard the records to avoid the inconvenience of responding to such requests?

Libraries serve as the repository of one's culture. They serve as the storeplace for the poetry, literature, scientific knowledge, religious dogma, art, and history that a society values. They reflect the sum and substance of a body of knowledge for each historical period during which they exist, and they hold the works that presage the body of knowledge for future generations. They are unique in this sense. For that reason alone, their records must be protected.

One scholar demonstrates clearly the significance of the data contained in library collections. She refers to the modern social history research, "which has emerged over the last twenty years as a dominant genre in historical research."[3] These historians study demographics to gain a "picture of society 'from the bottom up,' a picture that emphasize[s] the living conditions and collective mentality of the majority."[4] Clearly, library statistics can play an important role in such studies. Traditional historical research has focused on *political* figures and events (for example, presidents, elections, laws, wars, etc.)—and this research is greatly facilitated by the historical fact that persons in positions of great influence (the elite) are aware of their place in history and are inclined to save their papers, correspondence, and other documents for posterity. That is not true, however, for the nonelites upon whom the newer social history focuses. The focus of historical research on these groups is facilitated primarily by the retention of data that reflects their attitudes and behavior, data that is often gathered by governmental agencies, including public libraries.

The library profession has an additional motivation for retaining its records. As a profession struggling to define its role and demarcate its jurisdiction, the lack of adequate records deprives historians of opportunities to measure the historical role and significance of libraries, thus rendering them relatively invisible and eliminating their claim to a position of importance. Retaining library records would allow historians and other scholars to focus attention on libraries and would inevitably raise the prominence of libraries and enlarge their symbolic capital.

In addition to these lofty goals, there are of course more mundane reasons for protecting library records, particularly records that hold "primary" value. For purposes of valuing records as a step in determining how long they should be kept, records can be divided into two general groups: those with primary value and those with secondary value. Primary value means the importance that a record has to the agency that created it—for example, those records that have administrative, fiscal, budgetary, or legal significance to the agency.[5] Secondary value means records that have importance for reasons other than those for which they were created—for example, historical importance or evidentiary importance in a criminal or civil lawsuit. Many records have both primary and secondary value.

It is usually the case that an agency readily appreciates records of primary value, at least during the time for which they continue to have that value. A librarian or library director can easily understand why it is important to keep records relating to current employees or current budgets or current acquisitions and holdings. But after these records lose their primary value, they do not become "valueless." Instead, they may retain their secondary value and should be kept for that reason. They may, for example, prove helpful in demonstrating to a subsequent director or a subsequent generation how the library operated, what kinds of people served in it, why certain materials and not others were held there, what kinds of people utilized its materials and services, and how different kinds of materials or services were valued based on the percentage of its budget that was expended on them. Keeping library records that have lost their primary value contributes significantly to our knowledge of social, cultural, and community history.

In response to these concerns and specifically because agencies, whether federal, state, or local, are funded with tax money, both the federal and state governments have passed legislation governing the disposition of public records. Because public libraries are funded with state and local money, their records are governed by state statutes. Failing to follow the mandates of these statutes constitutes a violation of state law and can result in severe penalty. So if an appeal to one's social conscience does not encourage librarians to save their records, perhaps the threat of legal sanctions will.

STATE LAWS GOVERNING RECORD RETENTION AND DESTRUCTION

Every state has laws governing the disposition of public records. Some of them are very specific and some are very general. But for purposes of determining whether and how they apply to library records, it is important to ask a number of questions. What is a public record? Does the definition apply only to state records, or does it include county and local government (city, town, village, or other municipality)? Does it apply to electronically generated material? In the absence of specific directions for specific types of records, who determines when they can be destroyed? Who is responsible for establishing and enforcing retention schedules? Are guidelines provided for the establishment of such schedules? When can records be destroyed and what procedures must this entail? What happens when the statute is violated? Does the law provide penalties and, if so, what are they?

These questions may or may not be addressed by the state statute. If they are not, they should be. An examination of the laws reveals varying degrees of success in answering these questions.

What Is a Public Record?

The definition of "public record" encompasses several subquestions. What types of formats are included—written or electronic or both? Does the definition apply only to *state* records or does it include county and local records? Are any records excluded?

The vast majority of states have chosen to define public records in some version of the following:

Any document, paper, book, letter, photograph, drawing, map...or other document of any other material, regardless of physical form or characteristic, created or received under law or in connection with the transaction of official business... as evidence of the organization, function, policies, decisions, procedures, operations or other activities of the governing body.

Although this definition includes materials of any physical format, some states have made it clear that records stored on newer electronic media are included. Thus, some states have added the following language:

1. cards, tapes, disks, diskettes, recordings;[6]
2. microfilm, magnetic tape, or other material;[7]
3. card, tape, recording, microform, motion picture, sound recording, computer disk, tape or other machine-readable medium;[8]
4. a document, paper, letter or writing...prepared by handwriting, typewriting, printing, photostating, or photocopying; or a photograph, film, map, magnetic or paper tape, microform, magnetic or punch card, disc, drum, sound or video recording, electronic data processing material, or other recording medium, and includes individual letters, words, pictures, sounds, impulses or symbols, or combination thereof.[9]

Some states' definitions are fairly restrictive and may present problems in the future, given the increased reliance on computers and other electronic storage media. One such definition defines a public record as:

all written, typed or printed books, papers, letters, documents and maps made or received in pursuance of law.[10]

Indiana has one of the broadest and most unusual definitions of public records:

all documentation of the informational, communicative or decision-making processes of state government, its agencies and subdivisions made or received by any agency of state government or its employees in connection with the transaction of public business or government functions, which documentation is created, received, retained, maintained, or filed by that agency...as evidence of its activities or because of the informational value of the data in the documentation, and which is generated on:

1. Paper or paper substitutes;
2. Photographic or chemically based media;
3. Magnetic or machine readable media; or
4. Any other materials, regardless of form or characteristics.[11]

Recently, in a case involving the *federal* public records act, one judge determined that electronic messages are included in the definition of public records.[12] Definitions under state laws are often just as expansive.

Does the State's Public Records Law Apply to State, County, and Local Records?

This question is very important to libraries, because most of them (other than the State Library in each state) are considered county or municipal entities, funded with county or municipal treasuries. Forty-one states include the records of county and/or local agencies in their record retention laws.[13]

When a library falls within the definition articulated in state retention statutes, its records must be retained pursuant to the statute and may be destroyed only within the statute's parameters. Combined with the very broad definitions of "records" as set forth above, it is clear that in many states all writings, papers, computer records, and other recordations of official business, *including* patron registration and circulation records, constitute public records.

Which Records Are Excluded from the Definition?

From a library professional's perspective, it would be desirable to exclude records that are confidential. But that desire is not evident in the record retention laws.

Twenty-three states specifically exclude library and museum material developed or acquired and preserved solely for reference, historical, or exhibition purposes; extra copies of records; or stocks of publications and processed documents.[14] Georgia excludes "books in formally organized libraries."[15] Iowa excludes "miscellaneous papers or correspondence without official significance."[16] Utah excludes, among other things, temporary drafts, materials owned privately, proprietary software, books held by a public library, and computer programs developed or purchased by the government for its own use.[17] No state specifically excludes library patron records from its record retention law. In fact, both Indiana and Oregon specifically include confidential materials within the provisions of their record retention acts.[18]

Who Determines When Library Records May Be Destroyed?

State statutes delegate the responsibility of public record retention and destruction to various decision-making bodies. Pursuant to these laws, twenty-one states have established specialized commissions, boards, committees, or other governmental bodies to determine public records policy for the state and its counties and other political subdivisions, particularly as that policy relates to the retention and destruction of such records.[19] Laws vary as to the makeup of these decision-making bodies, but in most cases they are composed of various state, county, or local government officials. In the rarer case, historians and archivists are included. Seven states have placed this responsibility in the offices of the state libraries.[20] Nineteen states directly include a representative from a history or archival unit in the decision-making process.[21] Eight states delegate responsibility to various public administrators,[22] although it is likely that in practice these administrators have delegated the duties to specialized bodies.

How Are Record Retention/Destruction Decisions Made?

Some states have mandated specific step-by-step procedures to follow prior to the destruction of public records. Most states have at least provided guidelines or significant factors that must be considered. For example, seventeen states specify that the legal significance or value of records be considered prior to their destruction.[23] This requirement is a logical one, because it takes into account the necessity of preserving records that may play a role in litigation or in legal challenges to the governmental agency's conduct. The same concern for practical necessity has prompted sixteen states to include in their record destruction guidelines the administrative value of records[24] and twelve states to include records' fiscal value.[25]

Another concern has been expressed by seventeen states that list the historical value of a record as a factor to consider prior to authorizing the record's destruction.[26] This demonstrates a commitment to something other than the practical necessities mentioned above. It recognizes that some records should be retained simply because of their interest for a future generation. Clearly, some library records would fit within this category.

A few states have added to these factors a variety of other concerns: whether the information is available from another source,[27] whether the records are of public interest,[28] or whether the records hold research[29] or official value.[30] It is unclear how seriously any of these factors are considered when decisions are made to destroy public records, but the fact that they appear within the statutes demonstrates at least a legislative commitment to them.

Are Penalties Imposed for Improper Destruction?

Twenty-two states impose penalties for improper destruction of public records.[31] They range from fines of $500.00 up to $10,000.00 and jail time from ninety days up to ten years. In Nevada, for example, a public official who "willfully and unlawfully . . . destroys . . . a record, map, book, paper, document or other thing filed . . . in [his or her own] public office" faces imprisonment of up to ten years or a fine up to $10,000.00 or both.[32] In addition, a few states provide that a civil action can be filed against one who illegally destroys public records[33] or that the public official responsible for the destruction lose his or her public office.[34]

CURRENT LIBRARY PRACTICES

It is often the case that what the law *says* and what people *do* diverge significantly. In order to ascertain whether this is true in the library profession, I sent questionnaires to various offices in all fifty states.[35] These were sent during the last part of 1991 and the first half of 1992 to state offices responsible for local government records[36] and to the chief officers of State Library agencies.[37] Similar questionnaires were sent to the American Library Association (ALA) state chapter executives in all states and to library directors for the largest public libraries in all states. The questions, in varying form, asked the following:

1. Have you established (or are you aware of) a written record retention/disposition schedule that sets forth the length of time library records must be retained? Included in the questionnaire was this definition: "Public library records include circulation and registration records, correspondence, papers, and documents prepared or received by the library relating to the conduct of its public business." If such schedules existed, copies were requested.

2. Who determines when library records may be destroyed and how is that determination made? What procedures, if any, are required prior to destruction of public library records? Who must approve the destruction of library records? How long are public library records retained?[38]

3. Are you aware of any *local ordinances* in your state that govern the retention or disposition of library records? The questionnaire defined local ordinances as "laws enacted by cities, towns, villages, or other municipalities, but do *not* include *state* laws." The question was included because, although state laws are readily available through general legal research, local ordinances are not. The questionnaire requested copies of such ordinances, if applicable.

4. The library directors for major public libraries were also asked whether smaller public libraries in their state followed the same record retention/disposition schedule.

Forty-six states and the District of Columbia responded to the questionnaire. The state-specific responses are discussed in Chapter 2. They revealed various levels of knowledge about current laws governing the retention and destruction of library records.

For example, in Delaware the state archivist's office responded that county and municipal library retention schedules had been reviewed by county and municipal librarians, but the State Division of Libraries admitted that retention of library records is "[h]it or miss—every municipality is supposed to have a records officer, who has the responsibility for implementing the retention schedule. In reality, we don't know if this is consistently done." In Georgia, the Department of Archives and History has developed elaborate retention schedules for county and municipal agencies, including schedules specifically for public libraries, yet library boards of trustees continue to decide on their own when records may be discarded. Indiana law mandates that no public records be destroyed for three years except pursuant to an approved retention schedule. A step-by-step procedure is provided by law prior to a record's destruction, but as of late 1991, library directors continued to make such decisions, apparently without proper authorization. The Kansas local records archivist for the Historical Society complained that many public libraries "flagrantly" violated retention schedules. And in Nebraska, although records may not be destroyed unless they either appear on an approved retention schedule or have been approved for destruction by the state records administrator, the state's Library Commission reported that local library boards routinely make such decisions.

Perhaps this state of affairs can best be summarized by the response from one public library director, who said that, since there has not yet been any problem, he does not worry about record retention laws. He noted: "Regulation enforcement is most difficult where the targeted agency is a public agency. [A private corporation] may quail under the disapproving gaze of a [federal regulation] while almost any state agency or federal dept. yawns."[39]

Most librarians do not deliberately ignore the law. Some simply are unaware that the law applies to library records. This is particularly true in smaller libraries. For example, although the Boise (Idaho) Public Library follows a state-mandated procedure for library record destruction, other local library boards make their own determinations. Although Louisiana punishes the intentional destruction of public records with imprisonment for up to five years "with or without hard labor" or with a fine up to $5,000.00, or both, public library directors continue to decide on their own when library records should be destroyed. Similar unfamiliarity with the laws was demonstrated in many other states, including Massachusetts, Michigan, and New Jersey.

On the other hand, a few states appear light-years ahead of others.

Arizona has developed a detailed retention schedule for both county and municipal libraries, which provides retention periods for such records as accession lists, borrower's registrations, and circulation records. In Florida, not only have retention schedules been developed for library records, but the state distributes the schedules to the proper authorities and periodically conducts workshops for public libraries, covering such topics as public records law, records management basic principles, and preservation and disposition of records. Minnesota's retention schedules are distributed with detailed, comprehensible instructions for using the schedule. New York and North Carolina do the same. As of 1992, at least twenty-two states had developed record retention schedules for at least some of their library records.[40] Other states are advised to follow these examples if they hope to improve compliance with their laws.

Although many librarians are unaware that such laws include library records, others, like the librarian above, choose not to address the issue unless and until it becomes a "problem." Unfortunately, when it does, the penalties for violation can be very severe. Furthermore, by the time librarians realize the significance of wholesale record destruction, the records will be forever lost.

After reviewing the responses to the questionnaire and the provisions of the state statutes, it should become apparent that the library profession must act to strengthen its policies, its practices, and the state laws to ensure that valuable library records are not destroyed.

INTERSECTION OF RETENTION AND CONFIDENTIALITY LAWS

The library profession has to some extent directed its attention to both areas addressed in this book: the retention and destruction of library records, and confidentiality of library records. What has been missing, however, is the intersection of these two areas. Most librarians now assume that, because library circulation records are confidential, they may (and, some argue, *should*) be destroyed as soon as possible. However efficacious such an approach may seem, in some states it constitutes a violation of state law.

All states have public records laws that forbid the indiscriminate destruction of public records. Library records are public records and fail within this proscription. In a few states,[41] library records that are confidential (usually registration and circulation records) are specifically defined as nonpublic records for purposes of disclosure. But the definition of "public record" in the record retention statute does not specifically exempt confidential records; it is therefore unlikely that such records are exempt from retention laws. In most states, library records are either expressly or impliedly "public." This means they are subject to the state's retention laws and cannot be destroyed except pursuant to schedules in compliance with state law.

Nor can libraries rely on the excuse that the computer automatically purges the system of such records. Computer programs can, of course, be designed to do so or not. If libraries demand a system that stores such records, the system will do so. To appreciate the significance of the argument if taken to its logical conclusion, consider that any public official could order or self-design a computer program for storage of public records that purges the information automatically every year (or every month, or every day). Then record retention laws would be rendered meaningless, since the recordkeeper could determine unilaterally which records should be kept and which destroyed. In short, librarians do not have that kind of authority. They, like other public officials, are governed by state law. The key for libraries to operate lawfully is to create a retention schedule pursuant to state law that provides that the retention period for circulation records is very brief, perhaps no longer than until the materials are returned. But until such time as this type of schedule is approved by the responsible governmental agency, destruction of such records is a state law violation.

For now, it is only necessary that one appreciate the intersection between the two bodies of law. After examination of each of them, several proposals will be advanced to resolve the troubling current state of affairs.

NOTES

1. The library historian is my husband, Wayne A. Wiegand, who has researched in the area of library history for nearly twenty years. See, e.g., his Politics of an Emerging Profession: The American Library Association, 1876–1917 (1986) and "An Active Instrument for Propaganda": American Public Libraries During World War I (1989).

2. In fact, this problem arose recently when President George Bush was preparing to leave the White House. Members of his administration threatened to erase computer records before they left. A federal judge ordered that the records be preserved: "Such information can be of tremendous historical value . . . ," he said. He stated that such records are protected under the Federal Records Act, a law governing public records prepared by federal agencies. Armstrong v. Executive Office of the President, 61 U.S.L.W. 2427 (D.C. D.C. Jan. 26, 1993).

3. Heather MacNeil, Without Consent: The Ethics of Disclosing Personal Information in Public Archives 104 (1992).

4. Id. at 105.

5. Both Dearstyne and Jones discuss records in terms of primary and secondary value and offer the definitions I have adopted. See Bruce W. Dearstyne, The Management of Local Government Records: A Guide for Local Officials (1988); H. G. Jones, Local Government Records: An Introduction to Their Management, Preservation, and Use (1980).

6. Ky. Rev. Stat. Ann. § 171.410 (Michie/Bobbs-Merrill 1990).

7. Ga. Code Ann. § 50–18–91 (1984).

8. D.C. Code Ann. § 1–2901 (1981).

9. Mich. Comp. Laws Ann. § 18.1285 (West Supp. 1992).

10. Ala. Code § 41–13–1 (1975).

11. Ind. Code Ann. § 5–15–5.1–1 (West 1989).

12. Armstrong v. Executive Office of the President, *supra* note 2.

13. These states are: Alabama, Alaska, Arizona, Arkansas, California (state and county), Colorado, Connecticut, Delaware, Florida, Georgia, Hawaii, Idaho (state and city), Illinois, Indiana, Iowa (state and city), Kansas, Kentucky, Louisiana, Maine, Maryland, Massachusetts, Michigan, Minnesota, Missouri, Nebraska, Nevada, New Hampshire, New Jersey, New York, North Carolina, Ohio, Oregon, Pennsylvania (some counties and cities), Rhode Island, South Carolina, Texas, Utah, Vermont, Virginia, Washington, and Wyoming.

14. These states are Alaska, Arizona, Arkansas, Colorado, Idaho, Illinois, Indiana, Iowa, Kansas, Louisiana, Maryland, Minnesota, Missouri, New Hampshire, New York, North Dakota, Oklahoma, Oregon, Pennsylvania, South Dakota, Texas, Virginia, and West Virginia, plus the District of Columbia.

15. Ga. Code Ann. § 50–18–91 (1984).

16. Iowa Code Ann. § 304.2 (West 1988).

17. Utah Code Ann. § 63–2–103 (Supp. 1992). Computer programs are defined as "instructions that allow a computer system to function as designed to provide storage and retrieval of data . . . that explain how to use the program." *Id.*

18. See Ind. Code Ann. § 5–15–5.1–2 (West 1989); Or Rev. Stat. § 192.005 (1991).

19. These states are Alabama, Arizona, Colorado, Delaware, Illinois, Indiana, Maine, Maryland, Massachusetts, Minnesota, Missouri, Nebraska, New Hampshire, New Jersey, Ohio, Pennsylvania, Tennessee, Utah, Vermont, Washington, and Wyoming. In addition, several states have such bodies whose purpose is to determine policy for state records only. These states are Iowa, Montana, New Mexico, North Dakota, South Dakota, West Virginia, and Wisconsin.

20. These states are Connecticut (state librarian), Florida (Library and Information Services, Department of State), Kentucky (Department for Libraries and Archives), Nevada (state librarian and the local governing bodies), Oklahoma (state librarian—for state government records only), Texas (State Library and Archives Commission), and Virginia (State Library Board).

21. These states are Arizona (Department of Library, Archives and Public Records), Arkansas (History Commission and state historian), Colorado (Division of State Archives and Public Records), Georgia (Department of Archives and History), Kansas (state archivist—state government records only), Kentucky (Department of Libraries and Archives), Louisiana (state archivist), Maryland (Records Management Division, Department of General Services and state archivist), Massachusetts (supervisor of public records and Records Conservation Board), Mississippi (Department of Archives and History—state government records only), Missouri (Records Management and Archives Service), New Hampshire (Division of Records Management and Archives), New Jersey (Division of Archives and Records Management), Oregon (Secretary of State and state archivist), Pennsylvania (State Historical and Museum Commission), South Carolina (Department of Archives and History), Texas (State Library and Archives Commission), Utah

(Division of Archives and Records Service and State Records Committee), and Washington (Division of Archives and Records Management and Local Records Committee).

22. These states are Alaska (governing bodies of political subdivisions), California (County Board of Supervisors), Hawaii (state comptroller), Idaho (Department of Administration), Michigan (Department of Administration), New York (commissioner of education), North Carolina (Department of Cultural Resources), and Rhode Island (Department of Administration).

23. These states are Alabama, Alaska, Arizona, Colorado, Connecticut, Florida, Georgia, Louisiana, Missouri, Nebraska, New Hampshire, Oklahoma, Oregon, Rhode Island, Utah, Virginia, and Washington. Virginia law defines legal values as follows: "Records shall be deemed of legal value when they document actions taken in the protection and proving of legal or civil rights and obligations of individuals and agencies." Va. Code Ann. § 42.1–77 (Michie 1992).

24. Alaska, Arizona, Colorado, Connecticut, Florida, Georgia, Louisiana, Missouri, Nebraska, New Hampshire, Oklahoma, Oregon, Rhode Island, Utah, Virginia, and Washington. Virginia law defines administrative value as follows: "Records shall be deemed of administrative value if they have continuing utility in the operation of an agency." Va. Code Ann. § 42.1–77 (Michie 1992).

25. Arizona, Connecticut, Florida, Georgia, Louisiana, Missouri, Nebraska, New Hampshire, Oklahoma, Rhode Island, Utah, and Virginia. Virginia law defines fiscal value as follows: "Records shall be deemed of fiscal value as long as they are needed to document and verify financial authorizations, obligations and transactions." Va. Code Ann. § 42.1–77 (Michie 1992).

26. Alabama, Alaska, Colorado, Connecticut, Delaware, Georgia, Illinois, Indiana, Missouri, Nebraska, New Hampshire, New York, Oklahoma, Rhode Island, Texas, Utah, and Virginia. Florida has termed this "archival" value. Virginia law defines historical value as follows: "Records shall be deemed of historical value when they contain unique information, regardless of age, which provides understanding of some aspect of the government and promotes the development of an informed and enlightened citizenry." Va. Code Ann. § 42.1–77 (Michie 1992).

27. Alabama law includes this factor.

28. Delaware law includes this factor.

29. Georgia, Missouri, North Carolina, Oklahoma, and Oregon laws include this factor.

30. Indiana and North Carolina laws include this factor.

31. These are Arizona, Florida, Hawaii, Indiana, Kentucky, Louisiana, Maine, Maryland, Massachusetts, Minnesota, Nebraska, Nevada, New Hampshire, New Jersey, North Carolina, Ohio, Rhode Island, South Carolina, Texas, Utah, Vermont, and Virginia.

32. Nev. Rev. Stat. Ann. § 239.320 (Michie 1991).

33. These states are Kentucky, Ohio, and Utah.

34. These states are Kentucky, Utah, and Virginia.

35. See Appendixes A, B, and C for copies of the questionnaires.

36. As provided in Dearstyne, *supra* note 5, app. I.

37. In some cases, the chief officer of the State Library agency is the same officer responsible for local government records.

38. The ALA state chapter executives were not asked these detailed questions.

Instead, they were asked if they are aware of retention/disposition schedules for library records and, if not, whether public librarians in their states know when they can dispose of records.

In addition to these questions, state officers responsible for public records were asked if penalties are imposed for improper destruction of library records.

39. Response from Thomas H. Ballard, director, Jackson-Hinds Library System, Jackson, Mississippi.

40. These states are Alaska, Arizona, Arkansas (for some libraries), Colorado, Connecticut, Delaware, Florida, Georgia, Kentucky, Maryland (for some libraries), Minnesota, Missouri (in process), Nevada, New Jersey, New York, North Carolina, North Dakota (for city and state libraries only), Oregon (in process), Pennsylvania, Virginia, Washington, and Wyoming.

41. See, e.g., Ga. Code Ann. § 24–9–46 (1981); Mass. Gen. Laws Ann. ch. 78, § 7 (West 1982); Minn. Stat. Ann. § 13.02(12) & 13.40 (West 1988); Nev. Rev. Stat. § 239.013 (1981); R.I. Gen. Laws § 38–2–2 (1991); Utah Code Ann. § 63–2–103(11) & (14), § 63–2–302 (1992); Vt. Stat. Ann. tit. 1, § 317(b)(19) (1989); W. Va. Code § 10–1–22 (1990).

2

State-Specific Laws and Current Practices

This chapter includes a state-by-state summary of both the relevant state record retention laws and the responses to the questionnaire. The advantages to this approach are that readers can refer to their own states to review the current status of the laws and the practices there, and they can review the laws and practices in other states to ascertain how others have addressed the issues. This approach also demonstrates that the issue of record retention, particularly as it relates to library records, is in its infancy. Retention laws were not drafted with library records in mind, nor have they yet been interpreted by the courts. In some cases, it is unclear whether or how they relate to library records, and this confusion is noted in the Commentary following a description of each state's law. Some states have not done a very good job of informing librarians of their obligations nor of offering them assistance. As a result, the laws may be ignored or misunderstood or blatantly violated. Much work is needed in this area. Chapter 3 will propose possible solutions.

METHODOLOGY

The research methodology for this book is intentionally neither scientific nor statistical in its approach. It is, instead, based on legal research, anecdotal evidence, and a questionnaire sent to those who would be most likely to know the practices of libraries in their states. It does provide an accurate summary of record retention laws and it also provides a general overview of current library practices in all fifty states. Its primary value is to focus the profession's attention on the serious need for strong, clear record retention policies and laws that will provide the profession with the guidance needed to ensure that library records are retained, or destroyed, not haphazardly nor in response to the exigency of crowded storage rooms, but pursuant to a system established after careful thought and deliberation.

In November 1991, questionnaires were sent, along with a cover letter,[1] to state officers responsible for local government records[2] and to the chief officers of state library agencies (COSLA).[3] In some cases, the officers in both categories were the same. In June 1991, a follow-up letter was sent to COSLAs in states from which no response had been received. In all, forty-six states responded.

In January 1992, a cover letter and similar questionnaire[4] were sent to the directors of the largest public libraries in each state and to the state chapters of ALA in all states. Eleven ALA chapters and fourteen public library directors responded. Although the response for these groups was smaller, their responses were not deemed to be critical. In many cases, the failure to respond may have been due to lack of awareness of record retention schedules and laws. Such schedules do not ordinarily emanate from ALA chapters or public librarians, but from state librarians or other state or local officials. It was therefore more important to elicit responses from those persons.

RESULTS

The rest of this chapter will present selected portions of the record retention laws in all fifty states and the District of Columbia, along with the summarized responses to the questionnaire. Forty-six states and the District of Columbia are represented in the questionnaire responses, either by the COSLA, the state officer responsible for public records, the director of the largest public library in the state, the ALA state chapter executive, or by two or more of these persons. The name and title of the specific person responding are provided in footnotes. In only four states did none of these persons respond. In most cases, following the summarized response, I have included my comments.

Alabama

Law

A "public record" includes "all written, typed or printed books, papers, letters, documents and maps made or received in pursuance of law" by officers of the state, counties, municipalities and other subdivisions "in the transactions of public business."[5] A seven-member state records commission and a twelve-member local records commission are created by statute and they determine which records must be "permanently preserved because of historical value" and which may be destroyed.[6] No governmental official (state, county, municipal, or other local government) "shall cause any . . . government record to be destroyed or otherwise disposed of without first obtaining the approval of the . . . records commission."[7] The commissions are to issue regulations classifying all public records and prescribing the proper retention period.[8]

Prior to issuing the regulations, the commissions are required to consider several factors: (1) the necessity to save records for litigation, including state and federal statutes of limitation; (2) the availability of the information from other sources; (3) the historical value; and (4) "[s]uch other matters as the commissions shall deem pertinent in order that public records be retained for as short a period as is commensurate with the interests of the public."[9]

Alabama law requires public officers to "correctly make and accurately keep . . . all such . . . documents, files, papers . . . as at all times shall afford full and detailed information in reference to the activities or business required to be done or carried on by such officer. . . ."[10] When these papers cease to be current, public officers are directed to deliver them to the director of the Department of Archives and History (for state offices) or to the county probate judge and "mayor, president of the board of commissioners or other executive officer . . . " (for county and local offices).[11]

Response

State law authorizes the State Records Commission and Local Government Records Commission to oversee the disposition of public records, which includes public library records. The commissions are to develop and approve written record retention schedules that set up minimum retention periods for public library records prior to their destruction. The director of the Department of Archives and History, who serves as the chair for both commissions, must approve the destruction of public library records.

Specific schedules have not yet been established for public libraries, although some of their records are included in the State General Records Schedules. There are no penalties for improper destruction of library records. The respondent adds:

Although the State Legislature established legal responsibilities concerning the retention and disposition of public records, the centralized management of a records management program is relatively young and developing. Not all agencies have approved records retention schedules and many officials are unaware of the [Commissions'] legal responsibility to approve the destruction of public records.[12]

Commentary

The State General Records Schedules, included in the questionnaire response, are printed in a pamphlet and include the *minimum* retention periods for budgeting, purchasing, accounting, payroll, personnel, property inventory, administrative, and public information records. Although the schedules included apply to *state* records, the respondent indicated that they would also govern libraries, which in most cases are funded locally.

The law governs all public records in all formats, including automated information and videotapes. Although schedules are not provided for specific library records, "routine correspondence" ("answering questions of constituents or other agencies," correspondence not dealing "with policy or rule making decisions," "correspondence created in the office on a daily basis") must be retained for three years or "until no longer useful."[13]

Typical of state record retention laws, Alabama law does not create a category (series) specifically for library patron records. Furthermore, these records do not fit comfortably within any of the designated categories. The closest category included in the State General Records Schedules is one entitled "Information Request Files." This category allows destruction "annually or when no longer useful" of files that contain "routine requests" by the public "for information . . . regarding the activities and service performed by the agency."[14] Information sought by patrons does not literally concern library activities and services; such language is obviously directed at other kinds of records.

Alaska

Law

The state archivist, under the authority of the Department of Education, administers the state records management program. A "record" is

any document, paper, book, letter, drawing, map . . . magnetic or paper tape . . . or other document of any other material, regardless of physical form or characteristic, developed or received under law or in connection with the transaction of official business and preserved or appropriate for preservation by an agency or political subdivision, as evidence of the organization, function, policies, decisions, procedures, operations or other activities of the state or political subdivision or because of the informational value in them.[15]

This does not include "library and museum material developed or acquired and preserved solely for reference, historical or exhibition purposes, extra copies . . . or stocks of publications and processed documents."[16]

Officials of political subdivisions (i.e., counties, cities, towns, and villages) who have custody of public records that they believe have no legal, administrative, or historical value must submit a list of such records to "the governing body of the political subdivision." The governing body must approve *in writing* the destruction of such records.[17] The chief executive officer of a *state* agency (department, office, agency, commission, or other unit created under the state executive branch, excluding the University of Alaska) must preserve its public records, establish retention schedules in conformance with state procedures, and submit those retention schedules to the Department of Education for approval.[18]

Response

Although no written record retention schedule has been established for library records, the Archives and Records Management Section of the Division of Libraries, Archives & Museums has prepared general schedules for local governments, with suggested retention periods for some library records. They are:

Accession Records	Permanently retained
Circulation Records	1 year
Circulation Statistical Reports	5 years
Circulation Cards	Until superseded
Shelf List or Inventories	Until superseded plus 3 years
Catalogues	Until superseded
Purchasing Records	3 years
Fine and Lost Item Reimbursement Accounting Records	3 years

Local governments determine when public library records may be destroyed, but there are no penalties for improper destruction.[19]

Commentary

The definition of "record" includes all formats, which would clearly encompass electronic records. The definition also includes all library records. Circulation records are required to be kept for one year, precluding their automatic expungement.

Arizona

Law

The director of the Department of Library, Archives and Public Records administers the records management and preservation of public records law. It is his or her job to establish record management standards and procedures and to determine record retention schedules for "records of

continuing value" and for the destruction "of records no longer possessing
sufficient administrative, legal or fiscal value to warrant their further keeping."[20] The heads of each state and local agency must establish a records
management program for their agency and must submit to the director a
record retention schedule, in accordance with the director's standards,
"proposing the length of time each record series warrants retention for
administrative, legal or fiscal purposes." They must also submit a list of
public records that are no longer "needed in the transaction of current
business and that are not considered to have sufficient administrative, legal
or fiscal value to warrant their inclusion in established disposal schedules."[21]
An agency head who violates this section commits a class 2 misdemeanor,
which can result in a fine or in jail time up to four months.[22]

"All records made or received by public officials . . . in the course of their
public duties are the property of the state." Officials must preserve them
and may not destroy them without approval from the Department of Library, Archives and Public Records. "Records" include

all books, papers, maps, photographs or other documentary materials, regardless
of physical form or characteristics . . . made or received by any governmental agency
in pursuance of law or in connection with the transaction of public business and
. . . appropriate for preservation by the agency . . . as evidence of the organization,
functions, policies, decisions, procedures, operations or other activities of the government, or because of the informational and historical value of data contained
therein.

This does not include "[l]ibrary or museum material made or acquired
solely for reference or exhibition purposes, extra copies . . . and stocks of
publications or documents intended for sale or distribution to interested
persons. . . ."[23]

Response

The Records Management Division of the Department of Library, Archives and Public Records has established a general record retention schedule for library records, although some jurisdictions have developed a more
specific schedule for their own use. The schedule includes the following
retention periods for county libraries:

Accession Records	Official copy to Clerk of Board of Supervisors
Borrower's Register	2 years after expiration of card
Circulation Records	
a. Annual	10 years after calendar year compiled
b. Other (daily, monthly, etc.)	2 years after prepared
Policy and Procedures Files	1 year after revised

Shelf Lists (Indices)	After revised
Minutes-Library Advisory Board	3 years after calendar year created

Other record categories (series) listed have varying retention periods. For municipal libraries, a few of the retention periods are:

Accession Files	2 years after fiscal year created
Borrowers Registry	After revised or updated
Circulation Records & Activity Reports	2 years after calendar year created or received
Policies & Procedures	After revised or updated
General Correspondence	2 years after calendar year created or received
Shelf Lists	After revised or updated
Minutes of Library Board	3 years after calendar year prepared[24]

Commentary

The definition of "record" includes all formats, which would clearly encompass electronic records. As is obvious from the retention schedules, the definition also includes library circulation records, which are required to be kept for at least two years, precluding their automatic expungement. However, the State Records Management Division director believes that "circulation records" might now refer only to statistical compilations because of the confidentiality law passed after the retention periods were established.[25] If so, the retention schedules must be modified.

Arkansas

Law

Arkansas has a law known as the Public Records Management and Archives Act of 1973, whose purpose, among other things, is to prohibit the premature destruction of public records.[26] Under this law, the Arkansas History Commission and the state historian administer the state public records management program and an archives program, under the supervision of the Department of Parks and Tourism. The state historian's duty is to administer a state records management program, including the development of "uniform standards and principles to be utilized as guidelines to be followed in the preservation and management of agency records," subject to the approval of the Arkansas History Commission. The commission also determines which records should be transferred to the state archives. Each governmental agency official is to develop a management program for his or her agency records.[27]

"Before destroying or discarding outdated records, other than ephemeral materials," all officers of the state, county, or other local governmental body, must advise the commission, in writing, of their intention to destroy material. If the commission determines that any of the materials have historical value, they must be transferred to the commission.[28]

"Records" included are:

all papers, correspondence, memoranda, accounts, reports . . . or other documents, regardless of physical form, including records produced by or for use with electronic or mechanical data processing devices, and which have been or shall be created or received by any agency . . . or official thereof in the exercise of his office, or in the conduct, transaction, or performance of any business, duty, or function pursued in accordance with law.

This does not include "library and museum material made or acquired and preserved solely for reference purposes, extra copies . . . and stock of publications and reproduced documents." "Agency" refers to "any office, department, bureau, division, board, commission, or court of the State . . . or any of its political subdivisions. . . . "[29]

Response

The state historian indicated that the state "has no public records management system, so our agency is responsible for public records only to the extent that the offices and departments owning such records choose to give them to us. We have no records of public libraries and have nothing to do with the retention and disposition of such records."[30]

Some libraries have established their own record retention schedules. The Central Arkansas Library System, which serves the City of Little Rock, and Pulaski and Perry counties, provided the following schedule:

Circulation Records for overdue materials	3 years past due date
Other Circulation Records	No retention period
Registration Records	4 years

No schedule for correspondence, etc., but board minutes and similar documents are kept "forever."[31]

Commentary

The status of record retention in Arkansas is typical of that in many other states. Although the legislature has recognized the importance of saving public records, steps have not been taken to ensure that the records are saved. It appears that each state and local agency can decide autonomously which records should be saved and which ones destroyed. Nor does it appear that libraries are advising the Historical Commission prior to destruction of records.

The law obviously contemplates a management program for all public records, explicitly including electronic and mechanical records. The definition of "records" includes circulation records, although they are protected by a confidentiality statute. In fact, Arkansas is the only state that mandates that "[p]ublic libraries shall use an automated or Gaylord-type circulation system that does not identify a patron with circulated materials after materials are returned."[32] This law in effect mandates a zero retention period for library circulation records. Although such a law accommodates the interest in library confidentiality, it obviously creates dismay among library and social historians who urge that circulation records be opened to researchers after a suitable waiting period.

California

Law

California has enacted a State Records Management Act, which governs the retention and disposal of state records. It mandates each state agency head to establish a records management program in accordance with state standards and procedures.[33] More significantly for librarians, California law also addresses *county* records. It gives to the county board of supervisors the power to

authorize the destruction or disposition of any record, paper or document which is more than two years old and which was prepared or received in any manner other than pursuant to a state statute or county charter. The board may authorize the destruction or disposition of any record, paper or document which is more than two years old, which was prepared or received pursuant to state statute or county charter, and which is not expressly required by law to be filed and preserved if the board determines by four-fifths (4/5) vote that the retention of any such record . . . is no longer necessary or required for county purposes.[34]

The law also provides that, "[a]t the request of the county officer concerned, the board of supervisors of any county may authorize the destruction of" records under specified conditions.[35] County officers may destroy records if the board "has adopted a resolution authorizing the county officer to destroy records. . . ."[36]

Response

Record retention schedules have been established for state records, but they do not pertain specifically to libraries. They include retention periods for such things as correspondence, budgets, employee records, and work orders.[37] The State Library "has no authority over local public library practices, and has established no records retention/disposition schedule for local public libraries." Each library creates its own procedures and time limitations for record retention, but most of them destroy circulation records as soon as the materials are returned.[38]

Commentary

No law specifically governs local records, leaving the local libraries to make that determination autonomously. Although the law states that the board of supervisors "may" authorize destruction of certain county records, it does not clearly mandate that all county record destruction requires such authorization. County library records, including circulation records, are public records under the law, even though California's confidentiality law protects patron records from disclosure.[39] Regardless, it appears that both county and municipal libraries can simply destroy library records at will.

Colorado

Law

The Division of State Archives and Public Records is the official custodian of "all public records of whatever kind which are transferred to it . . . from any public office of the state or any political subdivision." The state archivist, chief administrative officer of the Division of State Archives and Public Records, is responsible for administering the state's records management program. The state's governor has authority to "direct any department, division, board, bureau, commission, institution, or agency of the state, or any political subdivision thereof, to designate a records liaison officer to cooperate with and assist and advise the state archivist" in his duties.[40] All public officers must consult periodically with the archivist and state attorney general to determine whether records in their possession have legal, administrative, or historical value. Only if all three (public officer, archivist, and attorney general) agree that the record has no such value may it be destroyed. A list of such records, signed by all three persons, must be filed in the office where the records were kept and in the archivist's office. Those records with legal, administrative, or historical value may be transferred to the Division of State Archives and Public Records.[41]

"Records" include

all books, papers, maps . . . or other documentary materials, regardless of physical form or characteristics, made or received by any governmental agency in pursuance of law or in connection with the transaction of public business and preserved or appropriate for preservation by the agency . . . as evidence of the organization, functions, policies, decisions, procedures, operations, or other activities of the government or because of the value of the official governmental data contained therein.

"Library books, pamphlets, newspapers, or museum material made, acquired, or preserved for reference, historical, or exhibition purposes" are excluded from the definition.[42]

Response

The state archivist has established a record retention/disposition schedule for public library records. Libraries are provided with yearly updates advising them of the schedules and the minimum retention periods for each kind of record, along with dates when records may be destroyed. Included in the archivist's response was a sample schedule for a city library. It provided retention periods for numerous records series, among which are:

Correspondence & General Documentation*	Permanent Retention
Annual Statistical Report	Permanent Retention
Circulation Statistics	Permanent Retention
Routine Correspondence & General Documentation*	1 year plus current
Registration Cards	1 year after expiration

*categories that included correspondence and general documentation are divided into two groups with two separate retention periods. Correspondence and documentation that has administrative, policy, legal, fiscal, historical or research of enduring value should be retained permanently; others may be destroyed after one year. Furthermore, "no record shall be destroyed . . . so long as it pertains to any pending legal case, claim, action or audit."[43]

Commentary

This law clearly covers both state and local public officers, including public librarians. It covers records regardless of their physical form or characteristics, thereby including electronic records. It allows for the destruction of public records only if the local officer, the state archivist, and the attorney general agree that destruction is appropriate. If the local officer no longer needs the record for transaction of his or her business, but is not authorized to destroy the record, it may be transferred to the state archives. To avoid the necessity of numerous meetings to determine whether a particular record may be destroyed, both the local officer and the state archivist will be encouraged to create record retention schedules, which determine in advance the retention period for record series, such as annual reports, minutes of board meetings, and so on. Circulation patron records are not included in the sample schedule provided, although they fall within the definition of "public record."[44] Presumably, they are treated as nonrecords because of the state's confidentiality law. States that wish to provide complete protection for such records would be well advised to include them in the retention schedule, stating explicitly that the retention period is zero.

Connecticut

Law

Under the state library board's supervision, the state librarian is "responsible for developing and directing a records management program for the books, records, papers and documents of all state agencies within the executive department [and for] the several towns, cities, boroughs, districts and other political subdivisions of the state. . . . " He or she may require each state or local agency to submit a proposed retention schedule for approval. The state librarian is also to appoint an assistant to serve as the public records administrator.[45]

If the public records administrator and the state archivist determine that certain books, records, papers and documents which have no further administrative, fiscal or legal usefulness are of historical value to the state, the state librarian shall direct that they be transferred to the state library. If the state librarian determines that such books, records, papers and documents are of no administrative, fiscal, or legal value, and the public records administrator and state archivist determine that they are of no historical value to the state, the state librarian shall approve their disposal. . . .[46]

Response[47]

A retention/disposition schedule has been established for library records. It contains numerous categories, such as Accounting, Administration, Contract, and Financial Records. Among these are the following:

Registration Records	Until superseded, or length of registration
Correspondence, Routine (Memos, Transmittals, etc.)	Discretion of filing officer
Library Board: Bylaws, Minutes, Policies, Reports	Permanent retention
Procedures, manual of	Until superseded/unless valuable as retrospective publication, refer to historical collection
Circulation Statistics	Current, plus 1 year

The schedule also provides that all records "created, received, or maintained" by local governments belong to the state "and shall not be . . .

disposed of without official authorization from the Public Records Administrator and the State Archivist."[48] If a particular record does not appear on the schedule, it may not be destroyed without permission from the Public Records Administration. "Irrelevant" or "unnecessary" records may not be destroyed without permission, either. The state has printed forms for such requests.[49]

Commentary

The state law as drafted is fairly ambiguous. It does not specifically set forth when local agencies may destroy records or the steps they must take before destruction. However, the state Public Records Administration has stepped in to clarify and flesh out the law's framework. It has established detailed retention schedules and has prohibited destruction of any state or local public records without authorization, thus transforming the law into a clear, specific mandate binding on all public officials. The law does not specifically refer to electronic records, although it does refer to "books, records, papers and documents." Presumably an electronic record or document is included.[50]

The library retention schedules do not include circulation patron records, undoubtedly because the state's confidentiality law protects them. However, because they are public records under the state's definition, their inclusion in the retention schedule would be advised, even if the retention period is designated as zero.[51]

Delaware

Law

The Delaware Public Records Law is "applicable to all public officers and employees" and is administered by the Department of State, which must authorize the destruction of any public record.[52] A State Records Commission advises the Department concerning state governmental records and a Local Records Commission advises concerning local records.[53] After consultation with these commissions, the Department of State must establish retention schedules for public records. It is "the responsibility of every public official and employee to adequately document the transaction of public business and the services and programs for which such persons are responsible; [and] to retain and adequately protect all public records in their custody."[54] The Department of State may transfer to the State Archives any records in the possession of state or local public officials that it deems to have historical or public interest.[55] All state and local government agencies must designate a records officer to serve as a liaison to the

Department of State and to assist in the implementation of a records management program.[56]

A "public record" is defined as:

any document, book, photographic image, electronic data recording, paper, sound recording or other material regardless of physical form or characteristics made or received pursuant to the law or ordinance in connection with the transaction of public business by an officer or employee of this State or any political subdivision thereof.[57]

Response

The State Archives office reports that a retention schedule "is developed through an inventory process and interviews with Division of Libraries staff." The schedule is then reviewed and approved by the Bureau of Archives and Records Management, the Attorney General's office, and the Office of the Auditor of Accounts. It is signed by the state archivist. "The schedule is then distributed to the Agency Head and Agency Records Officer for implementation." The county and municipal library schedule is a general one and was reviewed by county and municipal librarians, according to an employee of the state archives.[58]

However, the Department of State, Division of Libraries is more skeptical. It reports that retention of library records is "Hit or miss—every municipality is supposed to have a records officer, who has the responsibility for implementing the retention schedule. In reality, we don't know if this is consistently done."[59]

Included in the responses were three retention schedules, one for Department of Community Affairs, Division of Libraries; one for County Libraries; and one for Municipality Libraries. The first applies to the State Library. Although some of these records are confidential, they are included in the schedule. For example, the schedule contains the following information:

Circulation Records (books borrowed & borrowers for State Library, Books by Mail, Book Mobile)

   • Retain at agency 1 year, destroy (confidential)

Registration records for State Library, Books by Mail

   • Retain at agency until obsolete; destroy (confidential)

Computer Output: X-DDL1 Reader Enrollment and Delivery System (READS) (Contains reader records, including background, reading history, requests; talking book inventories and circulation records; statistical reports)

   • Retain at agency 1 year after updates; successful federal audit; destroy (confidential)

Both the County and Municipal Libraries retention schedules are identical and include the following:

Patron registration records

- Until obsolete. *Note*: Because of the confidential nature of this information, it is important to dispose of obsolete material in a manner that will ensure confidentiality.

Circulation Records (includes cards, computer entries, and statistical reports)

- Cards and computer entries: until superseded.
- Annual statistics: permanent.
- Other statistics: 2 years.

Acquisition Records

- Permanent

Publications (newsletters, brochures, flyers, programs, and other publications intended for general distribution to the public)

- Permanent; submit 2 copies to State Archives for *Delaware Documentation* as created.

Commentary

The law is quite explicit in terms of who is responsible for record retention schedules and how the schedules should be developed. The law also includes electronic records within its definition of public records. The retention schedules themselves are well detailed and include such items as computer records, ensuring that public officers in control of records understand the broad definition of "records." The schedules for libraries demonstrate considerable thought and care. For example, copies of library publications such as flyers and brochures must be submitted to the state archives, which will preserve them for historical purposes.

The schedules demonstrate an awareness that, even though library records are not "public records" for purposes of the state's freedom of information act,[60] they are public records under the laws pertaining to retention of public records. Thus, if a retention schedule were to order retention of circulation records for 100 years, libraries must retain such records for that period, albeit confidentially.

District of Columbia

Law

The D.C. Office of Public Records Management is headed by the Public Records administrator, who serves as the chief records manager for the

District.[61] The administrator serves as the secretary to the Records Disposition Committee, which helps oversee the retention and destruction of public records in the District. No public record may be destroyed unless authorized by a retention schedule or approved by the Committee and the administrator.

Each governmental agency (i.e., board, commission, department, division, institution, authority, or part thereof)[62] must develop its own records management plan in compliance with standards and procedures set by the administrator. Each agency must designate an employee to serve as the records management officer to develop the plan and serve as liaison with the administrator. "Any inactive public record of the District which is deemed to have continuing historical or other significance shall be transferred to the District of Columbia Archives to be properly preserved."[63]

"Public record" means:

any book, paper, map, photograph, card, tape, recording, microform, motion picture, sound recording, computer disk, tape or other machine-readable medium, or other documentary material, regardless of physical form or characteristics, created or received by any agency or unit of the District in pursuance of law or in connection with the transaction of public business.[64]

This excludes "library or other reference materials or records maintained solely for convenience or reference."[65] The head of each agency must submit to the administrator "at least 4 copies of each report, study, or publication of the agency and those prepared by independent contractors."[66]

Response

Although the District of Columbia law mandates that the D.C. public library establish retention schedules, the respondent indicated she did not believe it had done so.[67]

Commentary

The District of Columbia Public Records Management Act was enacted in 1985.

Florida

Law

Florida law provides: "All agencies shall establish a program for the disposal of records that do not have sufficient legal, fiscal, administrative, or archival value in accordance with retention schedules established by the records and information management program of the Division of Library and Information Services of the Department of State."[68] Agencies included are "state, county, district, authority, or municipal officer, department, division, board, bureau, commission, or other separate unit of government created or established by law and any other public or private agency, person, partnership, corporation, or business entity acting on behalf of any public agency."[69] The definition of "record" is also very broad: "documents, papers, letters, maps, books, tapes, photographs, films, sound recordings or other material, regardless of physical form or characteristics, made or received pursuant to law or ordinance or in connection with the transaction of official business. . . . "[70] This includes information stored on computers.[71]

Public records in Florida may not be destroyed without the approval of the Division of Library and Information Services of the Department of State pursuant to rules and regulations established by the Division. Every public agency must submit to the Division "a list or schedule of records in its custody that are not needed in the transaction of current business and that do not have sufficient administrative, legal, or fiscal significance to warrant further retention. . . . " The Division then decides which of those should be transferred to it and which should be destroyed.[72] Any public officer who violates the provisions of the Public Records Chapter is guilty of an infraction, resulting in a fine up to $500.00. Anyone who willfully and knowingly violates the Chapter is guilty of a misdemeanor of the first degree, which carries a fine up to $1,000.00 and prison term up to one year.[73]

Response

The State Library director included in his response several current retention schedules, registration information for a records management workshop for libraries, and other relevant publications.[74] Records management workshops for public libraries are held periodically in Florida. They include topics related to the public records laws, records management basic principles, scheduling, preservation and disposition of records, and records management in areas of emerging technology.

Record retention schedules for state and local agencies are developed in a two-step process. The Records Management Services, Division of Library and Information Services, Department of State issues standards for records common to several or all state or local agencies. These include retention schedules for such records as personnel, fiscal, accounting, procurement matters, and similar generalized areas. They provide the minimum time that all such records must be kept. For records unique to an agency—for example, library circulation or accession records—the agency itself must submit a form requesting approval of its own retention schedule for those records. When approved, records within the schedule must be kept for the stated retention period. After the expiration of the period, the agency must submit another form requesting permission to destroy the records. Only after permission is granted may records be destroyed. "The Request assures that there is no premature destruction of records, or that records to be destroyed do not have an immediate or urgent value beyond the original retention period."[75] To assist agencies in preparation of proposed retention schedules and to aid them in following the detailed requirements for obtaining approval for record destruction, the state publishes several handbooks.[76]

The general records schedule for local government agencies includes generic categories such as:

Accounts Payable/Receivable

- 3 years after final payment or receipt provided applicable audits have been released.

Budget

- Approved annual budget: permanent; microfilm optional.
- Supporting documents: 3 fiscal years provided applicable audits have been released.
- Duplicates: retain until obsolete, superseded or administrative value is lost.

Correspondence

- Routine not relating to policy or a particular project: 3 fiscal years provided applicable audits have been released.
- Nonroutine: Same as item it relates to.

The general schedules also include retention periods for library accession records and library shelf lists (life of book or other material). The schedules list a total of ninety-two different records series, including such detailed records as agendas (permanent), car logs (1 year), daily time sheets (2 years), and long-distance telephone call records (1 year).

Commentary

Florida has a very sophisticated, comprehensive procedure for records management. Not only is the law clear on who is responsible for retention schedules and how such schedules should originate, but it is also very comprehensive in its definition of agencies and records included. Furthermore, and more important, the state *supports* the establishment of sound records management through its distribution of numerous publications designed to educate and assist public officials in the creation of a records management program for their agencies. Workshops are also offered at low cost to participants.[77] No matter what the schedules require substantively, it is clear that much effort has gone into ensuring that public records are not carelessly and thoughtlessly destroyed. In this respect, Florida has much to offer to those states lagging behind.

Georgia

Law

The Department of Archives and History is responsible for ensuring "the retention and preservation of the records of any state or local agency with historical and research value."[78] The Department must develop records management and retention rules and standards and assist state and local agencies in implementing a records management program in conformity with the rules and standards.[79]

The State Records Committee reviews retention schedules submitted by agency heads or by county or municipal governments and either approves, disapproves, amends, or modifies the schedules, based on the records' administrative, legal, fiscal, or historical value. Once approved, the schedules are "authoritative . . . directive, and shall have the force and effect of law."[80]

Each state agency ("any state office, department, division, board, bureau, commission, authority, or other separate unit of state government created or established by law"[81]) must establish a records management program, designate an agency records management officer, and submit to the Department of Archives and History a recommended retention schedule for its records. Retention periods for records that are common to the various agencies may be determined by the Department.[82] "Records" include "all documents, papers, letters, maps, books (except books in formally organized libraries), microfilm, magnetic tape, or other material, regardless of the physical form or characteristics, made or received pursuant to law or ordinance or in performance of functions by any agency."[83]

For local governments, "[a]ll records created or received in the performance of a public duty or paid for by public funds" by the governing body of a county, municipality, or consolidated government, "are deemed to be public property. . . . "[84] Each local office must submit to the local governing body for its approval a proposed retention schedule for agency records, based on their administrative, legal, fiscal, and historical value. Local record retention schedules must be submitted to the State Records Committee for approval.[85] The Georgia secretary of state is to assist local governments, providing advice, coordination, and training.[86]

Response

The Department of Archives and History has developed and published common records retention schedules for both county and municipal governmental agencies, which include schedules specifically for public libraries.[87] The publications are available upon request and the state plans to make the schedules available on a statewide computer network.[88] Wider distribution is apparently necessary. A response from Public Library Services of the Department of Education indicates that library boards of trustees continue to determine how long library records must be retained, that such periods vary with local policy, and that destruction of library records can take place with the approval of the public library system board of trustees.[89]

The common records schedules established by the Department of Archives and History are organized by governmental unit and by general subject. For example, categories include tax assessor's records, fire department records, correctional institute records, but also general administrative records (accident reports, computer hardware maintenance records, litigation case files, etc.) and personnel records. But both the county and municipal schedules include a section for library records only, which lists identical retention periods for the following record series:

- Accession books: Permanent
- Borrower registration: Until expiration plus 2 years
- Circulation records (A record indicating the daily, monthly, and annual activity of the library. Shows circulation statistics, fees received, new borrowers, holding circulation statistics by category [i.e., nonfiction, fiction, adult, juvenile, paperbacks, magazines, visual aids] and totals. Usually arranged chronologically by date): 3 years except annual circulation statistics, which are retained permanently for historical purposes.
- Minutes of library board or commission: Permanent
- Shelf lists file: Retain until updated.

Commentary

Although Georgia has a fairly comprehensive records management program, apparently not all agencies are aware of its existence and mandates. Thus, although the retention schedules were published in 1984, at least some libraries remain unaware that their records are included within the schedules' coverage. This is a common problem.

The definition of records is broad enough to encompass all forms of records, including electronic materials. Although both registration and circulation records are confidential under Georgia law,[90] it is apparent that they constitute "public records" for purposes of retention laws. Thus, in the schedules, registration records, although confidential, must be kept two years after they expire. Circulation records are also kept (for three years), but it is not clear whether the *materials borrowed* are included in the definition. The definition above appears to focus on circulation statistics, although it includes new borrower names as records which must be kept.

It would be advisable to revise the circulation record retention schedules to resolve this question.

Hawaii

Law

The law concerning the retention and disposition of public records is very brief. It provides that "[e]ach public officer, except public officers of the judiciary having the care and custody of any government records shall submit to the state comptroller a list of records for disposal. . . . " The comptroller determines whether such records can be destroyed.[91] The law also penalizes one who destroys a public record, knowing he or she lacks authority to do so. This violation is a misdemeanor, carrying a fine up to $2,000.00 and jail time up to one year.[92]

Response. None.

Idaho

Law

The director of the Department of Administration is responsible for developing records management programs and retention periods for all state public records and for developing and distributing to all state agencies a records management manual. "Records" include: "any document, book, paper, photograph, sound recording, or other material, regardless of physical form or characteristics, made or received pursuant to law or in connection with the transaction of official state business." Not included in the definition are "[l]ibrary and archive material made, acquired, or preserved solely for reference, exhibition, or historical purposes, extra copies of documents preserved only for convenience of reference, and stocks of publications and of processed documents. . . . "[93]

City business records may be destroyed only by resolution of the city council after a regular audit. Permanent records—that is, "documents or records as may be deemed of permanent nature by the governing body"— must be kept at least ten years.[94]

Response

The state archivist reports that no written, specific retention schedule has been developed for public libraries. Individual cities and districts, in consultation with the state archivist, determine when library records will be destroyed. Final request for record destruction is directed to the state archivist, who must approve the destruction.[95]

The Boise Public Library demonstrates how this procedure operates. It reports that it "follows the directives of the city's Records Management Division of the City Clerk's office, complying with local policies and procedures, and state law." Prior to the destruction of any library records, they are transferred to City Archives and a request to destroy is made at the expiration of the retention period. Pursuant to Idaho law, the "City Council, after regular audit, passes a Resolution listing records to be destroyed, under City Clerk supervision. Written notice of intent to destroy must go to the Idaho State Historical Society 60 days prior to destruction." The respondent indicated that library records are retained for various periods, depending on their nature. " 'Permanent' records are kept for not less than ten years (annual report, minutes, etc.), ILL records and library card applications, 2 years; donor records, 7 years." She also indicated that circulation records are computerized "and are eliminated from attachment to a patron's record upon check-in of the item."[96]

However, it appears that the Boise Public Library, undoubtedly because of its size and connection with a large city, is the exception rather than the rule. A public library consultant for the State Library reports that local boards determine when library records may be destroyed, that there are no retention schedules, and that no approval is required prior to destruction.[97]

Commentary

The retention law of Idaho applies to state and city records. It applies to any form of record, which would include electronic records.

Although a city the size of Boise has in place a sophisticated process to ensure that valuable local records are preserved, apparently few other cities and towns do. Even a program the size of Boise's raises some questions: for example, if records are deemed to have such value as to require "permanent" retention, why are they kept only for "not less than ten years"? When does permanent mean permanent? For historians and other scholars, ten years is but an instant.

As with most state laws, the problem of confidential records reappears here. Under Idaho law, library circulation records are public records, but exempt from public disclosure.[98] Because they are public records, they cannot be ignored in the development of a public records management program. If a determination is made that they should have a retention period only until the materials are returned, such a provision should be written into the retention schedule.

Illinois

Law

Illinois has both State and Local Records Acts. The State Act governs the disposition of records in the custody of a state agency—that is, "all parts, boards, and commissions of the executive branch of the State government including . . . State colleges and universities and their governing boards. . . . " It mandates each state agency to establish a records management program[99] and to submit to the State Records Commission "lists or schedules of records . . . that are not needed in the transaction of current business and that do not have sufficient administrative, legal or fiscal value to warrant their further preservation," along with proposed retention periods.[100] The Commission determines which records "no longer have any administrative, legal, research, or historical value and should be destroyed or disposed of otherwise."[101] No record of any state agency can be destroyed without the Commission's authorization.[102] "Records" include:

all books, papers, maps, photographs, or other official documentary materials, regardless of physical form or characteristics, made, produced, executed or received by any agency in the State in pursuance of state law or in connection with the transaction of public business and preserved or appropriate for preservation by that agency . . . as evidence of the organization, function, policies, decisions, procedures, operations, or other activities of the State or of the State Government, or because of the informational data contained therein.

It does not include "[l]ibrary and museum material made or acquired and preserved solely for reference or exhibition purposes, extra copies of documents . . . and stocks of publications and of processed documents."[103]

The Local Records Act applies to "all parts, boards, departments, bureaus and commissions of any county, municipal corporation or political subdivision." The definition of "public record" is identical to that above, except that it applies to records made, produced, executed, or received by a local, rather than a state, agency.[104] The state archivist serves as the local records advisor,[105] but the Act is administered by Local Records Commissions organized by county. Written approval must be obtained from the appropriate Local Records Commission before any public records can be destroyed.[106] The Commission must issue regulations and procedures for the disposition of all records. Furthermore, even if the Commission determines that a record may be destroyed, the state archivist may keep it and deposit it in an appropriate library or museum if it has historical value.[107]

The heads of local agencies must submit to the appropriate Commission the same kinds of lists and retention schedules as state agencies must submit to the State Records Commission. As in the state agency framework, approval for destruction of public records on the local level must be sought from the appropriate records commission.

Response

The State Library reports that no written record retention schedules concerning library records have been established at the state level.[108] The executive director of the ALA chapter reports that "the Illinois State Library and each regional library system" handle record retention matters.[109]

Commentary

The definition of public records is broad enough to encompass all forms of materials, including computer-generated records. Although circulation and registration records are confidential under Illinois law,[110] they nevertheless constitute public records under the state retention laws. Presumably, prior to destruction of any library records, including circulation and registration records, libraries currently seek the approval of the Local Records Commissions. Obviously, if retention schedules have been approved by the local commission, the necessity for continuing requests to the Commission is alleviated, as long as the record to be destroyed falls within a record series in the schedule. It is possible, as in other states, that libraries are unaware of the Local Records Act and are therefore in violation of it. One problem with the Local Records Commission format is that record retention may vary substantially from one locale to another. A preferable scheme would involve some uniformity. It is to be hoped that the state archivist's advice to the local commissions is provided with this in mind.

Indiana

Law

Indiana has both State and Local Records Commissions. The State Commission on Public Records was created to administer the public records laws for the administrative and executive branches of state government. Its duties include the establishment of a state records management program and record retention schedules.[111] An oversight committee serves as the policymaking body for the Commission; this committee determines which records "have no apparent official value but should be preserved for research or other purposes" and it has "final approval of all record retention schedules."[112] "Records" include:

all documentation of the informational, communicative or decision-making processes of state government, its agencies and subdivisions made or received by any agency of state government or its employees in connection with the transaction of public business or government functions, which documentation is created, received, retained, maintained, or filed by that agency or its successors as evidence of its activities or because of the informational value of the data in the documentation, and which is generated on:

1. Paper or paper substitutes;
2. Photographic or chemically based media;
3. Magnetic or machine readable media; or
4. Any other materials, regardless of form or characteristics.[113]

"Records" do not include copies of original materials or reference books and exhibit materials held for reference or exhibition purposes only.[114] The provisions in this chapter of Indiana law specifically include confidential materials, but exclude records held by state-supported colleges and universities.[115]

Under this law, each agency (defined as "any state office, department, division, board, bureau, commission, authority, or other separate unit of state government established by the constitution, law, or by executive or legislative order"[116]) must submit to the Public Records Commission's oversight committee a proposed retention schedule for its records, although the Committee may determine the retention periods for records common to several agencies. Records requiring retention of several years are transferred to the records center.[117] Those records designated as confidential retain that designation after transfer. No record may be destroyed unless the Public Records Commission has approved such in writing or the record is included in a record retention schedule and the retention period has expired.[118]

Records other than those held by *state* agencies are governed by local public records commissions, organized county by county. The definition of local "public records" is the same as that for state records, except that local government documentation, rather than state government documentation, is included.[119] The local commissions determine which public records have official or historical value.[120] Those that have no such value should be destroyed. However, no records should be destroyed for three years unless their "destruction is according to an approved retention schedule."[121]

It is the duty of the county records commissions to establish retention schedules for local government officials. Prior to the adoption of any such schedules, they must be approved by the same oversight committee mentioned above.[122] No record may be destroyed unless either it is covered by an approved retention schedule or the county commission has approved the destruction.[123] Once the local commission approves the destruction of records and prior to the destruction, it must enter that order in its minutes and notify the Indiana state archivist and any county "active genealogical society" or "active historical society" of the impending destruction to give them an opportunity to procure the records.[124] The law makes it a Class D felony to improperly destroy public records, including library records. This carries a penalty of one-and-one-half years in prison, plus up to $10,000.00 in fines.[125]

Response

As of November 1991, no state-originated retention schedules had been designed for public libraries. Legislation then pending (later passed) placed such responsibility clearly in the hands of local agencies and records commissions.[126] Both the State Library and State Archives noted that local county commissions determine retention schedules for public libraries.[127] The Indiana State Archives program director for Local Government Records Program noted that his office is currently developing retention schedules for public libraries. As envisioned under the law, public libraries must file a request with the local records commission seeking permission to destroy any of its records. The commission reviews the request, votes to approve or disapprove the request, and then notifies the State Archives (and county genealogical and historical societies). The Archives reviews the request to determine if it wants to procure any of the records. If not, then the records may be destroyed. All records must be retained for at least three years, according to the program director.[128]

It is obvious that retention schedules have not yet reached the public librarians. As of the beginning of 1992, the Allen County Public Library in Fort Wayne had no such schedule. The library director alone determined "case by case" when records should be destroyed.[129] The new law governing destruction of records became effective July 1, 1991.

Commentary

Indiana's law is unique in many respects. Destruction of library records without written approval or in accordance with a mandated retention schedule constitutes a felony, carrying a penalty of one-and-a-half years in prison and a fine up to $10,000.00, yet retention schedules had not yet been developed for public libraries and the director of the second largest public library in Indiana determined unilaterally when records should be destroyed. Criminal penalties for violation of the retention laws were only recently adopted in Indiana. It is hoped that this will prompt both state and local officials to make all reasonable efforts to inform public officers of their duties under the law. The imposition of a criminal penalty, particularly a felony, is fairly rare among state public records laws.

Another unique feature of Indiana's law is that it states specifically that records that are confidential are nevertheless included in the retention law, which means that they must be preserved as any other public records. The law also states specifically that they retain their confidential nature even after transfer to a central facility. This is especially important in those states where confidentiality laws may bind public library employees, but not others. Obviously this would not be a problem if retention schedules allow destruction of such records after only a brief retention period.

As in many other states, the definition of records is broad, clearly en-

compassing computer and micro-records. But in Indiana, the law specifically excludes coverage of the records held by state-supported colleges and
universities.

What is somewhat troublesome about Indiana's law is that the retention
of library records will vary from county to county, depending upon the
county records commission. Each county commission is composed of a
circuit court judge, the president of the board of county commissioners,
the county auditor, the circuit court clerk, the county recorder, the school
superintendent, and the city controller (if none, then the clerk-treasurer
of the county seat). Depending upon the focus of each particular commission, especially if none of the commissioners has a historical or scholarly
perspective, emphasis may be given to minimizing record storage space
rather than to preservation of valuable historical information. Historians
and other scholars may well find it frustrating to have some records available from some counties and not from others, particularly for comparison
purposes. It is to be hoped that this problem will be somewhat alleviated
by the State Archive review of all destruction schedules and that this review
will be more than perfunctory.

Iowa

Law

The state Records Management Act is administered by the state records
commission. The commission determines "what records have no administrative, legal, fiscal, research or historical value and should be disposed
of or destroyed." It establishes standards and procedures for the "selective
retention of records of continuing value."[130] A "record" means "a document, book, paper, photograph, sound recording or other material, regardless of physical form or characteristics, made, produced, executed or
received pursuant to law in connection with the transaction of official
business of state government." It does not include "library and museum
material" whose purpose is for reference or exhibition only, nor does it
include "miscellaneous papers or correspondence without official significance, extra copies of documents, . . . and stocks of publications and processed documents."[131]

This law applies only to state government agencies, defined as "executive
department, office, commission, board or other unit of state government."[132] Thus, it would not apply to county, city, or other municipal
public libraries.

Response. None.

Commentary

This law is extremely skeletal. It clearly envisions some form of supervision over public records but places such responsibility in the hands of

the State Commission and gives to the Commission almost total discretion to establish standards, procedures, and other guidelines for implementation of the law. It envisions that agencies and the Commission will work together to determine which records should be destroyed and which retained. Fortunately, the Commission is composed of representatives with varying interests and concerns: secretary of state, director of the Department of Cultural Affairs, state treasurer, director of Revenue and Finance, director of the Department of Management, state librarian, state auditor, and director of the Department of General Services.[133]

It is unclear from that law what happens to records of cities and other municipalities. Presumably, because the law does not address their retention, they can be destroyed at will.

Kansas

Law

"All government records made or received by and all government records coming into the custody, control or possession of a state or local agency, in the course of its public duties" are public property and cannot be destroyed "except as provided by law, or as may be authorized in the retention and disposition schedules."[134] A "government record" means:

all volumes, documents, reports, maps, drawings, charts, indexes, plans, memoranda, sound recordings, microfilms, photographic records and other data, information or documentary material, regardless of physical form or characteristics, storage media or condition of use, made or received by an agency in pursuance of law or in connection with the transaction of official business or bearing upon the official activities and functions of any governmental agency.[135]

It does not mean reference material, extra copies of documents, or stocks of publications.[136]

It is the state archivist's duty to assist state agencies in preparing retention schedules, which must be approved by the state records board. The board must also approve requests for authority to destroy state and county records not included in the schedules. "No records of state agencies or counties shall be disposed of before retention periods designated in the schedules have elapsed without the approval of the board." The retention schedules for local agencies other than counties "shall be recommendations and shall not alter or replace current statutes authorizing or restricting the disposition of government records by local agencies."[137] Local agencies are instructed to "[g]ive careful consideration to the recommended retention and disposition schedules prepared by the state archivist when considering the disposition of government records."[138]

Response

The Kansas State Historical Society has established a written record retention/disposition schedule for public library records, which is included in a published manual on retention schedules. It provides the following retention periods:

Accession registers	Retain permanently
Annual reports to state library	Retain permanently
Borrower registers	Retain until obsolete or superseded
Circulation records (individuals)	2 years
Circulation records (statistical)	Retain permanently
Community services directories	Retain permanently
Overdue book charges record	2 years after settled or written off
Scrapbooks (history of library)	Retain permanently

However, the local records archivist for the Historical Society notes that many public libraries "flagrantly" violate retention schedules.[139]

Commentary

There is confusion in the law. For example, while state agencies are provided with specific procedures for implementing retention schedules, counties are given less guidance and local agencies (e.g., public libraries supported by cities, towns, or other municipalities) even less. Local agencies are told only to "give careful consideration" to *recommended* retention schedules. Does this mean they are free to ignore such schedules? Not so, according to the local records archivist who responded. In short, the law is too sketchy to offer much guidance, leaving it to county and local governmental officials to act on their own, or not act at all. However, the law does prohibit destruction of any county record unless it is included in a retention schedule or the state records board approves, thus encouraging the establishment of detailed retention records. Under Kansas law, library patron records are public records, albeit confidential.[140] Thus they may not be destroyed unless they are included in a retention schedule and the requisite time has elapsed or the board approves their destruction. The public library retention schedule prepared by the Kansas State Historical Society provides for a retention period of two years.

Kentucky

Law

The Department for Libraries and Archives is responsible for public records management, with the advice of the State Archives and Records

Commission. The Commission has "authority to review and approve schedules for retention and destruction of records submitted by state and local agencies." The Commission determines which public records may be destroyed and its decision is binding.[141] "Public records" include "all books, papers, maps, photographs, cards, tapes, disks, diskettes, recordings, and other documentary materials, regardless of physical form or characteristics, which are prepared, owned, used, in the possession of or retained by a public agency." A "public agency" refers to a

state or local office, state department, division, bureau, board, commission and authority; . . . every county and city governing body, council, . . . municipal corporation, and any board, department, commission, committee, subcommittee, ad hoc committee, council or agency thereof; and any other body which is created by state or local authority and which derives at least twenty-five percent (25%) of its funds from state or local authority.[142]

The Department for Libraries and Archives is responsible for establishing procedures and standards for the retention and destruction of public records and for implementing and enforcing them. The Department is also responsible for furnishing a copy of the procedures and standards to all public officials affected by them.[143]

The Department is to "prescribe the policies and principles to be followed by state and local agencies in the conduct of their records management programs, and make provisions for the economical and efficient management of records by state and local agencies."[144] Although the law is not clear, an Attorney General Opinion states that, in the absence of a State Archives and Records Commission rule or regulation concerning a particular record, a county must obtain Commission approval before destroying the record.[145] The Commission also has the responsibility of establishing "standards for the selective retention of records of continuing value."[146]

Heads of state and local agencies, in accordance with the standards and procedures established by the Department and Commission, must "establish and maintain an active, continuing" records management program.[147] "When there is a question whether a particular record or group of records should be destroyed, the Commission shall have exclusive authority to decide whether or not the record or group of records are to be destroyed."[148] A person who knowingly violates certain portions of this law has committed a Class A misdemeanor carrying a penalty of up to $500.00 and/or twelve months in jail[149] and may face civil liability for damages to the state. In addition, if the person is a state employee who knowingly violates the law, he or she may face dismissal from employment.[150]

Response

The state's Department for Libraries and Archives has established a written record retention/disposition schedule for public library records. These schedules are routinely distributed to public officials. The schedule, which applies to county public libraries and library boards, provides retention periods for forty-four different record series. Some of them are generic—for example, board meeting minutes, audits, annual reports, personnel folders, official correspondence, and receipts/disbursements (all retained permanently). Others are unique to public libraries and include

Donors' Register or List	Permanent
Cataloging Card	Destroy when obsolete
Shelf List Cards	Destroy when obsolete
Accession Register of Acquisitions (for libraries using this process)	Destroy after 10 years & when no longer useful
Check-out slips or cards	Destroy when matched with returned book & when no longer useful
General correspondence	Retain no longer than 2 years
Daily Circulation Report	2 years
Monthly Circulation Report	5 years
Patron Registration Records	Destroy when obsolete
Patron Circulation Records	Destroy when books are returned[151]

Commentary

Kentucky law addresses a couple of issues that many states overlook. In its definition of records included in the record retention laws, it specifically includes both state and local governmental records and even an agency that receives 25 percent or more of its funding from a state or local government. Clearly public libraries fall within this definition. The definition of "record" is also broad enough to cover computer and microrecords.

The state has also recognized that patron records, although confidential, are nevertheless public records that must be included in the retention laws. Here, it is the state's intention that such records not be retained beyond the time that library materials are being used. If the state had failed to include such records, as many states do, their destruction would result in the commission of a Class A misdemeanor, civil liability, and even loss of one's job. With such high stakes, it is clearly necessary to include such records in an approved retention schedule. It is also helpful to keep public officials advised of the law's requirements, as is the practice of the state's Department for Libraries and Archives.

Louisiana

Law

The state archivist, who serves as director of the Division of Archives, Records Management, and History, is responsible for records management in both state and local agencies. Acting on behalf of the secretary of state, the state archivist must establish rules, regulations, and standards for the retention and destruction of all public records.[152] "Public records" include:

all documents, papers, letters, books, drawings, maps, plats, photographs, magnetic or optical media, microfilm, microphotograph, motion picture film, or other document or any other material, regardless of physical form or characteristic, generated or received under law or in connection with the transaction of official business, or preserved by an agency or political subdivision because of other informational or legal value.

This does not include "library and museum material developed or acquired and preserved solely for reference or stocks of standard publications, or processed documents."[153]

The state archivist, acting on behalf of the secretary of state, must establish retention standards for the "selective retention of records of continuing value" and ensure that state and local agencies follow the standards. State and local agencies must submit to the archivist proposed retention schedules for those records that have administrative, legal, or fiscal values. The archivist must approve or disapprove the retention schedules. For those records that have no such value and are no longer necessary to the agency, the agency head must seek the archivist's authorization for destruction.[154] Records that are no longer necessary to the agency but must be retained pursuant to a retention schedule may be transferred to a central records center. If the records were by law confidential in the agency's custody, they remain confidential at the records center.[155]

The heads of both state and local agencies have a statutory obligation to notify all agency officials and employees that no records may be destroyed unless the procedures set forth above have been followed and to inform them of the penalties for violation of the law.[156]

The law mandates that public officials "shall exercise diligence and care in preserving the public record for the period . . . of time specified . . . in formal records retention schedules." If no formal retention schedule has been developed and approved by the archivist for a particular public record, those records must be retained for a minimum of three years from the date on which they were made.[157] Louisiana law makes the intentional destruction of any record filed in any public office punishable by imprisonment for up to five years "with or without hard labor" or a fine up to $5,000.00 or both.[158]

Response

The associate state librarian was aware of no record retention laws that pertain to public libraries, nor was he aware of any penalties for violation. He indicated that currently public library directors determine when library records are destroyed, that the retention periods vary, depending upon the director's discretion, and that he was aware of no regulations governing the retention of library records. He stated that, several years ago, when directing a public library in the state, he sought assistance in this area from parish (county) officials but received little help.[159]

Commentary

Obviously the most significant problem is that public librarians apparently are unaware of the law. This is of special concern since Louisiana is one of the few states that criminally penalizes violation of the retention statutes. It is probable that public librarians do not believe that libraries fall within the public record retention laws and thus ignore them. However, Louisiana's definition of agencies governed by the law is very broad. It includes "any state, parish and municipal office, department, division, board, bureau, commission, authority, or other separate unit of state, parish or municipal government created or established by the constitution, law, resolution, proclamation, or ordinance."[160] Numerous references to state subdivisions appear in the various laws governing public record retention. Furthermore, the law that governs confidentiality of library patron records appears within the same title, Title 44—Public Records and Recorders.[161] Clearly, library records are governed by the public record retention laws.

Also clear is that public libraries are not only unaware of the law but also in violation of it. Louisiana has included in its law a "default" retention period of three years. Thus, if public records do not appear on an approved retention schedule they must be retained for three years. It would be a rare library indeed that retained all of its records for three years, particularly under the broad definition of "record" that Louisiana law provides. Not only are written records included, but also magnetic and optical media, microfilm, and any other material "regardless of physical form or characteristic."

Maine

Law

Prior to 1989, public record retention laws in Maine applied only to the records of state agencies, not to county or local agencies. In 1989, the Local Government Records Law was enacted.[162] Under the law pertaining to *state* records, the state archivist, operating within the Department of the Secretary of State, has the duty to establish policies and procedures for sound records management in the executive branch of state government and to supervise their implementation.[163] Upon request of either the legislative or judicial branches, the archivist has authority to "assist and advise" them in establishing a records management program. The archivist establishes retention schedules for each state department, retaining only those records with administrative, legal, or fiscal value, and authorizing the destruction of the others.[164] The Archives Advisory Board, consisting of "9 persons especially interested in the history of the State," advises the state archivist in his or her implementation of the Archives and Records Management Law.[165]

The newer Local Government Records Law applies to "any government entity that is not an agency of the State or of the United States, specifically including counties, municipalities, school districts, special purpose districts and similar government entities." Records are defined as "all documentary material, regardless of media or characteristics, made or received and maintained by a local government in accordance with law or regulation or in the transaction of its official business."[166] The law provides that no local public records may be destroyed "except as provided by the Local Government Records Board,"[167] consisting of seven members, including the state archivist, the state registrar of vital statistics, and five other local and county officials appointed by the governor.[168] The Local Government Records Board is directed to establish standards and procedures for the disposition of local records and "shall, as far as practical, follow the program established" for state record disposition.[169] Any person violating this law is guilty of a Class E crime[170] and subject to a fine of $1,000.00 and one year in jail.[171]

Response

No written record retention schedule exists for public library records. The state librarian determines when public library records may be destroyed and must approve destruction of such records. Library registration records are retained for two years and circulation records are kept on an automated system, which clears the record upon return of the materials.[172]

Commentary

Apparently, the Local Government Records Board has not yet established retention periods for library records, leaving that task in the hands of the state librarian. One notable component of the state records law is the requirement that the Archives Advisory Board consist of nine persons with an interest in the state's history. This might offset the frequent focus of public officials on ways to save money; it might prevent the mass destruction of public records simply to minimize storage costs.

Maryland

Law

The Records Management Division of the Department of General Services and the state archivist share responsibility for records management of state office public records. They establish standards and procedures for the disposal of such records and arrange for either destruction of the records or their transfer to state archives. Each unit of state government must develop a record retention schedule for its records in accordance with established standards and procedures.[173]

For both state and local records (including counties, cities, and towns),[174] when a record is no longer needed, the public official in charge of the agency must offer it to the archivist for storage. If the retention period for that record has expired and the archivist declines to accept it, only then may it be destroyed.[175] "Record" includes an original paper, book, and file. But it does not include books, magazines, newspapers, or "other library or museum material that was made or acquired for reference or exhibition purposes," extra copies of documents, stocks of publications, a public officer's acceptance or refusal of an invitation, or his or her personal materials.[176] It is a criminal offense to willfully destroy, without proper authority, any public record, which includes the "official books, papers, or records whether kept on a manual or automated basis, which are created, received, or used by the State or any agency thereof, a bicounty or a multicounty agency, any county, municipality, or other political subdivision." Violation could result in imprisonment of up to three years or a fine up to $1,000.00 or both.[177]

Response

No state written record retention schedule has been established for public libraries, but schedules have been developed for three libraries within Maryland's twenty-four jurisdictions. Each library unit, "working with Records Management, and with the final approval of Archives, develops records retention and disposal schedules. . . . Once a retention schedule has been approved, each unit must notify Records Management of any destruction of records."[178]

Based on the statutory authority outlined above, Maryland has adopted a Code of Regulations, binding on public officials, which outlines in detail the procedure for retaining and destroying state government records. It specifies, for example, that "record" includes "any documentary material in any form or format including paper, microform, computerized record, or other medium, that is . . . [c]reated . . . or . . . [r]eceived by an agency or office in connection with the transaction of public business."[179] It also provides that a "public record may not be disposed of without authorization from the

State Archivist. The authorization shall be obtained by means of filing the [retention and disposal] schedules and obtaining approval of the State Archivist." It instructs all agencies and offices to prepare such schedules.[180]

Based on the law and regulations, three libraries have developed schedules. The schedule for Anne Arundel County Public Library includes primarily financial records. Under the general heading of "accounting records," the schedule provides retention periods for payroll records, accounts payable, accounts receivable, and miscellaneous. A subheading refers to "General Office & Correspondence Files," defined as files that "contain general information such as copies of letters and memoranda, personnel information . . . and other information of a housekeeping nature which has a temporary reference value." These are to be retained for three years and then destroyed.

Baltimore County Public Library has organized its retention schedule somewhat differently. It divides its records by both subject matter and length of time retained. For example, three categories focus on retention periods. "Permanent Records" include minutes of Board of Library Trustees meetings, correspondence regarding legal matters, insurance records, books of original entry, general ledgers, annual financial statements, and audit reports. "Intermediate Records" (records that should be saved for seven years and then destroyed) include accounts receivable and payable, inventory records, payroll records, time sheets, check stubs and bank statements, expired contracts, leases, and purchase orders. "Short-term Records" (records that should be saved for two years and then destroyed) include petty cash vouchers, purchase order work sheets, expense reports, and mileage reports.

Subject matter record series include budget records, personnel records, leave and time sheets, and general correspondence. This last category includes "original incoming letters, copies of outgoing letters, memoranda, studies, reports, directives, policies, and other materials related to the administration of the agency." These are screened annually. Material no longer needed is destroyed, but "[d]irectives, policies, and other materials related to the planning and policy that illustrate the development of the agency" are retained permanently.

Montgomery County Department of Public Libraries arranges its schedule by subject matter. It includes the following:

Library Board Minutes	Permanent
Shelf List Cards	Permanent

| Borrower Registration Slips | "Retain until replaced by new registration slip (three years), and then destroy." |
| General Files (correspondence, financial records, personnel records, records of fines collected, etc.) | "Retain for three years and then destroy all material not having continuing administrative value." |

In the absence of a retention and disposal schedule, public libraries are apparently free to determine autonomously when records are destroyed. The assistant state superintendent for libraries responded that library boards of trustees determine when library records may be destroyed and that retention "varies from system to system. The circulation record is generally erased when the item is returned to the library."[181]

Commentary

Twenty-one library jurisdictions have no state-approved retention schedules, despite the law's obvious design and intent for such schedules to govern the retention and destruction of all public records. In fact, the criminal penalty for destroying records without proper authority is severe. Those schedules that do exist do not address patron circulation records, although they are public records within the law's definition.[182] The law provides confidentiality for such records and an unusual provision of Maryland's law provides that state and local government agencies "may keep only the information about a person that ... is needed ... to accomplish a governmental purpose that is authorized or required to be accomplished under" a state law, a governor's executive order, an executive order from the local jurisdiction's chief executive, or a judicial rule and "is relevant to accomplishment of the purpose."[183] Thus, the state apparently would approve a retention schedule that allows destruction of circulation records as soon as the materials are returned. However, none of the libraries have as yet received such approval.

Although the statute itself does not carefully and broadly define "public record" to include all formats, the regulations adopted by the state do and the statute specifically gives the state archivist authority to adopt such regulations.[184] They are thus binding on public officials.

Massachusetts

Law

The supervisor of public records is responsible for preserving the records of the commonwealth and its counties, cities, and towns. The law states that the following records must be "preserved and safely kept":

1. "Every original paper belonging to the files of the commonwealth or of any county, city or town, bearing date earlier than eighteen hundred and seventy";

2. "every book of registry or record, except books which the supervisor of public records determines may be destroyed";

3. "every report of an agent, officer or committee relative to . . . state, county or municipal interests not required to be recorded in a book and not so recorded."

[E]very other paper belonging to such files shall be kept for seven years after the latest original entry . . . , unless otherwise provided by law or unless such records are included in disposal schedules approved by the records conservation board for state records or by the supervisor of public records for county, city, or town records; and no such paper shall be destroyed without the written approval of the supervisor of records.[185]

"Record" is defined as "any written or printed book or paper, or any photograph, microphotograph, map or plan."[186] Violation of these provisions can result in a fine of $10.00 to $500.00 or imprisonment up to one year, or both.[187]

For state records, a Records Conservation Board, whose members include the supervisor of public records, the state librarian, and the state archivist, has authority to destroy or sell "all records in accordance with disposal schedules which shall have been submitted to said board and either approved or modified by said board or the board may authorize such sale or destruction."[188] "State records" include "all books, papers, maps, photographs, recorded tapes, financial statements, statistical tabulations, or other documentary materials or data, regardless of physical form or characteristics, made or received by any officer or employee of any agency, executive office, department, board, commission, bureau, division or authority of the commonwealth. . . . " When in doubt, the agency is directed to inquire of the Records Conservation Board in writing.[189]

Response

The assistant archivist for records management and acquisitions responded that the supervisor of public records determines when public library records may be destroyed. A library that wishes to destroy its records must file a written request and await the supervisor's authorization. No written retention schedule has been established for all libraries, but authorization is granted as the requests are received. Penalties apply as set forth above.[190]

However, the librarian for the State Board of Library Commissioners responded that no state regulations apply to library record retention, that local libraries determine when their own records may be destroyed according to their own procedures, and that the only penalties that apply are those developed by each local library.[191]

Commentary

The responses demonstrate a common failing in record retention law. Although the law seems clear, it apparently is not communicated to the library profession. And the fact that the law applies to "public records" generally means that librarians may not even be aware that library records are included. They certainly are not aware of the criminal penalties imposed for violation of the law.

The definition of "public record" is not very broad, including only written or printed papers; this definition might be interpreted to exclude computer records. It is also arguable that confidential library patron records are not included by definition. In contrast to the law of most other states, Massachusetts law specifically states in Chapter 78: "That part of the records of a public library which reveals the identity and intellectual pursuits of a person using such library shall not be a public record...."[192] This would mean that retention schedules for public records need not include this particular record series. However, Chapter 66, which defines public records for purposes of retention, does not mention library records as an exception. A cautious interpretation would include patron records in the retention schedule.

Michigan

Law

The Department of Administration is responsible for records management in state agencies. The head of each agency must "cause the records to be listed on a retention and disposal schedule." "Records" include:

documents, papers, books, letters, or writings prepared by handwriting, typewriting, printing, photostating, or photocopying; or a photograph, film, map, magnetic or paper tape, microform, magnetic or punch card, disc, drum, sound or video recording, electronic data processing material, or other recording medium, and includes individual letters, words, pictures, sounds, impulses or symbols, or combination thereof, regardless of physical form or characteristics. Record may also include a record series, if applicable.[193]

The Department of Administration must maintain a records management program that provides for the "development, implementation, and coordination of standards, procedures, and techniques" for retention of state agency records. It is the Department's duty to establish retention schedules "for the official records of each state agency with consideration to their administrative, fiscal, legal, and archival value." The Department submits its proposed schedules for approval to the secretary of state, the auditor general, the attorney general, and the state administrative board.[194]

Although the law applies only to *state* agencies, the Michigan Historical Commission has some control over the records of *county* and *local* agencies. The Commission has the power "to collect from the public offices in the state, including state, county, city, village, school and township offices, such records, files, documents, books and papers as are not in current use, and are of value" to the Commission. Prior to the destruction of records, "the directing authority of each state, county, multicounty, school, municipal agency, department, board, commission and institution of government" must provide to the Historical Commission a retention schedule or list of records that it no longer needs and that have no value. The Commission may retrieve those it believes have value. As for those records remaining, the directing authority must submit the schedule of documents to be destroyed to the state administrative board for its approval of the destruction.[195] Any person who willfully destroys any "official books, papers or records created by or received in any office or agency of the state of Michigan or its political subdivisions" in violation of the above laws is guilty of a misdemeanor, which could result in a fine up to $1,000.00 or imprisonment up to two years.[196]

Response

A written record retention schedule has been adopted for the State Library. In addition four county libraries have "prepared/submitted" schedules, but none of them include records series of circulation related materials.[197] The schedule for the State Library consists of thirteen pages of instructions for the retention of numerous records series. It is classified into major groups such as State Librarian's Office, Law Library Division, Information & Government Services Division, Business & Technical Services Division, and Library Development & Special Service. Included are circulation records for materials from the Law Library Division, which provide that such records are retained only until the materials are returned. However, circulation records that consist of service requests "made by an individual to the library" must be kept for two years.

The Detroit Public Library responded that it had no written retention schedule "except for schedules and other documents for biennial audit."[198] Nor was the executive director of the ALA state chapter aware of any library record retention schedules.[199]

Commentary

Michigan has an unusually comprehensive definition of what materials constitute a "record," including such items as "individual letters, words, pictures, sounds, impulses or symbols." This is apparently designed to include the latest technological developments in record keeping.

Although the law envisions a process whereby the Michigan Historical Commission and the State Administrative Board have the power to retain certain public records and prevent their destruction, it appears that few libraries follow the process or are even aware of it, despite the criminal penalties imposed for violation.

Minnesota

Law

Minnesota has a Records Disposition Panel, consisting of the attorney general, the legislative auditor (for state records), the state auditor (for local records), and the director of the Minnesota Historical Society. The panel has power to authorize the destruction of government records that have no further value and to order that records with value be transferred to the Historical Society for preservation. "Government records" include:

state and local records, including all cards, correspondence, discs, maps, memo-randa, microfilms, papers, photographs, recordings, reports, tapes, writings, optical disks, and other data, information or documentary material, regardless of physical form or characteristics, storage media or conditions of use, made or received by an officer or agency of the state and an officer or agency of a county, city, town, school district, municipal subdivision or corporation or other public authority or political entity within the state pursuant to state law or in connection with the transaction of public business by an officer or agency.[200]

"Record" does not include "data and information that does not become part of an official transaction, library and museum material made or ac-quired and kept solely for reference or exhibit purposes, extra copies . . . and stock of publications and processed documents."[201] Nor does this def-inition include records of the University of Minnesota, the Minnesota State Agriculture Society, the Minnesota Historical Society, or the Minnesota State Library (except with the state librarian's consent).[202]

The commissioner of administration administers a records management program, but the "head of each state agency and the governing body of each county, municipality, and other subdivision of government" have a duty to cooperate with the commissioner in establishing a records man-agement program. "When requested by the commissioner, public officials shall assist in the preparation of an inclusive inventory of records in their custody, to which shall be attached a schedule, approved by the head of the governmental unit or agency," for the retention or destruction for each record series. When the Records Disposition Panel has unanimously ap-proved the schedule, then the records may be destroyed in accordance with the retention times set forth in the schedule. A list of records destroyed must then be sent to the commissioner and to the state archivist.[203]

Prior to destruction of records that are not included in an approved retention schedule, "[a]n officer, department, or agency of the state or an officer or agency of a county, city, town, school district, municipal subdivision or corporation, or other public authority for political entity shall apply in writing to the archivist for an order" approving such destruction. The Records Disposition Panel acts upon each request,[204] but no records may be destroyed without the panel's approval, either by means of an approved retention schedule or on an ad hoc basis. Violation of this law constitutes a misdemeanor,[205] resulting in jail time up to ninety days, a fine up to $700.00, or both.[206]

Response

Both the state's deputy archivist and the director of the Office of Library Development and Services enclosed the record retention schedule that "would apply to all varieties of public libraries in Minnesota."[207] The schedule was developed with the assistance of the Department of Administration and was distributed to each city.[208]

Instructions for using the schedule are detailed and specific. For example, cities are advised that the schedule "applies to any form of the record (paper, computer tape or disk, microfilm, etc.)." Furthermore, "[r]ecords not listed on this schedule cannot be destroyed without submitting" a written request for authorization. Appropriate forms are provided for this process.[209] Cities that adopt the schedule avoid the paperwork and time involved in each unit of government repeatedly requesting authorization for destruction of specific documents. The schedule allows destruction of the records included therein on a continuing basis.

The schedules are divided into separate classifications for library, payroll, personnel, and administration. Included in the library schedule are:

Circulation Records (which includes cards, computer entries, and statistical reports): Retain cards and computer entries until superseded. Retain annual statistics permanently or transfer to the State Archives for selection and disposition; other stats 2 years.

Director's/Librarian's Files: Retain permanently or transfer to State Archives for selection and disposition.

Minutes of the Library Board: Retain permanently or transfer to State Archives.

Minutes - Tape Recordings of Library Board: Tapes may be reused or discarded 1 year after formal approval of written minutes of board. Tape recordings cannot be the permanent record.

The state's largest public library, the Minneapolis Public Library, is in the process of establishing its own retention schedule for the state's approval. Most of its records are kept permanently. The library is fully aware of the law and is relying on a variety of sources for development of its own schedule, including journal articles about records management and the city's own "Guide to Records Management Service."[210]

Commentary

Minnesota's record retention law and practices are very well developed. In contrast to the practices of many states, local libraries are aware that their records are included in the law and that library records cannot be destroyed without state authorization. This authorization may be in the form of a written request each time an agency wishes to destroy a particular record or, for efficiency, by means of the adoption of a written retention schedule for record series.

On both state and local levels, governmental units have developed detailed written assistance for their agencies, not only to advise them of the law, but also to assist them in following it. This kind of support and advice is rare and is badly needed. Minnesota's law is also very broad, clearly including all local units of government and all record formats. The law classifies circulation records as "not public" records under the state's open record act,[211] arguably exempting them from retention laws. However, they are included in the schedule prepared by the state archivist's office, a wise safeguard in any event.

Mississippi

Law

The Mississippi Archives and Records Management Law of 1981 applies only to records in the custody of a *state* "office, department, division, board, bureau, commission, institution of higher learning or other separate unit or institution of state government created or established by law."[212] Each state agency head must submit to the Department of Archives and History a proposed record retention schedule. The State Records Committee must review all such schedules, either approving or disapproving them, basing its decision on the records' administrative, legal, fiscal or historical value. The Committee's decision is binding on the agency.[213]

Response

All state agencies must either submit retention schedules for approval by the State Records Committee or receive permission to destroy records from the director of the Department of Archives and History. The Department has no authority over local public libraries, only over "public library records of state management agency for public libraries,"[214] and the Department's director was unaware of the length of time local libraries retain their records.

The state's largest public library has no written retention schedule. It retains some records permanently ("those which EEOC, Labor Dept., etc. might ever wish to see" and general business records, such as payroll, financial, and personnel records). The library director retains archived computer disks of his correspondence. For the remaining records, the "common sense" of the responsible department head dictates the retention period.[215] The director notes: "This subject is critical only if libraries begin to have trouble for failures. Thus far—not a problem. . . . I don't worry about records retention policies because it's not a problem." He also notes that "[r]egulation enforcement is most difficult where the targeted agency is a public agency. [A private corporation] may quail under the disapproving gaze of an OSHA GS 11 while almost any state agency or federal dept. yawns."[216]

Commentary

Honesty is a virtue. The library director captures precisely the problem with record retention laws in public libraries. Until attention is focused on the problem, libraries will give little thought to resolving it. That is not to say it is not a problem, only that it remains unresolved.

In Mississippi, regulation is minimal, applying only to state agencies, leaving public libraries free to determine on their own how long they wish to retain any records. Until 1992, those librarians concerned about patron record confidentiality in this state had reason to be concerned: such records were not confidential and the public could view them on request.[217] Thus it was of great advantage to those who value confidentiality that local libraries were free to destroy such records without state interference. It was, of course, of great *disadvantage* to historians. However, 1992 brought a change in Mississippi law, which now protects patron records from public access.[218] Whether this encourages libraries to save such records is questionable, particularly since the state's retention law applies only to state agencies.

Missouri

Law

The State and Local Records Law governs the retention and destruction of any state or local "document, book, paper, photograph, map, sound recording or other material, regardless of physical form or characteristics, made or received pursuant to law or in connection with the transaction of official business." It does not include "library and museum material made or acquired and preserved solely for reference or exhibition purposes, extra copies . . . and stocks of publications and of processed documents."[219]

The Records Management and Archives Service is responsible for administering the Act. Its director is to establish standards and procedures for records management and, "[w]ith approval of the state records commission or local records board, establish standards for the preparation of" retention schedules for state and local records "of continuing value" and for the destruction of records "no longer possessing sufficient administrative, legal, historical or fiscal value to warrant their future keeping." The director must "[p]ublish lists of records authorized for disposal or retention."[220] The State Records Commission is composed of various state officials;[221] the Local Records Board is composed of at least twelve members, representing a cross-section of local interests: school boards, communities of various sizes, higher education, counties, and historical societies.[222]

The head of each state agency must establish a records management program and submit to the State Records Commission proposed retention schedules.[223] The head of each local agency must "[s]ubmit within six months after a call to do so from the secretary of state" proposed record retention schedules in accordance with standards developed by the Local Records Board and the director of Records Management and Archives. "No record shall be destroyed or otherwise disposed of by any agency unless it is determined by the [state records] commission or [local records] board that the record has no further administrative, legal, fiscal, research or historical value."[224] Until such time as the Commission or Board promulgate rules and regulations for record destruction, agencies may follow "the provisions of existing law and administrative regulations."[225]

Response

The State Library has established no written record retention schedule for library records, but it is in the process of recommending such a schedule in a revised edition of *Guidelines for Missouri Libraries.* That publication lists nearly seventy record series, including the following:

Borrower Registration File: Retain until expiration plus 2 years.

Circulation Records (a record indicating the daily, monthly, and annual activity of the library. Documents circulation statistics, fees received . . . , lists of new borrowers, holding circulation statistics by category [fiction, nonfiction, juvenile, etc.] and totals): Retain 3 years except annual circulation statistics, which should be retained permanently for historical purposes.

Correspondence and Reports (two categories):

   a. Policy and Program Development Records: 5 years

   b. General Housekeeping Files: Until no longer needed

Minutes and Supporting Documents: Permanently for historical purposes

Shelf Lists File: Retain until revised or updated[226]

Commentary

Although Missouri law applies to both state and local agencies, only the state agencies must automatically submit proposed record retention schedules. Local agencies, which include public libraries, need do so only in response to a "call" from the secretary of state. In the meantime, the State Library has taken the initiative to develop schedules for the state's public libraries, although they serve as guidelines only.

Missouri's law, like those in Alabama, Alaska, and some other states, requires that governmental agencies take into account "historical" value, rather than just administrative, legal, and fiscal value. That emphasis is demonstrated in the guideline prepared by the State Library, which also suggests that certain records be retained for historical purposes.

The State Library's guideline recognizes that, although registration and circulation records are confidential,[227] they are nevertheless public records for purposes of the State and Local Records Law and must be included in the retention schedule.

Montana

Law

Montana's records management act applies only to "executive branch agencies of the state," thus excluding county and local agencies (i.e., public libraries). For the state agencies included, a state records committee administers the act and must approve, modify, or disapprove the proposed retention schedules submitted by state officials.[228] Except for categories of records included in retention schedules, "no [state agency] public record may be disposed of or destroyed without the unanimous approval of the state records committee."[229]

Response. None.

Nebraska

Law

The state's Records Management Act applies to both state and local agencies. The secretary of state is the state records administrator, responsible for establishing and administering a records management program, with assistance from the State Records Board.[230] The "head of any state agency, department, board, council, legislative or judicial branch, and political subdivision" must submit to the administrator proposed retention schedules for records in his or her custody, setting forth the time each record series should be retained for "administrative, legal, historical or fiscal purposes" and listing records that it no longer requires and that have no such value and therefore may be destroyed.[231] "Records" include "any book, document, paper, photograph, microfilm, sound recording, magnetic storage medium, or other material regardless of physical form or characteristics, created or received pursuant to law, charter, ordinance or in connection with any other activity relating to or having an effect upon the transaction of public business."[232]

Each retention schedule submitted to the administrator must be reviewed by the state archivist for the selection of archival and historical material. After the archivist approves the schedule, he or she returns it to the administrator for further review and either approval or disapproval.[233] State and local agency heads may dispose of agency records in accordance with the approved retention schedules. If a record does not appear on an approved retention schedule, the agency head must submit a written request to the administrator for authority to destroy it.[234] Anyone who willfully destroys a public record in contravention of the law commits a Class III misdemeanor and is subject to jail time up to three months, a fine of $500.00, or both.[235]

Response

The State Historical Society's role in records management is to examine proposed retention schedules "to identify historically valuable records which should be deposited in the state archives." The Records Management Division in the secretary of state's office is responsible for establishing the schedules.[236]

The Nebraska Library Commission responded that no written record retention schedule for public libraries has been established and that local library boards make such decisions. The Commission was also unaware of any penalties for improper destruction.[237] The Omaha Public Library agreed with this assessment, noting that library administrators make decisions about record destruction on an "as needed basis."[238]

Commentary

The most significant aspect of the law and survey responses is their discrepancies. The law clearly provides for retention schedule standards, procedures, and penalties, but libraries are apparently unaware that the law applies to them. Thus, records are destroyed autonomously, without the knowledge or approval of the Records Management Division or the State Historical Society.

Nevada

Law

Nevada has a public records law that is comprehensive and applicable to all public records: state, county, and local. The law mandates that *state* records "may be disposed of only in accordance with a schedule for retention and disposition which is approved by the state board of examiners."[239] Each state agency, board, and commission must submit to the board a proposed retention schedule for its approval. A "state record" is one "made or received by the officers or employees of a state agency in the performance of their public duties; and . . . whose preparation or maintenance was supported by public money."[240] The University of Nevada's records are specifically included.[241]

The records of local government, defined as "a county, an incorporated city, an unincorporated town, a township, a school district or any other public district or agency designed to perform local governmental functions,"[242] may not be destroyed without following state law, either. "Unless destruction of a particular record without reproduction is authorized by a [retention] schedule . . . , any custodian of public records in this state may destroy documents, instruments, papers, books and any other records or writings . . . only if those records or writings have been" first reproduced or entered into a computer system.[243] The law specifically permits local governmental entities to adopt retention schedules for approval by their governing bodies. The schedules must comply with applicable law, including regulations developed by the state librarian that provide for minimum retention periods for local records.[244] If the special charter of an incorporated city authorizes a different procedure for the disposition of its records, state law allows the city to follow that procedure rather than the one set forth above.[245]

"Old records," defined as local governmental entity records "which are retained for any purpose by the local governmental entity beyond the minimum period for retention established . . . or for 5 years or more, whichever is earlier," may be submitted to the Division of Archives and Records of the State Library and Archives, in lieu of destruction.[246]

The wrongful destruction of public records results in criminal sanctions. A person who "willfully and unlawfully . . . destroys . . . a record, map, book, paper, document or other thing filed or deposited in a public office" faces imprisonment of one to six years, or a fine up to $5,000.00, or both.[247] When the person committing the offense is a public officer destroying records of his or her own office, the penalty increases: imprisonment up to ten years or a fine up to $10,000.00, or both.[248]

Response

The state has developed retention schedules for public libraries in its administrative code, which is also published in the *Nevada Local Government Records Manual*.[249] The Nevada Administrative Code is binding on agencies in the state. In addition to minimum retention periods for records common to local governmental entities, the following periods are among those that apply to public library records:

Records pertaining to services provided to a patron of a library: 1 year after the date of last activity

Requests for material to be ordered through interlibrary loan: 1 year

Requests that patron pay a fine on an overdue book: 1 year

Renewals and book loans: Until annual audit is completed[250]

The state library association is aware of the retention schedules, but responded that it is in the process of revising them.[251] The Las Vegas-Clark County Library District responded that it followed state statutes in determining when library records are destroyed and that the library director must approve the destruction.[252] Presumably, this means that the library follows the mandate of the administrative code.

Commentary

Although Nevada gives local governmental entities authority to establish their own retention schedules, the law does mandate that such schedules be established. Pursuant to the law that permits the state librarian to develop regulations for local governments, the state has established retention schedules for public libraries, which are binding on them.

Although circulation records are confidential and not "public" for purposes of public inspection,[253] they are public for purposes of the retention laws and are therefore included in the state-established retention schedule. Thus, even though confidential, libraries must keep them for one year.

New Hampshire

Law

The state's Records Management and Archives Act is designed to apply to both state and local records.[254] It provides that the director of the Division of Records Management and Archives (of the Department of State) is responsible for establishing "standards, procedures, and techniques for effective management of records."[255] A "record" includes a "document, book, paper, manuscript, drawing, photograph, map, sound recording, microform, or other material, regardless of physical form or characteristics, made or received pursuant to law or in connection with the transaction of official business." It does not include "[l]ibrary and museum material made or acquired and preserved solely for library use or exhibition purposes, extra copies . . . and stocks of publications and of processed documents."[256] Records that do not have a permanent or historical value may be destroyed after seven years, unless a specific law or regulation or specific approved retention schedule provides otherwise.[257]

The director of the Division of Records Management and Archives is responsible for establishing retention schedules for *state* records, based on the administrative, legal, or fiscal value they hold. Each state agency head must submit to the director a proposed retention schedule for records in his or her custody, in accordance with the standards developed by the director.[258]

Municipal records (i.e., the records of a city, town, county, or precinct) may be destroyed only in accordance with standards, procedures, and regulations promulgated by the Municipal Records Board. "Municipal records" are "all municipal records, reports, minutes, tax records, ledgers, journals, checks, bills, receipts, warrants, payrolls, deeds and any other written or computerized material that may be designated by the board."[259] The Municipal Records Board consists of various state officials, including the director of the Division of Records Management and Archives, the director of the New Hampshire Historical Society, the state librarian, a professional historian, and other persons representing fiscal concerns.[260] The Board establishes standards, procedures, and regulations for the retention and destruction of municipal records, but a local municipal committee is responsible for administering those standards, procedures, and regulations.[261] The purposeful and unlawful destruction of a public record constitutes a misdemeanor, which could result in up to one year in jail and $2,000.00 in fines.[262]

Response

The state librarian responded that public library records are destroyed pursuant to a retention schedule established by the Municipal Records Board, but "to date only minutes of the board of trustees and financial records have been dealt with."[263]

Commentary

The definition of "municipal records" is ambiguous and circular. It includes "all municipal records, . . . ledgers, journals, checks . . . receipts . . . and any other written or computerized material that may be designated by the board." It does not define "records." Referring to another title and chapter of New Hampshire law provides guidance. The Records Management and Archives Act sets forth general guidelines for both state and local records and broadly defines "record" without restricting the definition to *state* records.[264] It thus becomes apparent that municipal records would include all library records, including circulation records, even though they are designated "confidential."[265] The state librarian indicated that, although the issue of retention/destruction of circulation records had never before been considered, it would be brought forward now.[266]

New Jersey

Law

New Jersey's Destruction of Public Records Law governs the disposition of both state and local public records. "Public records" are defined as

any paper, written or printed book, document or drawing, map or plan, photograph, microfilm, sound-recording or similar device, or any copy thereof which has been made or is required by law to be received for filing, indexing, or reproducing by an officer, commission, agency or authority of the State or of any political subdivision thereof, including subordinate boards thereof, or that has been received by any such officer, commission, agency or authority of the State or of any political subdivision thereof, including subordinate boards thereof, in connection with the transaction of public business and has been retained by such recipient or its successor as evidence of its activities or because of the information contained therein.[267]

The Division of Archives and Records Management in the Department of State is responsible for promulgating rules and regulations to effectuate the Act and for preparing proposed record retention schedules for the State Records Committee's approval. The schedule does not become "operative" until the Committee approves it.[268]

Any person who maliciously destroys a public record without the consent of the record's custodian commits a "high misdemeanor" and is subject to three to five years in prison and a fine of $7,500.00.[269]

Response

A written record retention/disposition schedule has been established for both general public records and for specific library records.[270] They were mass mailed by the State Library to those governmental entities affected. The general retention schedule for counties and municipalities includes the minimum retention periods for five major record series: financial records; personnel records; general administrative records; agency-related policy, legislation, and operating procedures; and reports and publications. The schedule for public libraries consists of six pages of record series, including:

Circulation Statistics (on-line and manual; contains date, Dewey Decimal System classification, and statistics): 3 years

Friends and Donors File (contains information pertaining to patrons donating money and texts and purchasing memorial bookplates): 20 years after final action

Interlibrary Loan Request (Interlibrary Loan System, New Jersey State Library, State Colleges, Community Colleges, and School Districts; contains borrower's name, signature, address, phone, status, and social security number; text title, publisher, and date; and journal title, publisher, and date. Copy is retained by the borrower): 1 year

Material Circulation Statistics (monthly and annual statistics of materials borrowed. Contains amount referenced and subject classification): 10 years

Patron Registration—Temporary: As updated, upon expiration of card

Patron Statistics—Annual: 10 years

Reference Referral List (contains name, date, telephone, topic request, requesting library, request answer, and in-house office referral): 3 years

Search Service Log (contains name, date, subject, and pages printed): 1 year

Text Reserve List (contains requestor's name and telephone number, and text call number, author, and title): 1 year

Videotape Borrower's File: 1 year[271]

The Request and Authorization Form "must be completed by all State, County, and Municipal agencies prior to the disposition of any public records." It is submitted to the Division of Archives and Records Management for approval.[272]

The Newark Public Library responded that the newer automated circulation system it uses breaks the links between patron and item records when the items are returned.[273] "In the future the head of Technical Services may direct that expired patron records be purged from the system." The head of personnel "periodically" destroys outdated personnel records. Correspondence is sent to the local history collection when it is no longer needed, and the collection's librarians determine if it should be preserved. Board minutes and resolutions are stored permanently.[274] The library neither seeks the approval of the Division of Archives and Records Management nor does it file the requisite forms.[275]

Commentary

Based on the response from the Newark Public Library, it appears that in New Jersey, as in so many other states, the state-issued retention schedule for public libraries has not been given much, if any, attention.

The schedule itself demonstrates certain anomalies. Although it includes a record series for circulation *statistics*, it does not include a series for circulation records that would include the patron's name and materials checked out, even though such information constitutes a "public record." Under the state's confidentiality law, "[l]ibrary records that contain the names or other personally identifying details regarding the users of libraries are confidential."[276] Patron use would include reference requests, searches, videotape checkouts, and interlibrary loan requests—and yet the retention schedule requires that *this* information, including the patron's name, be retained. It is clear from the definition of "public record" that all such information may be destroyed only in accordance with an approved retention schedule.

It also appears that the retention schedule focuses on minimizing the amount of storage space for public records rather than on preserving a record for the future. The retention periods are fairly brief; *none* of the records listed in the library retention schedule are required to be kept permanently. In the general schedule for local agencies, even correspondence is required to be kept for only a few years and very few records are required to be kept permanently. Any scholar seeking information about public libraries fifty years from now will find very little information in New Jersey.

New Mexico

Law

New Mexico's Public Records Act applies only to records kept by a *state* agency, department, bureau, board, commission, institution or other state government organization.[277] Although the state records administrator "may advise and assist county and municipal officials in the formulation of programs for the disposition" of county and municipal records,[278] each county and municipality controls the disposition of its own records. "What the municipality has power to create, it has power to destroy."[279]

Under this law, a State Commission of Public Records administers the Public Records Act, establishing standards, procedures, and techniques for a state records management program. The Commission's administrator also develops record retention schedules for the various state agencies.[280] Knowingly destroying any public record without lawful authority is a fourth-degree felony, resulting in a fine up to $5,000.00 and jail time up to eighteen months.[281]

Response

The state librarian verified that "[t]here is no state-level procedure, policy, or law regarding public library records," except for the law that provides that they are confidential.[282] Thus, each local public library decides for itself when records may be destroyed.

New York

Law

New York's public records law is divided into two parts, one for state agencies and one for local agencies. The commissioner of education is responsible for both.

For state agency records, the state archives "shall acquire, appraise . . . [and] preserve . . . those official records that have been determined to have sufficient historical value or other value to warrant their continued preservation. . . . " It is up to the commissioner to promulgate rules and regulations to effectuate this provision. Furthermore, once the records are transferred to the archives, the commissioner has authority to authorize their destruction. But at least forty days prior to the destruction of state records, the commissioner must send a list of such records to the attorney general, the comptroller, and the state agency that originally had custody of the record to allow any of them to object to the destruction. No destruction will take place if there is an objection.[283]

The Local Government Records Law, enacted in 1987, begins with a clear statement of legislative intent:

The legislature finds that public records are essential to the administration of local government. Public records contain information which allows government programs to function, provides officials with a basis for making decisions, and ensures continuity with past operations. Public records document the legal responsibility of government, protect the rights of citizens, and provide citizens with a means of monitoring government programs and measuring the performance of public officials. Local government records also *reflect the historical development of the government and of the community it serves*. Such records need to be systematically managed to ensure ready access to vital information and to promote the efficient and economical operation of government.[284]

"Local government" includes "any county, city, town, village, school district, board of cooperative educational services, district corporation, public benefit corporation, public corporation, or other government created under state law that is not a state department, division, board, bureau, commission or other agency. . . . " A local government "record" means a "book, paper, map, photograph, or other information-recording device, regardless of physical form or characteristic, that is made, produced, executed, or received by any local government or officer thereof pursuant to law or in connection with the transaction of public business." It does not include "library materials, extra copies of documents . . . and stocks of publications."[285]

Each local government must designate a records management officer to oversee the records management program.[286] The state commissioner of education appoints a local government records advisory council to advise the commissioner about local records policies and procedures.[287] It is the commissioner's responsibility to advise local governments about proper records management and he or she "is authorized to establish requirements for the proper creation, preservation, management and protection of records," including authorization to develop record retention schedules.[288]

"No local officer shall destroy . . . any public record without the consent of the commissioner of education."[289]

Response[290]

The Local Government Records Bureau responded by sending numerous state-issued record retention schedules applicable to various local governmental units, along with a pamphlet entitled "Retention and Disposition of Library System Records."[291] The pamphlet illustrates the kinds of questions likely to be raised in other states. The five-page pamphlet notes that the Local Government Records Law prohibits all public libraries and public or school library systems covered by the law from destroying their records "until the governing body passes a resolution adopting the appropriate 'records retention and disposition schedule.' " It also states that "[r]ecords may include audio and computer tapes, microfilm and optical disks." The pamphlet's primary focus is on the *types* of libraries included in the law's coverage.

Public libraries (which include municipal, public school district, special district, and joint municipal libraries) must adopt a state-established record retention schedule prior to the destruction of any records. Thereafter, they must follow the minimum retention periods set forth in the schedule.

Association libraries (those " 'established and controlled . . . by a group of private individuals operating as an association' and are *not* created by governmental actions") need not follow a state-established retention schedule and may destroy their records at will.

School district and BOCES libraries (Boards of Cooperative Educational Services) may destroy their records only pursuant to the state-established retention schedule mandated for them.

Public library systems must follow the mandated retention schedule unless they are cooperative (i.e., created by the action of member libraries and not governmental units).

School library systems must also follow the mandated retention schedule.[292]

Various published retention schedules apply to these library groups, depending upon whether they are agencies of county, city, or other local governmental units. For example, a separate 50-page retention schedule applies to school districts and BOCES, another 100-page schedule applies to counties, still another 88-page schedule to municipalities (cities, towns, villages, and fire districts).

Public libraries are most likely to be bound by the schedule for counties or municipalities. In addition to retention periods for records common to all county or municipality agencies, both of the schedules have specific chapters for library records. They are identical and consist of the following:

1. Incorporation, chartering, and registration records: Permanent
2. Accession records: 1 year after accessioning procedure becomes obsolete

3. Directory of public library system and member libraries, prepared by public library system (member library's copy): 0 after superseded

4. Borrowing or loaning records, including interlibrary loan: 0 after no longer needed

5. Catalog of holdings
    a. Manuscript or printed catalog: Permanent
    b. Continuously updated catalog: 0 after superseded or obsolete

6. Individual title purchase requisition which has been filled or found to be unfillable: 1 year

7. Records documenting selection of books and other library materials: 1 year

8. Library material censorship and complaint records, including evaluations by staff, patron's complaints and record of final decision: 6 years after last entry

9. Patron's registration for use of rare, valuable, or restricted noncirculating materials: 6 years

The schedule notes that "[s]ome library censorship records deal with serious constitutional issues and may have value for future research" and suggests that these be kept permanently.[293]

The State Archives and Records Administration noted that libraries for *state* agencies are bound by the state public records law. This means that each agency must request authorization from the commissioner of education to destroy its own library records, as with any other agency record.[294]

Commentary

Little more need be said of New York's records management program. It is sophisticated, comprehensive, published, clear, and accessible. It is one of the few programs that recognizes that library circulation and registration records are public records that must be included in the retention schedule. It is also unique in its statement of legislative intent, recognizing the value of keeping some records "simply" because of their historical value. Unfortunately, for historians, the retention periods of library records seem to be designed more for efficiency than for history.

North Carolina

Law

The state's public records law governing the destruction of governmental records applies not only to state agencies but also to "every public office, ... institution, board, commission, bureau, council, department, authority or other unit of government of the State or of any county, unit, special district or other political subdivision of government."[295] It applies to "all documents, papers, letters, maps, books, photographs, films, sound recordings, magnetic or other tapes, electronic data-processing records, artifacts, or other documentary material, regardless of physical form or characteristics, made or received pursuant to law or ordinance in connection with the transaction of public business."[296]

No person may destroy a public record without the consent of the Department of Cultural Resources. Doing so is a misdemeanor, resulting in a fine of $10.00 to $500.00.[297] Obtaining the Department's consent requires the custodian of the record to certify that the record has "no further use or value for official business"; the Department must then certify that the record has "no further use or value for research or reference." Then the governing body of the county, city, municipality, or other subdivision may authorize destruction. The governing body's minutes must contain this certification and authorization.[298]

The law also provides for the preparation of retention schedules to make the authorization process more efficient. The Department of Cultural Resources must approve the schedule and it thereafter authorizes the destruction of records contained in it.[299]

Response

The State Archives and Records administrator included in his response a copy of the retention and disposition schedule for North Carolina's public libraries, approved in 1987. Because of its status as a state agency, the State Library is governed by a different schedule.[300] The state offers various workshops to assist governmental agencies in the administration of the records management program. The retention schedule for libraries contains six categories, the first five of which are common to many governmental agencies: administrative and management records, budget and fiscal records, legal records, office administration records, personnel records, and programs operational records.

The administrative and management records series includes retention periods for "[o]fficial records and materials created and accumulated during operations of public libraries." They include, among other materials, the governing/advisory board records (minutes, bylaws, correspondence, etc.). The schedule mandates that minutes and bylaws be transferred to the State Records Center for microfilming and then returned. One duplicate copy goes to the State Records Center for security and the original is retained permanently. Remaining records in this series are destroyed when their "administrative value" ends.

The programs operational records series includes "[o]fficial records and materials created and accumulated in the performance of routine administrative tasks in the public libraries." They include, among other materials, circulation records in manual or electronic form. The schedule provides that patron overdue records are destroyed "in accordance with local board policy" and other records are destroyed when the "transaction is completed." Statistical materials concerning intercounty or interlibrary loans are destroyed when their "reference value ends." Remaining intercounty or interlibrary loan materials are destroyed when the "transaction has been completed." Patron registration records are destroyed when "superseded or obsolete." Statistics for circulation, voter and patron registration, reference questions answered, and such are destroyed when their "administrative value ends and after 5 years, whichever is later." The *only* programs operational records of the thirty-four listed that must be retained permanently are check-in records for federal documents.

Commentary

The state law is comprehensive, including governmental units at all levels and records of any format. Furthermore, the retention schedule designed specifically for public libraries is very helpful. It also recognizes that circulation and registration records are public records and must be included in the schedule. Unfortunately, the retention periods appear to focus on record efficiency and privacy at the expense of research and historical value.

North Dakota

Law

North Dakota's Records Management Act applies to state agencies only, thereby excluding county and municipal libraries. It places records management in the hands of the state records administrator, who has responsibility for establishing standards, procedures, and techniques for records management and for establishing standards for the preparation of retention schedules for state records.[301] The head of each state agency must submit to the administrator proposed record retention and disposition schedules for agency records, proposing the minimum time records should be retained because of their administrative, legal, or fiscal value. The agency head must also submit a list of records that no longer have any such value.[302] The administrator, in consultation with the agency head, the attorney general, and the state archivist, must determine which records have continuing value so as to be retained, and which records no longer possess "administrative, legal, or fiscal value" and thus may be destroyed.[303] The agency or department head and the state archivist must review any records prior to destruction; "[a]ny records found to be of permanent value for research, reference, or other use appropriate to document the organization, function, policies, and transactions of government must be transferred to the state archivist for preservation as archival resources."[304]

A state "record" includes a "document, book, paper, photograph, sound recording or other material, regardless of physical form or characteristics, made or received pursuant to law or in connection with the transaction of official business." It does not include "[l]ibrary and museum material made or acquired and preserved solely for reference or exhibition purposes, extra copies of documents . . . and stocks of publications and of processed documents."[305]

As for governmental records that are not state records, the state records administrator must adopt "rules . . . for a uniform system of . . . retention, and final disposition of county, city, and park district records." County, city, and park district offices, departments, and agencies *may* adopt these schedules, but they are not required to.[306]

Response

The chief librarian for the State Historical Society included in her response a copy of the *North Dakota City Records Management Manual*.[307] She also indicated that no library schedules appear in the county records manual. The city manual contains three pages of retention periods for various record series. Many categories are typical of any agency: budget, cancelled checks, receipt and disbursement ledgers, accounts payable, and so on. Others unique to the library include:

Library Board Minutes: Retain permanently (archival and administrative value)

Monthly Newsletters: Retain for 3 years, then transfer to archives (archival and administrative value)

Book Reserved Program (borrower's name, phone number, and title of book on reserve): Retain until request filled, then dispose by shredding (administrative value)

Interlibrary Loan Program (requests made and received logs, list of program participants, etc.): Retain for 2 years, then dispose by shredding (administrative value)

Patron List (card number, name, address, zip, phone number, date of birth): Retain until updated, then dispose by landfill (administrative value)

Annual Reports (usage statistics for the year, synopsis of employees, list of board members, financial status, etc.): Retain for 10 years, then transfer to archives (archival and administrative value)[308]

A separate record retention schedule has been established for the State Archives & Historical Research Library. It includes retention periods for such records as microfilm order forms, donor files, accession records, reading room register, researcher's registration form, statistical reports, and other administrative records. The only materials that circulate from this library are microfilmed rolls of newspapers.[309]

Commentary

The retention periods for library records in North Dakota reflect a concern that certain records have a historical or archival value beyond the period of time when they may no longer be needed for administrative purposes. Thus, a number of records are kept permanently. The schedule also reflects an awareness that some records, though confidential, are still public records that must be included in retention schedules. However, circulation records are inexplicably absent from the list, even though interlibrary loan, patron register, and book reserve records are included. Under North Dakota law, all of these are considered "private" for purposes of public access under the open records act,[310] but are included in the definition of "record" in the retention act.

Ohio

Law

The state's records management laws vary, depending upon whether the records are held by *state* or *local* governmental units. "Records," whether state or local, include "any document, device, or item, regardless of physical form or characteristic, created or received by or coming under the jurisdiction of any public office of the state or its political subdivisions, which serves to document the organization, functions, policies, decisions, procedures, operations, or other activities of the office."[311] The Department of Administrative Services is responsible for establishing and administering a records management program for all *state* records. These are records of state agencies only. The Department, in consultation with the state archivist, is to establish standards and procedures for the retention and destruction of state records and to promulgate record retention schedules for the various agencies, providing for the retention of those records that have "sufficient administrative, legal, fiscal, or other value to warrant their further preservation by the state."[312]

The law also provides for the creation of local records commissions. County records commissions are to "provide rules for retention and disposal of records of the county and to review applications for one-time records disposal and schedules of record retention and disposal submitted by county offices." When the commission approves records for disposal, it must send a list of such records to the state auditor for approval. If the auditor does not approve, the records must be retained. Furthermore, before the records are destroyed, the Ohio Historical Society must be given an opportunity to select records "of continuing historical value" for its collection.[313]

Records commissions for cities (municipal corporations), townships, and school districts function in the same way as county commissions, including the notification to the state auditor and Ohio Historical Society.[314] No public records may be destroyed "except as provided by law or under the rules adopted by the [local] records commissions." Any person who is "aggrieved" because of the wrongful destruction of a record or the threat of wrongful destruction may bring a civil action for an injunction to prevent the destruction or may bring a civil action to recover $1,000.00 for each violation, or both. Both actions also include an award of attorney fees.[315]

Response

There is no state-established record retention schedule for public libraries. The library boards of trustees are responsible for establishing record retention "policies."[316] Public officials in the state point to a 1960 Attorney General's Opinion, which states: "[A] library board of trustees may destroy nonpermanent records of the library when the records have served their entire useful purpose or are in a state of ruin beyond the possibility of use." The state auditor, in a 1988 bulletin to all public libraries, stated: "[I]t is the State Auditor's position that a formal records retention policy be established and followed."[317] He suggested that library boards of trustees establish record retention policies and provided guidelines:

1. Activate a Records Commission
2. Designate a "Records Officer"
3. Conduct a Complete Records Inventory
4. Determine a Retention Period for Records Being Created by Each Department
5. Prepare a Disposal List
6. Approval of the Disposal List. The law does not require libraries to have the disposal list approved; however, it is *suggested* that the list be sent to the Auditor of State (district office) and the Ohio Historical Society prior to actually disposing of the records.
7. Prepare a Certificate of Records Disposal. This certificate serves as the official record of the action. The original could be submitted to the Ohio Historical Society and a copy maintained for the library files.
8. Copies of All Documents Should Be Maintained by Records Commission. A central file will serve as the official record of all actions taken by the records commission. This file should contain the minutes of the commission's meetings and all inventory records disposal lists, approvals and certificates related to the retention of records. These documents should be scheduled for permanent retention.[318]

The 1988 bulletin also includes examples of the kinds of records that should be kept permanently (for example, audit reports, administrative policy and procedure files, board minutes, financial reports) and those for which retention schedules should include nonpermanent periods of retention (for example, insurance policies, bank deposit receipts and cancelled checks, invoices, budgets). This guideline, however, does not include the records unique to public libraries.[319]

The Ohio Historical Society included in its response its own archives-library retention schedule.[320]

Card Catalogs (reading room)	Permanent
Researcher Registers	10 years
Daily Researcher Sign-in Sheets	10 years
Researcher Registration Forms	10 years
Reference Correspondence	5 years
Interlibrary Loan Request Forms	5 years
Interlibrary Loan Correspondence	3 years
State Documents Shelflist	Permanent
Periodical Check-In	Permanent

Commentary

Despite the law's provision for county, city, and township records commissions, public libraries in Ohio are advised to develop their own record retention policies. They are given very little *substantive* guidance; the guidance they are given is primarily *procedural* and clearly advisory only. Thus each library is free to devise its own retention schedule, if at all.

Unfortunately, the law is not as clear as it could be. The local records commissions are to provide rules for the retention and destruction of records and review applications for retention schedules submitted by local offices. But the law does not mandate that all local offices submit such schedules. The responsibility rests with the local records commissions, which apparently have chosen not to act. Furthermore, inexplicably, it has been determined that public libraries are not subject to the local records commissions, as other local offices are. No clear reasons have been provided.

The law's provision for a civil action should records be wrongfully destroyed is a curious one. Although the action for an injunction can be very effective when one knows that destruction is imminent, an action for money damages after the destruction is of little benefit. When is one "aggrieved" by such destruction? It is extremely doubtful that any case could be made that one is directly harmed when a library record is destroyed. Although historians and other scholars argue that such destruction injures society generally, this type of injury is generally not recognized in our legal system. A more effective deterrent would be the imposition of a criminal sanction—that is, a fine or jail time.

Oklahoma

Law

Oklahoma's Records Management Act applies to *state* records only—records in the custody of a state agency, department, office, or other unit of state government. It does not apply to records of political subdivisions in the state,[321] therefore excluding county and municipal public libraries. However, the "governing body of each county, city, town, village, township, district, authority or any public corporation or political entity whether organized and existing under charter or under general law shall promote the principles of efficient records management for local records." The local governing bodies are directed to follow "as far as practical" the records management program established for state records.[322]

That program places responsibility for records management in the hands of the state librarian, designated for this purpose the state records administrator.[323] A "record" includes

document, book, paper, photograph, microfilm, computer tape, disk, record, sound recording, film recording, video record or other material, regardless of physical form or characteristics, made or received pursuant to law or ordinance or in connection with the transaction of official business the expenditure of public funds [sic], or the administration of public property.

It does not include "[l]ibrary and museum material made or acquired and preserved solely for reference or exhibition purposes and stocks of publications."[324]

The administrator's job is to develop standards and procedures for records management and for the preparation of record retention schedules, establishing which records should be retained because of their "continuing value" and which can be destroyed because they no longer possess "sufficient administrative, legal, or fiscal value to warrant their further keeping."[325] The head of each state agency must submit to the administrator proposed retention schedules for the records in its custody and a list of records no longer "needed in the transaction of current business and that do not have sufficient administrative, legal or fiscal value to warrant their further keeping."[326]

The agency must "consult with the State Librarian [the administrator]" to determine if the records should be deposited in the State Library Archives. If so, the agency must apply to the Archives and Records Commission for transfer to the archives. If not, the agency must apply to the Commission for permission to destroy the records.[327] No record can be destroyed unless the Archives and Records Commission determines it "has

no further administrative, legal, fiscal, research or historical value."[328]
Once the Commission receives the application for transfer or destruction,
the Commission can either authorize the destruction or order the record
transferred to the State Library archives. But the Commission may not
order the destruction of any record less than five years old "except upon
a showing of good cause by the [state] agency or the Archives and Records
Division of the . . . Department of Libraries and a unanimous vote of the
members of the Commission, or their designees, present."[329]

Response

The director of the state Department of Libraries indicated that, although state records management practices are strong, local practices are
in disarray, primarily because of the lack of a state law that governs local
records.[330]

The state's largest public library follows its "established but unwritten
retention policies" in determining when to destroy library records. Department managers must approve the destruction. The library's "unwritten" retention policy is as follows:

1. Circulation records are automatically erased by computer upon return of the
   material.
2. Circulation records for unreturned materials are erased after three years.
3. Unused patron cards are erased after five years.
4. Employee personnel files are retained permanently; the files of unsuccessful
   applicants are retained for three years.
5. Financial records relating to purchases and payroll are retained for five years,
   upon the advice of the library's auditors.[331]

Commentary

Obviously, a state law governing the retention of county and city records
would assist public librarians in determining when library records may be
destroyed. Although attempts have been made to pass such laws, they have
died in committee.[332] Until that time, each public library may toss records
at will.

One obvious advantage in passage of a local records law is demonstrated
in the current statute that applies to state records. In determining which
records may be destroyed, state agencies must consider the records' "administrative, legal, and fiscal" value. But the state's Archives and Records
Commission must authorize destruction of any state record, taking into
account not only the administrative, legal, and fiscal value of a record, but
also its research and historical value. This scrutiny should prevent the
sweeping destruction of records that appear to be of no further value to
administrators, but that may hold value for historians and other scholars

in the future. Such scrutiny is just as important for local records as it is for state records. As demonstrated in the retention policy of the state's largest library system, the focus of record retention policies is most likely to be on administrative, legal, and fiscal values.

Oregon

Law

The public records *policy* is more clearly defined in Oregon than in any other state. The introductory statute to the Oregon public records law states that the legislature finds:

(a) The records of the state and its political subdivisions [cities, counties, districts, or other municipal or public corporations] are so interrelated and interdependent, that the decision as to what records are retained or destroyed is a matter of state-wide public policy.

(b) The interest and concern of citizens in public records recognizes no jurisdictional boundaries, and extends to such records wherever they may be found in Oregon.

(c) . . . the state and its political subdivisions have a responsibility to insure orderly retention and destruction of all public records . . . and to insure the preservation of public records of value for administrative, legal and research purposes.[333]

A "public record" is defined as "a document, book, paper, photograph, file, sound recording, machine readable electronic record or other material, . . . regardless of physical form or characteristics, made, received, filed or recorded in pursuance of law or in connection with the transaction of public business, *whether or not confidential or restricted in use.*"[334] It does not include "[l]ibrary and museum materials made or acquired and preserved solely for reference or exhibition," "[e]xtra copies" of documents, "[a] stock of publications," Legislative Assembly records, or certain archaeological records.[335]

The secretary of state serves as the public records administrator, with the state archivist serving under his or her control and supervision.[336] It is the state archivist's responsibility to provide instructions and forms for various state and local officials to obtain authorization to destroy records in their custody. The archivist may give either "specific or continuing authorization for the retention or disposition of public records" in the officials' custody.[337] Continuing authorization would be granted by means of a retention schedule approved by the archivist. Authorization for destruction may be given only after the archivist considers the record's administrative, legal, or research purpose.[338]

Response

The state archivist's office stated: "The Oregon State Archives Division has responsibility for scheduling of public records at all levels of government. . . . We have a general schedule that is part of our administrative rules. Public libraries within the state can apply the general schedule to applicable record series that they create. We are developing a general schedule for cities," which includes a section for libraries. The archivist's office included a draft of that schedule. The office also approves special schedules submitted by various governmental units. Some cities adopt their special schedules as an ordinance.[339]

The proposed retention schedule for cities included the following retention periods specifically for library records:

Accession registers, catalogs, circulation cards, master shelf lists/inventories: Until superseded or obsolete

Borrower registration records: Until superseded or 1 year after expiration

Interlibrary loan records: 30 days after materials returned to owner library

Library board meeting records:

    Minutes, agendas, indexes, exhibits: Permanent

    Significant related records: 10 years

    Tape recordings of meetings: 1 year after minutes approved

Library publications (publications distributed to advertise library services, programs, and activities. May include brochures, activities calendars, bookmobile schedules, special events flyers, and other records): Contact the State Archives for appraisal assistance

Monthly library reports: 5 years

Annual reports to Oregon State Library: Permanent

In addition to this proposed city schedule, the archivist's office also included a copy of an approved special records retention schedule for the City of Salem Library. This schedule contains thirty-six record series and includes both "common" records (fiscal, personnel, general administrative records) and records unique to public libraries.

Commentary

Two provisions of Oregon law are striking. First of all, it is rare to have such a clear, comprehensive statement of legislative policy as appears in this state. It is notable that the policy includes emphasis on the *research* value that records have. Second, the definition of "public record" specifically includes confidential records, mandating that such records may not be destroyed merely because they are confidential.

The development of record retention schedules in Oregon is obviously in flux. But the state is well on its way to developing a sound retention schedule for all governmental units. Included in its proposed city schedule is a directive that librarians seek archivist assistance before destroying library publications. This advice is sound for many of the record series, because an archivist is more likely to consider the historical or research value of a record than another administrator might.

Pennsylvania

Law

Pennsylvania has both municipal and county records acts. The Municipal Records Act applies to cities of the third class, boroughs, incorporated towns, townships of the first and second class, and "any municipal authority created by any of these municipalities." The Act governs the retention and destruction of municipal public records, defined as "any papers, books, maps, photographs or other documentary materials, regardless of physical form or characteristics, made or received by a municipality or a municipal government agency in pursuance of law or in connection with the exercise of its legitimate functions and the discharge of its responsibilities."[340]

The law provides that "[c]ertain public records . . . shall be destroyed . . . if the disposition is in conformance with schedules and regulations which shall be . . . promulgated by the Local Government Records Committee."[341] That committee is established under the Pennsylvania Historical and Museum Commission and is composed of various state and local governmental officials.[342] The Commission is responsible for submitting proposed retention schedules to the Committee for its approval and for advising the municipalities of the applicable approved schedules.[343] Once any schedule has been approved by the Committee and the Commission has advised the municipalities of the approval, the schedule "may be acted upon by the municipalities until superseded. . . . Each municipality shall declare its intent to follow such schedule by municipal ordinance or resolution. . . ."[344]

A County Records Committee consists of various state and county officials. The Pennsylvania Historical and Museum Commission is to assist the Committee as far as possible and to enforce any retention schedules that the Committee develops.[345] The records governed by this statute are defined in the same way as municipal records, except that they are in the custody of the county. Specifically excluded are "[u]nofficial published material used solely for reference purposes; extra copies; . . . drafts, work copies and notes made merely as a matter of convenience by county officers . . . ; and stocks of publications."[346]

The County Records Committee is responsible for preparing retention schedules for county records.[347] "County officers in counties of the second,

second A, third, fourth, fifth, sixth, seventh and eighth class may dispose
of all county records in their custody, provided they follow the schedules
... and provided that the Pennsylvania Historical and Museum Commission ... certifies that such disposal is in accordance with the established
schedules."[348]

Response

Schedules prepared by the Pennsylvania Historical and Museum Commission do not apply to libraries in Philadelphia, which has its own Records
Department, nor do they apply to second class cities such as Pittsburgh.[349]
The county government schedule applies to counties of the second to eighth
class. It provides instructions about record retention and destruction and
includes retention periods for common records, such as financial, payroll,
and purchasing records. In addition, a specific library record retention
schedule is included, which provides the following retention periods:

Library Board Rules and Regulations: Retain 5 years after revoked or superseded.

Minutes of the Library Board: Retain permanently for administrative, legal and
historical purposes.

Patron Registration Files: Retain 3 years after expiration of card.

Records of Library Use (these records usually contain daily, weekly, and monthly
circulation statistics): Retain 2 years.[350]

Retention schedules for municipal libraries are similar, but records of
library use must be retained for *five* years, rather than for two, and the
schedule contains no record series for patron registration files. Operating
and maintenance records must be kept for five years.[351]

Commentary

The county and municipality record retention laws do not govern cities
of the first or second class, nor do they govern counties of the first class.
They govern only those libraries defined under the local and county records
laws. Moreover, the law regarding *municipalities* sounds advisory only.
Although the county records act states that the defined county officers may
dispose of their records only if they follow the established schedules, the
municipality act provides that municipalities "may" act upon the schedule.

Rhode Island

Law

Rhode Island has a comprehensive public record retention and disposal
scheme. The law applies to

any executive, legislative, judicial, regulatory, administrative body of the state or any political subdivision thereof; including, but not limited to any department, division, agency, commission, board, office, bureau, authority, any school, fire or water district, or other agency of Rhode Island state or local government which exercises governmental functions, or any other public or private agency, person, partnership, corporation, or business entity acting on behalf of any public agency.[352]

The law governs the disposition of "public records," which include "all documents, papers, letters, maps, books, tapes, photographs, films, sound recordings, or other material regardless of physical form or characteristics made or received pursuant to law or ordinance or in connection with the transaction of official business by any agency."[353]

No public record may be destroyed without the consent of the public records administration program in the Department of Administration.[354] The Public Records Administration Act provides that the Department of Administration is responsible for establishing a record retention and destruction program and may appoint an administrator (then designated the public records administrator) for that purpose.[355] The Department and its administrator are to develop standards, procedures, and techniques for proper and efficient records management and are to educate and train all agencies in such management.

Each state and local agency must prepare a "record control schedule" and submit it to the Department of Administration for approval.[356] A "record control schedule" is defined as a "document establishing the official retention, maintenance, and disposal requirements" for each record series, "based on administrative, legal, fiscal, and historical values" of the records.[357]

The state archivist is responsible for the administration of records that have "permanent historical or other value."[358] All public officers who have custody of public records have an obligation to consult periodically with the archivist, the state auditor, and the attorney general to determine which of its records have permanent value. Those without permanent value should be destroyed pursuant to an established record control schedule.[359] Each agency must "[e]stablish and maintain an active and continuing program for the preservation of records of permanent legal or historical value," designating an agency records officer for such purpose.[360] Any officer or employee violating these provisions is guilty of a misdemeanor, subject to a fine up to $1,000.00 or jail time up to one year.[361]

Response

Responses indicate that libraries in the state are aware of the state law governing record retention.[362] The Providence Public Library reports that it keeps auditors' reports for ten years and that patron records are purged if there is no activity for three years. Circulation records are deleted upon completion of each transaction.[363]

Commentary

Rhode Island's statute is very comprehensive, including even *private* agencies, persons, or business entities acting on behalf of a public agency. It also includes all records, regardless of format, thus by definition applying to computer and other electronic records. It appears that librarians are aware of the statute and have established retention schedules for library records. Presumably, circulation and other patron records have been incorporated into such schedules. Although library records are *not* public for purposes of the state's open records act,[364] they are public records for purposes of retention laws. In fact, researchers who might otherwise have access to records in the state archives are bound by open records restrictions that protect library records from disclosure, even while held in the archives.[365] Obviously, if the records have a state-approved retention period of zero, the problem becomes moot. The real question is whether such records retain any permanent value such that they should be preserved. Currently, the state's answer is no.

South Carolina

Law

The South Carolina Department of Archives and History is responsible for administering the state's records management program. The program applies to all public records, including "all books, maps, photographs, cards, tapes, recordings, or other documentary materials regardless of physical form or characteristics prepared, owned, used, in the possession of, or retained by a public body."[366] A "public body" refers to

any department of the State, any state board, commission, agency, and authority, any public or governmental body or political subdivision of the State, including counties, municipalities, townships, school districts, and special purpose districts, or any organization, corporation, or agency supported in whole or in part by public funds or expending public funds, including committees, subcommittees, advisory committees, and the like of any such body by whatever name known, and includes any quasi-governmental body of the State and its political subdivisions.[367]

The State Archives has the responsibility of developing a records management program for all agencies, which includes the establishment of standards, procedures, techniques, and schedules for record disposition. The head of each agency is mandated to cooperate with the Archives in pursuance of this goal.[368]

"When requested by the Archives, agencies and subdivisions must assist . . . in . . . establishing records schedules mandating a time period for the retention of each series of records." The "governing body of each subdivision or the executive officer of each agency or body having custody of the records, the Director of the Archives, and in the case of state or regional agencies, the State Budget and Control Board," must approve the schedules. The Archives has authority to prepare general record retention schedules for records common to agencies and subdivisions, but agencies and subdivisions must be given power to "opt out" of the general schedule in favor of their own approved schedule. "No records of long term or enduring value . . . including those filed, kept, or stored electronically . . . may be . . . destroyed, or erased without an approved records schedule."[369] Any person who unlawfully destroys a public record is guilty of a misdemeanor and subject to a fine of $200.00 to $5,000.00.[370]

Response

The state's public records act underwent major amendment in 1990. Because the changes are fairly recent, retention schedules have not yet been completed for many of the agencies. The state Department of Archives and History reports that no general retention schedules have been prepared. The Department has had "very limited experience with local libraries" because most county governments are more interested in other types of records and "[m]ost libraries in the state have yet to seek our services."[371] Two libraries that have sought assistance with particular record series are the Richland County Public Library Reference Department and the Beaufort County Library. Both of them involved the retention of specific newspaper articles. Both of them established permanent retention of the articles by means of microfilm storage.[372]

The State Records Center responded by sending fifty-nine different Record Series Retention/Disposition Schedules approved by the Department of Archives and History for the South Carolina State Library.[373] Most of these originated in the library's administrative department and provided retention periods for such items as State Library Board Monthly Reports (retain in Library for six years, then send to Department of Archives and History for screening for disposal or permanent retention), correspondence (three years), personnel files (thirty years after termination), and various fiscal and budget files. Some of the schedules originated in divisions in charge of field service and services to the blind and handicapped. The technical services division has approved retention schedules for various record series, including book orders (five years) and accessions by class (retain in the Library for five years after disposal of the book, then transfer to Department of Archives and History for screening for disposal or permanent retention).

In addition to including these schedules, the State Records Center responded that records may be destroyed only in accordance with approved schedules and that, before destruction, the agency must submit to the State Archives a records destruction authorization form.[374]

Commentary

Several features of South Carolina law are unique. First, the definition of public records for retention laws is the same as that for the state's Open Records Act. Under this Act, library records are public records but "are not considered to be made open to the public."[375] Given this wording, it is clear that such records should be destroyed only pursuant to an approved retention schedule. Second, the use of an automated circulation system would not excuse the destruction of such records; the law specifically provides that records stored electronically cannot be destroyed without an approved schedule. Finally, the law provides a unique "opt out" provision, which allows county and municipal agencies to exclude themselves from a general schedule if they choose to develop and submit for approval their own schedules.

South Dakota

Law

South Dakota's records management program is mandatory for state records but discretionary for county and municipal records. Thus, libraries supported by counties and municipalities are bound only by the mandates of their local units. "State records" include any "document, book, paper, photograph, sound recording, or other material, regardless of physical form or characteristics, made or received pursuant to law or ordinance or in connection with the transaction of official business." They do not include "[l]ibrary and museum material made or acquired and preserved solely for reference or exhibition purposes, extra copies of documents . . . and stocks of publications."[376]

A state records board under the direction of the Bureau of Administration administers the program for state records. "No record shall be destroyed . . . by any agency of the state unless it is determined by majority vote of such board that the record has no further administrative, legal, fiscal, research or historical value."[377] The head of each state agency must submit to the Bureau of Administration for approval a proposed record retention schedule.[378]

Although South Dakota's records management program applies only to state records, the governing bodies of counties, cities, towns, townships, districts, authorities, and any public corporations and political entities are directed to "promote and implement the principles of efficient records management for local records." These local governing bodies "may, as far as practical, follow the program established for the management of state records."[379]

Any person who intentionally destroys a public record, knowing that he or she lacks authority to do so, commits a Class 6 felony, which is punishable by up to two years in prison or $2,000.00 in fines, or both. If the crime is committed by a public official who has custody of the record, it is a Class 5 felony, punishable by up to five years in prison and, in addition, a $5,000.00 fine may be imposed.[380] If the criminal perpetrator is a public official or employee, he or she will also be discharged.[381]

Response

The state librarian responds that public libraries in the state are governed by local decision in the determination of library record retention.[382] The Sioux Falls public librarian reports that state law covers all financial, personnel, and historical information. "Rigid steps" adopted by the city must be taken prior to destruction of library records, and the City Commission must approve such destruction. The librarian also reports that "[c]omputerized circulation files are not covered by . . . state laws" and the library has established its own guidelines for purging them.[383]

Commentary

The definition of public record would ordinarily encompass circulation records even though they are by law confidential;[384] such records are documents or papers or other materials made in connection with the transaction of official business. But here the record retention laws apply only to the records of *state* agencies, thereby excluding county and local library records. If local governmental entities adopt the definition for their records management programs, circulation records would be included. If libraries believe that such records have no retention value, they should be included in the retention schedules with a retention period of zero. Simply excluding them from consideration opens the way for potential abuse in other agencies, which may determine that certain records are also excluded, and may inadvertently subject a public official to criminal liability.

Tennessee

Law

The State Public Records Commission is responsible for the proper disposition of state records, defined as "all documents, papers, letters, maps, books, photographs, microfilms, electronic data processing files and output, films, sound recordings, or other material regardless of physical form or characteristics made or received pursuant to law or ordinance or in connection with the transaction of official business by any governmental agency."[385] When a state agency head certifies that records in his or her custody have reached the end of their retention period, the Commission then either approves or disapproves their destruction. "No record . . . shall be scheduled for destruction without the unanimous approval of the voting members of the public records commission."[386]

In addition to the state Commission, "[t]he county legislative body of each county may create within the county a county public records commission"[387] whose responsibility it is to administer a records management program for the "documents, papers, records, books, and books of account in all county offices" and the "documents, papers, records, books of account and minutes of the governing body of any municipal corporation . . . or of any office or department of such municipal corporation. . . ."[388] "No record of any municipal corporation required by law to be kept shall be ordered destroyed by the county records commission except with the concurrence of the governing body of the municipality."[389] The county records commission has authority to develop procedures for the disposition of public records,[390] relying for assistance upon guides prepared by the University of Tennessee's Institute for Public Service, in cooperation with the State Library and the state Division of Records Management.[391]

Response

The only response came from the State Library Association. Its executive secretary was not aware of any retention schedules that apply to library records. She believes that large public libraries in the state have some knowledge about when library records can be destroyed, but she was not so sure about small county libraries in rural areas.[392]

Commentary

In a telephone interview, an official of the State Library and Archives provided additional information.[393] He indicated that counties may establish their own public records commissions and that approximately one-half of the counties had done so. In those counties, the commissions meet regularly to decide which records could be destroyed in compliance with schedules established by the county technical assistance service, a unit of the University of Tennessee's Institute for Public Service. The commissions then send a request to destroy records to the state archivist. If the archivist approves, the records are destroyed. Counties without public records commissions destroy records whenever they so choose, as do municipal agencies. A bill introduced in the state legislature in January 1993 would have protected all county and municipal records, but it failed to pass.

An unusual provision of Tennessee law mandates that records that are confidential (which would include library records[394]) "shall be so treated by agencies in the maintenance, storage and disposition of such confidential records." Their destruction "shall be in accordance with an approved records disposition authorization from the public records commission."[395] This provision demonstrates clearly that a record which by law is confidential is nevertheless governed by records management laws.

Texas

Law

Texas records management law is divided into two major sections: one applies to state records and one to county and local records. Both of them require some form of authorization before public records can be destroyed. The head of any *state* department or institution may destroy a record in his or her custody only with the approval of the chief executive of the State Library and Archives Commission and only if the record has no further legal, administrative, or historical value. In addition, the state auditor must approve the destruction of fiscal or financial records.[396] A "record" includes "a document, book, paper, photograph, sound recording, or other material, regardless of physical form or characteristics made or received... according to law or in connection with the transaction of official state business." It does not include "library or museum material made or acquired... solely for reference or exhibition purposes, an extra copy of a document... or a stock of publications."[397] Under this law, the heads of state agencies, including the Texas State University System and the State Library, must examine all their records dated earlier than 1952, classify and index them, name a retention period for each, and "request destruction of any worthless record or material."[398] For other records, the agency heads must submit to the director of the Records Management Division of the Texas State Library proposed retention schedules, based on the administrative, legal, or fiscal value of each record series.[399]

Records management laws for *local* governments include counties and district and precinct offices of counties, municipalities, public school districts, and other special-purpose districts or authorities.[400] According to the State Government Code, retention schedules must pass through several steps before they become binding upon local governments. First, the retention schedule, including schedules for records common to the various types of governmental entities, must be prepared by the director/librarian of the Texas State Library and Archives Commission. Second, it must be approved by the Local Government Records Committee, a committee composed of state, county, and municipal officials. Next, the Texas State Library and Archives Commission must adopt the schedules. Finally, the director/librarian of the Commission has the responsibility of distributing the retention schedules to local governments.[401]

The Local Government Records Act was enacted subsequent to the Government Code provisions set forth above. It provides more detailed directions for the establishment of retention schedules for local governments and provides that local governments prepare retention schedules for their own records. In developing the Act, the state legislature specifically found that "the preservation of local government records of permanent value is necessary to provide the people of the state with resources concerning their history."[402] The Act provides that the governing body of all local governments establish a records management program.[403] On or before January 2, 1995, the records management officer of each local governmental unit must submit to the director/librarian of the Texas State Library and Archives Commission a proposed retention schedule for records in his or her custody.[404] If the director approves the schedule, it thereafter governs the disposition of the included records without further notice to the director.[405] "Before the filing of a records control schedule . . . a local government record may be destroyed only with the prior approval of the director and librarian. . . . After the filing . . . a record that does not appear on a . . . schedule . . . may be destroyed only with the prior approval of the director and librarian."[406] A local government officer or employee who knowingly or intentionally destroys a public record in violation of this law commits a Class A misdemeanor, punishable by up to $3,000.00 in fines, one year in jail, or both.[407]

Response

The director of the Local Records Division of the Texas State Library responded that, although general administrative record retention schedules have been established, no retention schedules have yet been established specifically for local libraries; such schedules will be established in the next year or two.[408] The general schedules already prepared include such records as personnel and fiscal documents.[409]

Commentary

Obviously Texas is well on its way to establishing retention schedules for all library records. The legislature, in its statement of intent, has reminded custodians of public records that efficiency is not the only deciding factor in record disposition; historical value also should play a role. The state has also begun to address in its laws the *electronic* storage of public records, setting forth mandates for the establishment of standards and procedures in a new chapter entitled "Electronic Storage of Records."[410] Certainly, this area will receive substantial attention in the future.

Utah

Law

Utah has recently passed a comprehensive Government Records Access and Management Act, which became effective April 1, 1992. The law creates a Division of Archives and Records Service and a State Records Committee, both within the Department of Administrative Services.[411] The Archives administers the state's records management program and establishes standards, procedures, and effective techniques for the program. This includes the development of standards for record retention schedules that provide for the retention of records of continuing value and for the destruction of records that no longer possess "sufficient administrative, historical, legal, or fiscal value to warrant further retention."[412] The Records Committee is responsible for reviewing and approving retention and destruction of records.

As defined by the law, a "governmental entity" includes all state officials and offices in the executive branch that are publicly funded or are "established by the government to carry out the public's business," and it also includes "any political subdivision of the state and any state-funded institution of higher education or public education." If a political subdivision has adopted an ordinance or policy of its own relating to information practices, it is excluded from the coverage of this act.[413] A "record" includes "all books, letters, documents, papers, maps, plans, photographs, films, cards, tapes, recordings, or other documentary materials, and electronic data regardless of physical form or characteristics, prepared, owned, used, received, or retained by a governmental entity." It does *not* include the following:

1. Temporary drafts prepared for personal use;
2. Materials owned by an individual in his private capacity;
3. Materials with copyright protection unless the copyright is owned by a governmental entity;
4. Proprietary software;
5. Junk mail or commercial publications;
6. Books and other cataloged, indexed, or inventoried materials held by a library open to the public;
7. Personal notes made by members of the judiciary as part of their deliberative process;
8. Computer programs (defined as instructions that allow a computer system to function as designed to provide storage and retrieval of data and other materials that explain how to use the program) developed or purchased by the government for its own use.[414]

A "*public* record" does not include a record classified as "private"; library patron records are classified as private.[415]

The chief administrative officer of each governmental entity must establish a records management program in his or her office, appoint a records officer, and submit to the state archivist a proposed retention schedule for approval by the Records Committee.[416] No record created by a govern-

mental entity can be destroyed except as provided in this law.[417] Violation
of the law is a Class B misdemeanor, which carries a penalty of up to six
months in jail and $1,000.00 in fines.[418] In addition, any public employee
who willfully violates the Act is subject to suspension without pay or discharge (after a hearing). The state may also face a civil action for damages,
including exemplary damages, court costs, and attorney fees.[419]

Response

The Director of the Utah State Archives responds that the development
of a record retention schedule applicable to public libraries is in progress
and that libraries are working with his office to establish the schedules. As
envisioned by the new law, the State Records Committee will have authority to approve the destruction of library records.[420]

The Director of the Salt Lake County Library System is also well aware
of the new law and anticipates that retention schedules applicable to public
libraries will be developed within the next year. She has been involved
with the development of the new law over the past few years and anticipates
some revisions as the need develops. She states that, under the new law,
library records that identify an individual patron are classified as private.[421]

Commentary

As in Texas, this law is recent and the development of retention schedules
is in transition. Most likely because the law is so new, it defines in more
detail than older laws the kinds of records that are not included in the
law's coverage and specifically defines electronic data as a "record."

The definition of library records as "private" raises questions. Although
"records of publicly funded libraries that . . . identify a patron" are classified as "private,"[422] they are nevertheless "records." They are not *public*
records.[423] But in determining whether records can be destroyed without
approval by the Records Committee, the law repeatedly refers to "records," not merely to "public" records. Therefore, all library retention
schedules should include retention periods for private records as well as
others. Otherwise, destroying them by means of a computerized purging
system constitutes a Class B misdemeanor.

Vermont

Law

A custodian of public records in Vermont cannot destroy any of those
records without first submitting to the commissioner of General Services
a list of those records and an application for permission to destroy them.
Within sixty days of the application, the commissioner, with the advice of
the state Public Records Advisory Board, will order the preservation or

destruction or other disposition of the listed records.[424] The Public Records Advisory Board consists of the secretary of state, the director of the state historical society, the auditor of accounts, and two other members representing municipal or public interests.[425] The commissioner may adopt rules "necessary for the effectual preservation of all public records in this state."[426] Anyone who willfully destroys public records, without authority to do so, will be fined $50.00 to $1,000.00.[427]

The head of each *state* agency or department must establish a records management program, including in it "justifiable retention periods for all records." The commissioner must approve the program.[428]

Response. None.

Commentary

Although the brief statute does not mandate that county and municipal governmental agencies develop record retention schedules, doing so would surely facilitate the procedure for obtaining permission to destroy records from the commissioner of General Services.

Although library patron records are not "public records" for purposes of the state's open records law,[429] they do fall within the records management law, therefore requiring the commissioner's approval prior to destruction.

Virginia

Law

In enacting the Virginia Public Records Act, the state's legislature intended to "establish a single body of law applicable to all public officers and employees on the subject of public records management . . . and to ensure that the procedures used to manage and preserve public records will be uniform throughout the Commonwealth."[430] The law binds "all boards, commissions, departments, divisions, institutions, authorities, or parts thereof, of the Commonwealth or its political subdivisions." It applies to all public records, including

all written books, papers, letters, documents, photographs, tapes, microfiche, microfilm, photostats, sound recordings, maps, other documentary materials or information in any recording medium regardless of physical form or characteristics, including electronically recorded data, made or received in pursuance of law or in connection with the transaction of public business by any agency or employee of state government or its political subdivisions.

It does not include "reference books and exhibit materials made or acquired and preserved solely for reference use or exhibition purposes, extra copies of documents . . . and stocks of publications."[431]

The State Library Board is responsible for records management programs in the state,[432] with the advice of the State Public Records Advisory Council consisting of eleven public officials.[433] The Council proposes to the Board rules, regulations, and standards to serve as uniform guidelines for records management. The Board then issues regulations, establishing records management procedures throughout the state. Each public official having custody of public records must designate a records officer in his or her office and prepare for the Board a suggested retention schedule for his or her records.[434]

"No agency shall destroy or discard public records without a retention and disposition schedule approved by the State Librarian." If anyone does so, he or she is guilty of a Class 6 felony, carrying a penalty of jail time up to one year or $2,500.00, or both, or a prison term of one to five years.[435] If he or she is a public official having custody of the record, then wrongful destruction constitutes a Class 1 misdemeanor, carrying a penalty of up to one year in jail, a fine of $2,500.00, or both.[436] Furthermore the public official "shall forfeit his office and be forever incapable of holding any office of honor, profit or trust under the Constitution of Virginia."[437]

Response

The state archivist in the Virginia State Library and Archives responded that retention schedules for library records have been developed. He reports that "all agencies must report their intention to dispose of records on a prescribed form that must be approved before the records can be disposed of by the agency." Copies of the records management manual were sent to all public and institution librarians and to school records managers.[438]

The state archivist included the records retention schedules applicable to public libraries. They consist of schedules designed for county and municipal government and are divided into the following categories: fiscal, personnel, administrative, and library records. The first three apply to all county and municipal departments (including libraries), but the last applies only to public libraries. It includes the following record series:

Catalog Cards, Entries, or Listings: After last copy withdrawn, delete entry or destroy card. Delete or destroy entire catalog when replaced in its entirety.

Circulation Records

    a. Item history: Retain 1 year after last entry, then delete or destroy.

    b. Patron history: After return of item, delete or destroy ... by burning, shredding, or pulping.

Information Requests: Retain until response is completed, then destroy if no longer useful. Destroy any records containing personal information by burning, shredding, or pulping.

Interlibrary Loan Records: Retain 1 year or until completion of reimbursement cycle, whichever is longer, then delete or destroy. Destroy any personal information by burning, shredding, or pulping.

Overdue Notices: Retain until return of item or resolution with patron, then destroy by burning, shredding, or pulping.

Patron Identification or Registration Records: Retain until replaced or inactive, then destroy by burning, shredding, or pulping.

Commentary

The established retention schedules are somewhat unique in recognizing that library records, although confidential in Virginia,[439] are nevertheless public records subject to the records management laws. The law specifically includes electronically recorded data in its definition of "record." The law is also unique in that it defines terms that are commonly used in records management statutes. "Administrative value" means a record that has "continuing utility in the operation of an agency." "Legal value" means that a record documents "actions taken in the protection and proving of legal or civil rights and obligations of individuals and agencies." "Fiscal value" means that a record is "needed to document and verify financial authorizations, obligations and transactions." And "historical value" means that a record contains "unique information, regardless of age, which provides understanding of some aspect of the government and promotes the development of an informed and enlightened citizenry."[440] This broad definition of historical value should encourage record custodians to propose retention schedules that focus on long-term value, rather than simply on administrative value of library records. Unfortunately, the library record retention schedule does not reflect this emphasis.

Washington

Law

Washington divides its records management statute into two parts, one for *state* records and one for *local* records. However, both sections share a common definition for relevant terms. For both, a "public record" includes

any paper, correspondence, completed form, bound record book, photograph, film, sound recording, map drawing, machine-readable material, or other document, regardless of physical form or characteristics, and including such copies thereof, that have been made by or received by any agency of the state . . . in connection with the transaction of public business, and legislative records.[441]

The state subdivides public records into official public records and other public records. An "official public record" includes

all original vouchers, receipts, and other documents necessary to isolate and prove
the validity of every transaction relating to the receipt, use, and disposition of all
public property and public income from all sources whatsoever; all agreements and
contracts to which the state . . . or any agency thereof may be a party; all fidelity,
surety, and performance bonds; all claims filed against the state . . . or any agency
thereof; all records or documents required by law to be filed with or kept by any
agency . . . ; all legislative records . . . ; and all other documents or records determined by the records committee . . . to be official public records.[442]

"Office files and memoranda" are not official public records. They include
"such records as correspondence, exhibits, drawings, maps, completed
forms, or documents" that are *not* classified as official public records. They
also include duplicate copies of official records filed with any agency, "documents and reports made for the internal administration of the office to
which they pertain but not required by law to be filed or kept with such
agency; and other documents or records as determined by the records
committee to be office files and memoranda."[443]

All public records, both official and nonofficial, may be destroyed only
pursuant to the records management law. The Division of Archives and
Records Management, under the direction of the state archivist, is responsible for establishing record retention schedules for all *state* departments and other agencies of *state* government.[444] Every department or other
agency of state government must designate a records officer, who has
responsibility for coordinating the records management program and reviewing annually the established retention schedule to ensure its currency
and thoroughness.[445] The Records Committee, consisting of various state
officials, is responsible for approving, modifying, or disapproving all retention schedules.[446]

Destruction of any *official* public record must be pursuant to a retention
schedule approved by the Records Committee. Official records cannot be
destroyed unless (1) they are six or more years old; or (2) the record
custodian has "made a satisfactory showing . . . that the retention of the
records for a minimum of six years is both unnecessary and uneconomical . . . "; or (3) the originals have been copied or reproduced by a state-
approved method. In addition, if any official record is to be destroyed *prior*
to six years, the director of financial management, the state auditor, and
the attorney general must also approve of the destruction, unless federal
law establishes shorter retention periods for the record.[447]

When an agency or department wishes to destroy *nonofficial* records, it
must recommend such destruction to the Records Committee on approved
forms and the Committee must determine the retention period for such
records.[448]

A separate provision in the law relates to the records of county, municipal, and other local government agencies. Under this provision, the agen-

cies "may request authority to destroy noncurrent public records having no further administrative or legal value by submitting to the Division of Archives and Records Management lists of such records" on state-approved forms. The Local Records Committee—consisting of the state archivist, the chief examiner of the Division of Municipal Corporations, and one other member appointed by the attorney general—reviews the submitted list and may "veto the destruction of any or all items contained therein."[449]

In lieu of this rather inefficient process, these agencies can instead develop a records management program that includes record retention schedules. The schedules are then submitted to the Local Records Committee, which may approve, modify, or disapprove the schedule. Approval must be unanimous. Once approved, the agency need not seek subsequent approval for the destruction of any record included in the schedule. No public record may be destroyed without the approval of the Local Records Committee, either on an ad hoc basis or by means of the approved retention schedule.[450]

In addition, *official* public records less than six years old in the custody of local, municipal, or other local government agencies may be destroyed only if one of the three conditions set forth above for state records has been met.

Response

Although the State Library indicated it has established a retention schedule that governs library records, it did not include the schedule in its response.[451] The state's library association is aware of the law concerning record retention.[452]

Commentary

It is notable that, in requesting approval for the destruction of specific records, county and municipal officials need weigh only the administrative and legal value. However, because the state archivist sits on the Local Records Committee, presumably he or she will weigh the historical value of the records prior to approving destruction. The state archivist is also responsible for developing retention schedules for state records, thereby ensuring that historical values will be considered there as well.

West Virginia

Law

The state's Records Management and Preservation of Essential Records Act is administered by the secretary of the Department of Administration, designated the state records administrator. The Act focuses primarily on *essential* government records, defined either as "containing information necessary to the operation of government in the emergency created by a disaster" or "containing information necessary to protect the rights and interest of persons or to establish and affirm the powers and duties of governments in the resumption of operations after a disaster."[453] The records administrator's job is to "establish and administer . . . a records management program, which will apply efficient and economical management methods to the . . . preservation and disposal of state records."[454]

A "record" includes a "document, book, paper, photograph, sound recording or other material, regardless of physical form or characteristics, made or received pursuant to law or ordinance or in connection with the transaction of official business." It does not include "[l]ibrary and museum material made or acquired and preserved solely for reference or exhibition purposes, extra copies of documents . . . and stocks of publications."[455]

The records administrator establishes standards, procedures, and techniques for a records management program. He or she develops "standards for the preparation of schedules providing for the retention of *state* records of continuing value and for the prompt and orderly disposal of state records no longer possessing sufficient administrative, legal, or fiscal value to warrant their further keeping."[456] To assist in this goal, state officials must submit to the administrator a list of records in their custody with a recommendation as to which of those are *essential* records[457] and a proposed retention schedule for all records in their custody.[458] No state record may be destroyed unless both the records administrator and the director of the section of archives and history of the Division of Culture and History determine that the record has no further administrative, legal, fiscal, research or historical value.[459]

A "*local* record" is a record of a "county, city, town, authority or any public corporation or political entity whether organized and existing under charter or under general law."[460] Those local records that are essential fall under the purview of the state records administrator, whose job it is to "advise and assist in the establishment of programs for the selection and preservation of essential local records."[461] For local records that are not essential, the local entities are directed to "promote" efficient records management and *may* follow the management program established for state records.[462]

If any public officer destroys any record in his or her custody without proper authority to do so, he or she has committed a misdemeanor, subject to jail time up to one year, and a fine up to $1,000.00, in addition to losing public office and being "forever incapable of holding any office of honor, trust or profit in this State."[463]

Response

No written retention schedule has been established that applies to library records. The library boards and librarians of each public library determine when records may be destroyed.[464]

Commentary

The legislature's declared policy in passage of this law involves "economy and efficiency" and the preservation of records in the face of "all forms of disaster."[465] In determining whether records should be retained, state and local agencies focus on administrative, legal, and fiscal values of records.[466] Fortunately, the records administrator and director of the section of archives and history are directed to weigh the research and historical value of state records prior to their destruction, but this does not apply to local records. Unless a particular library board or director has interest in the research or historical value of particular records, records will most likely be destroyed after they have lost their administrative, fiscal, and legal values.

Wisconsin

Law

Wisconsin has established a records management program for *state* agencies. Counties, cities, towns, villages, and other municipal entities may by ordinance establish a program and retention schedules for their public records, but they are not bound by law to do so.[467] If they do enact an ordinance, the retention period must be at least seven years, unless another law provides for a shorter period or the state Public Records and Forms Board has approved a shorter period.[468] Prior to the destruction of any county or local records, sixty days' notice must be given to the state historical society to allow it to retrieve for preservation any records it deems to have historical value.[469]

The Public Records and Forms Board is responsible for the preservation of important state records. Such "records" include

all books, papers, maps, photographs, films, recordings, or other documentary materials or any copy thereof, regardless of physical form or characteristics, made, or received by any agency of the state or its officers or employees in connection with the transaction of public business, except the records and correspondence of any member of the state legislature.[470]

No state record can be destroyed without the written approval of the Board.[471] To effectuate this provision, state agencies must submit to the Board proposed retention schedules for all records in their custody. Once approved, the schedules are effective for ten years, at which time the agency must resubmit a proposed schedule for the Board's approval.[472]

As for local records, the Board "[u]pon the request of any ... county, town, city, village or school district, may order upon such terms as the board finds necessary to safeguard the legal, financial and historical interests of the state in public records, the destruction, reproduction . . . , temporary or permanent retention . . . of public records." Without such request, the Board *may* establish retention periods for the records of local governmental entities.[473]

"Whoever with intent to injure or defraud destroys . . . any public record is guilty of a Class D felony," punishable by a $10,000.00 fine, five years in prison, or both.[474]

Response

The state has not established written retention schedules applicable to public library records. They are considered municipal records and, "[a]ccording to the Wisconsin Public Records and Forms Board, very few municipalities have local ordinances covering destruction of records or preservation."[475] The state historian reports that retention periods vary from one county to another. The larger counties and cities have their own records management committees that draft retention schedules. Before destruction of any records, the historical society is to be notified, but the state historian noted that library records are not generally among those submitted to him.[476]

Commentary

Because the state's records management laws are mandatory only upon state records, no general retention statutes currently protect valuable library records from destruction. The only safeguard appears to be the sixty-day notice to the state historical society. The criminal penalty applies only when one destroys public records with "intent to injure or defraud."

Wyoming

Law

The director of the state Archives, Museums, and Historical Department is responsible for records management programs in the state. The director must "catalog and arrange retention and transfer schedules on all record files of all state departments and other agencies of state government."[477] Each state department or agency must designate a records officer to work with the director in implementing a records management program.[478]

Before any public record can be destroyed, whether state or local, the state Records Committee, chaired by the director, must approve. When a proposed record retention schedule is submitted to the Committee by state or local departments and agencies, it may approve, disapprove, or modify it. All modifications must be approved by the department or agency that made the request for approval.[479]

A "public record" is defined as "the original and all copies of any paper, correspondence, form, book, photograph, photostat, film, microfilm, sound recording, map, drawing or other document, regardless of physical form or characteristics, which have been made or received in transacting public business by the state, a political subdivision or an agency of the state." Political subdivisions include counties, municipalities, special districts, and other local governmental entities.[480] Public records are classified as either official or as office files and memoranda, but all public records are state property and are subject to the state's retention laws.[481] "Official" public records include

(A) All original vouchers, receipts and other documents necessary to isolate and prove the validity of every transaction relating to the receipt, use and disposition of all public property and public income . . . ;

(B) All agreements and contracts to which the state or any agency or political subdivision thereof is a party;

(C) All fidelity, surety and performance bonds in which the state is a beneficiary;

(D) All claims filed against the state or any agency or political subdivision thereof;

(E) All records or documents required by law to be filed with or kept by any agency of the state; and

(F) All other documents or records determined by the records committee to be official public records.

"Office files and memoranda" include "[a]ll records, correspondence, exhibits, books, booklets, drawings, maps, blank forms, or documents" not classified as "official," all duplicate copies of official records, "[a]ll documents and reports made for the internal administration of the office to which they pertain but not required by law to be filed or kept with the office; and all other documents or records, determined by the records committee to be office files and memoranda."[482]

There is an implied presumption that official public records will be kept for a minimum of ten years, but a shorter retention period will be approved "upon proper and satisfactory showing" that the ten-year period is "unnecessary and uneconomical."[483]

Response

The state has established retention schedules for county library records, included in the state's Records Management Manual.[484] The Manual advises record custodians that all "records dated prior to 1920 should not be destroyed until they have been thoroughly appraised for historical significance by Archives staff." It adds: "Age is not the sole criteria for permanent retention," and offers the services of the state's archivists to assist in an historical appraisal of records. The retention schedule itself consists of forty-one record series, including administrative, fiscal, personnel, and

specific library records. They include, among others, the following retention periods:

Annual Report: 5 years

Bank Statements: 3 years

Board Minutes: Permanent or transfer to state archives.

General Correspondence: 3 years. Evaluate for legal, administrative, and historical
value for transfer to State Archives. Destroy remaining records at discretion of
agency director.

Newsletters/Public Fliers: Destroy at discretion after information becomes noncurrent.

Patron Records: Destroy when superseded or no longer needed, or microfilm and
destroy.

Policy Statements: Retain 5 years after superseded or rescinded.

Commentary

The state-established retention schedules apply to all county libraries.
Wyoming has no city public libraries. The state has an obvious interest in
the historical value of its records, as demonstrated in its Records Management Manual. It recognizes that an "old" record may have historical
value and demonstrates its commitment by offering the services of its
archivists to evaluate the records.

Although patron records are confidential,[485] they are nevertheless public
records for purposes of the records management law. Patron records are
to be retained only for so long as they are "no longer needed," or they
may be microfilmed and then destroyed.

NOTES

1. See Appendix A for a copy of the questionnaire.
2. This list was obtained from Bruce W. Dearstyne, The Management of Local
Government Records: A Guide for Local Officials app. I (1988).
3. This list was obtained from the American Library Association.
4. See Appendix B for a copy of the questionnaire to public librarians and
Appendix C for a copy of the questionnaire to state ALA chapter executives.
5. Ala. Code § 41–13–1 (1975).
6. *Id.* at § 41–13–20, –21, –22.
7. *Id.* at § 41–13–21, –23.
8. *Id.* at § 41–13–24.
9. *Id.* at § 41–13–24.
10. *Id.* at § 36–12–2.
11. *Id.* at § 36–12–5.
12. Response from Richard Y. Wang, appraisal archivist, Records Management
Division, Department of Archives and History.

13. Alabama Department of Archives & History, State General Records Schedules 27 (1990).

14. *Id.* at 39.

15. Alaska Stat. § 40.21.150 (1970).

16. *Id.*

17. *Id.* at § 40.21.080.

18. *Id.* at § 40.21.060.

19. Response from George V. Smith, acting director, Division of Libraries, Archives & Museums, Department of Education.

20. Ariz. Rev. Stat. Ann. § 41–1345 (1992).

21. *Id.* at § 41–1346.

22. *Id.*; Ariz. Rev. Stat. Ann § 13–707 (1989).

23. Ariz. Rev. Stat. Ann. § 41–1347 (1992).

24. Response from Martin Richelsoph, CRM, division director, Department of Library, Archives & Public Records, Records Management Division.

25. Telephone interview with Martin Richelsoph, January 14, 1993.

26. Ark. Code Ann. § 13–4–101, –102 (Michie 1987).

27. *Id.* at § 13–4–105.

28. *Id.* at § 13–3–107.

29. *Id.* at § 13–4–103.

30. Response from John L. Ferguson, state historian, Arkansas History Commission.

31. Response from Linda Bly, assistant director, Central Arkansas Library System.

32. Ark. Code Ann. § 13–2–703 (Michie 1987).

33. Cal. Gov't Code § 14740 et seq. (West 1992).

34. *Id.* at § 26202.

35. Cal. Gov't Code § 26205 (West 1988).

36. *Id.* at § 26205.1.

37. Response from Nancy Zimmelman, archivist II, California State Archives, including in her response retention schedules for the state archives.

38. Response from Cy Silver, consultant, Library Development Services, California State Library.

39. See Cal. Gov't Code § 6254 (West 1980).

40. Colo. Rev. Stat. Ann. § 24–80–102 (West 1990).

41. *Id.* at § 24–80–103, –104.

42. *Id.* at § 24–80–101.

43. Response from Terry Ketelsen, state archivist.

44. See Colo. Rev. Stat. § 24–72–204 (West 1990).

45. Conn. Gen. Stat. Ann. § 11–8, –8a (West 1986).

46. *Id.* at § 11–8a.

47. Response from Office of the Public Records Administrator. The response was in the form of a pamphlet, Records Retention/Disposition Schedules: Municipalities/Towns (1991).

48. *Id.* at iii.

49. *Id.* at vii.

50. One can imply that electronic records would be included because section 9b of this same Title 11 defines a state publication as one that is "printed" or

published, and "printed" is defined as including "all forms . . . regardless of format." See Conn. Gen. Stat. Ann. § 11–9b (West 1986).

51. The state's library confidentiality law can be found in Conn. Gen. Stat. § 11–25 (West 1986). "Public records" is defined in Conn. Gen. Stat. § 1–18 (West 1988).

52. Del. Code Ann. tit. 29, § 503, 504 (1992).

53. *Id.* at § 522, 523.

54. *Id.* at § 504.

55. *Id.* at § 512.

56. *Id.* at § 521.

57. *Id.* at § 502.

58. Response from Penelope A. Rainey, coordinator of Records Services, Delaware State Archives.

59. Response from Charlesa Lowell, deputy state librarian, Delaware Division of Libraries.

60. See Del. Code Ann. tit. 29, § 10002(d) (1992): "For purposes of *this chapter*, the following records shall not be deemed public: . . . Any records of a public library which contain the identity of a user and the books, documents, films, recordings or other property of the library which a patron has used." (emphasis added).

61. D.C. Code Ann. § 1–2902, –2903 (1981).

62. *Id.* at § 1–2901.

63. *Id.* at § 1–2906.

64. *Id.* at § 1–2901.

65. *Id.*

66. *Id.* at § 1–2904.

67. Response from Roxanna L. Deane, chief, Washingtoniana Division, American Library Association (Martin Luther King Memorial Library, Washington, D.C.).

68. Fla. Stat. Ann. § 119.01 (West 1982).

69. *Id.* at § 119.011.

70. *Id.*

71. Seigle v. Barry, 422 So. 2d 63 (Fla. Dist. Ct. App. 1982).

72. Fla. Stat. Ann. § 257.36 (West 1991).

73. Fla. Stat. Ann. § 119.10, 775.082, 775.083 (West 1992).

74. Response from Barratt Wilkins, director, State Library of Florida.

75. General Records Schedule for Local Government Agencies vi (BC–1 Revised).

76. See, e.g., Starting a Records Management Program. See also Basics of Records Management Handbook. They are available from the Records Management Program, Division of Library and Information Services, Florida Department of State.

77. The two-day 1991 Records Management Workshop for Public Libraries had a $40.00 registration fee.

78. Ga. Code Ann. § 45–13–41 (1990).

79. Ga. Code Ann. § 50–18–93 (1975).

80. Ga. Code Ann. § 50–18–92 (1988).

81. Ga. Code Ann. § 50–18–91 (1984).

82. Ga. Code Ann. § 50–18–94 (1974).

83. Ga. Code Ann. § 50–18–91 (1984).

84. Ga. Code Ann. § 50–18–99 (1981).

85. Ga. Code Ann. § 50–18–92 (1988).

86. Ga. Code Ann. § 50–18–99 (1981).

87. Response from Peter E. Schinkel, Schedule Section, Department of Archives and History, Secretary of State. Mr. Schinkel included two publications: Managing Public Records: Common Records Retention Schedules for Municipal Governments (1984), and Managing Public Records: Common Records Retention Schedules for County Governments (1984). Both are published by the Department of Archives and History, Office of Secretary of State.

88. Response from Peter E. Schinkel, Schedule Section, Department of Archives and History, Secretary of State.

89. Response from Joe Forsee, director, Public Library Services, Georgia Department of Education.

90. Ga. Code Ann. § 24–9–46 (1981).

91. Haw. Rev. Stat. § 94–3 (1988).

92. *Id.* at § 710–1017, 706–640, 706–663.

93. Idaho Code § 67–5751, –5752 (1974).

94. Idaho Code § 50–907 (1988).

95. Response from William E. Tydeman, state archivist, Idaho State Historical Society.

96. Response from Marilyn Poertner, assistant director, Boise Public Library.

97. Response from Karen Strege, public library consultant, Northern Field Office, Idaho State Library.

98. Idaho Code § 9–340 (1992).

99. Ill. Ann. Stat. ch. 116, para. 43.5, 43.12 (Smith-Hurd 1991).

100. *Id.* at para. 43.21.

101. *Id.* at para. 43.19.

102. *Id.* at para. 43.20.

103. Ill. Ann. Stat. ch. 116, para. 43.5 (Smith-Hurd 1992).

104. *Id.* at para. 43.103.

105. *Id.* at para. 43.105.

106. *Id.* at para. 43.106, 43.107.

107. *Id.* at para. 43.107.

108. Response from Marlene Devel, deputy director, Illinois State Library.

109. Response from Barbara Cunningham, executive director, Illinois Library Association.

110. Ill. Ann. Stat. ch. 81, para. 1201, 1202; ch. 116, para. 207 (Smith-Hurd 1992).

111. Ind. Code Ann. § 5–15–5.1–3, –5 (West 1989).

112. *Id.* at § 5–15–5.1–19.

113. *Id.* at § 5–15–5.1–1.

114. *Id.*

115. *Id.* at § 5–15–5.1–2.

116. *Id.* at § 5–15–5.1–1.

117. *Id.* at § 5–15–5.1–10.

118. *Id.* at § 5–15–5.1–13, –14.

119. Ind. Code Ann. § 5–15–6–1.5 (West Supp. 1992).

120. *Id.* at § 5–15–6–2.

121. *Id.* at § 5–15–6–3.

122. *Id.* at § 5–15–6–2.5.

123. Ind. Code Ann. § 5–15–6–2.5 (West Supp. 1991).

124. Ind. Code Ann. § 5–15–6–7 (West Supp. 1992).

125. Ind. Code Ann. § 5–15–6–8, 35–50–2–7 (West 1992).

126. Response from Sandi Thompson, public library consultant, Indiana State Library.

127. Responses from Stephen E. Towne, assistant archivist, program director for Local Government Records Program, Indiana State Archives; and Sandi Thompson, public library consultant, Indiana State Library.

128. Response from Stephen E. Towne, assistant archivist, program director for Local Government Records Program, Indiana State Archives.

129. Response from Jeffrey R. Krull, director, Allen County Public Library.

130. Iowa Code Ann. § 304.3, .7 (West 1988).

131. *Id.* at § 304.2.

132. *Id.*

133. *Id.* at § 304.3.

134. Kan. Stat. Ann. § 45–403 (1986).

135. *Id.* at § 45–402.

136. *Id.*

137. *Id.* at § 45–404.

138. *Id.* at § 45–409.

139. Response from Dan Fitzgerald, local records archivist, Kansas State Historical Society.

140. See Kan. Stat. Ann. § 45–221(23) (1986).

141. Ky. Rev. Stat. Ann. § 171.420 (Michie/Bobbs-Merrill 1990).

142. *Id.* at § 171.410.

143. *Id.* at § 171.450.

144. *Id.* at § 171.520.

145. Ky. Op. Att'y Gen. 60–835 (1960).

146. Ky. Rev. Stat. Ann. § 171.530 (Michie/Bobbs-Merrill 1990).

147. *Id.* at § 171.680.

148. *Id.* at § 171.670.

149. *Id.* at § 171.520, 534.040, 532.090.

150. *Id.* at § 171.990.

151. Response from Diana Moses, manager, State Records Branch, Public Records Division, Department for Libraries and Archives; with letter from Richard N. Belding, state archivist and records administrator, Department for Libraries and Archives.

152. La. Rev. Stat. Ann. § 44:401, :402, :405 (West 1992).

153. *Id.* at § 44:402.

154. *Id.* at § 44:411.

155. *Id.* at § 44:407, :408.

156. *Id.* at § 44:422.

157. La. Rev. Stat. Ann. § 44:36 (West 1982).

158. La. Rev. Stat. Ann. § 14:132 (West 1986).

159. Response from Gary O. Rolstad, associate state librarian.

160. La. Rev. Stat. Ann. § 44:402 (West 1992).

161. See *id.* at § 44:13.

162. Me. Rev. Stat. Ann. tit. 30-A, § 1701 (West Supp. 1991).

163. Me. Rev. Stat. Ann. tit. 5, § 92, 94, 95 (West 1983).

164. *Id.* at § 95.

165. *Id.* at § 96.

166. Me. Rev. Stat. Ann. tit. 30-A, § 1702 (West Supp. 1991).

167. *Id.* at § 1703.

168. *Id.* at § 1704.

169. *Id.* at § 1705.

170. *Id.* at § 1707.

171. *Id.* at § tit. 17-A, 1304 & § 4-A (West 1983).

172. Response from Benjamin F. Keating, division director, Maine State Library.

173. Md. Code Ann., State Gov't § 10–632, –633 (1984).

174. *Id.* at § 10–637.

175. *Id.* at § 10–639.

176. *Id.* at § 10–639, –640.

177. Md. Code Ann., Crim. Law § 27–45A (1992).

178. Response from Kevin Swanson, director, State and Local Records Program, State Archives.

179. Md. Regs. Code tit. 14, § 18.02 (Supp. 1987).

180. *Id.*

181. Response from J. Maurice Travillian, assistant state superintendent for libraries, State Department of Education.

182. See Md. Code Ann., State Gov't § 10–616 (1992).

183. *Id.* at § 10–602.

184. Md. Code Ann., State Gov't § 9–1007 (1984).

185. Mass. Gen. Laws Ann. ch. 66, § 8 (West 1991).

186. *Id.* at § 3.

187. *Id.* at § 15.

188. Mass. Gen. Laws Ann. ch. 30, § 42 (1991).

189. *Id.*

190. Response from Kathryn Hammond Baker, assistant archivist for records management and acquisitions, Massachusetts Archives at Columbia Point.

191. Response from Brian Donoghue, librarian, Massachusetts Board of Library Commissioners.

192. Mass. Gen. Laws Ann. ch. 78, § 7 (West 1991).

193. Mich. Comp. Laws Ann. § 18.1284, .1285 (West Supp. 1992).

194. *Id.* at § 18.1287.

195. Mich. Comp. Laws Ann. § 399.5 (West 1988).

196. Mich. Comp. Laws Ann. § 750.491 (West 1991).

197. Response from David J. Johnson, state archivist, State Archives, Department of State.

198. Response from Florence R. Tucker, associate director for support services, Detroit Public Library.

199. Response from Marianne Gessner, executive director, Michigan Library Association.

200. Minn. Stat. Ann. § 138.17 (West 1987).

201. *Id.*

202. *Id.*

203. *Id.*

204. *Id.* at § 138.19.

205. *Id.* at § 138.225.

206. *Id.* at § 609.02.

207. Response from Duane P. Swanson, deputy state archivist, Division of Library and Archives, Minnesota Historical Society. See also response from William G. Asp, director, Office of Library Development and Services.

208. *Id.*

209. "City General Records Retention Schedule," available from the Department of Administration, Data and Records Management Division, St. Paul, Minnesota.

210. Response from Deborah Struzyk, administrative assistant, Minneapolis Public Library and Information Center.

211. Minn. Stat. Ann. § 13.02, 13.40 (West 1987).

212. Miss. Code Ann. § 25–59–3 (1991).

213. *Id.* at § 25–59–7, –15.

214. Response from H. T. Holmes, director, Archives & Library Division, Mississippi Department of Archives and History.

215. Response from Thomas H. Ballard, director, Jackson-Hinds Library System, Jackson, Mississippi.

216. *Id.*

217. Miss. Op. Att'y Gen. May 10, 1985.

218. Miss. Code Ann. § 39–3–365 (1992).

219. Mo. Ann. Stat. § 109.210 (Vernon 1992).

220. *Id.* at § 109.230.

221. *Id.* at § 109.250.

222. *Id.* at § 109.255.

223. *Id.* at § 109.240.

224. *Id.* at § 109.260.

225. *Id.* at § 109.310.

226. Response from Monteria Hightower, associate commissioner for libraries, State Librarian.

227. Mo. Ann. Stat. § 182.815, .817 (Vernon 1991).

228. Mont. Code Ann. § 2–6–201, –202, –204 (1991).

229. *Id.* at § 2–6–212.

230. Neb. Rev. Stat. § 84–1203, –1204 (1989).

231. *Id.* at § 84–1207.

232. *Id.* at § 84–1202.

233. *Id.* at § 84–1212.01.

234. *Id.* at § 84–1214.

235. *Id.* at § 84–1212.02, –1213; 28–106.

236. Response from Steven R. Wolz, public records officer, Nebraska State Historical Society.

237. Response from Rod Wagner, director, Nebraska Library Commission.

238. Response from Michael Phipps, director, Omaha Public Library.

239. Nev. Rev. Stat. Ann. § 239.080 (Michie 1991).
240. *Id.*
241. Nev. Op. Att'y Gen. 906 (April 12, 1950).
242. Nev. Rev. Stat. Ann. § 239.121 (Michie 1991).
243. *Id.* at § 239.124, .051.
244. *Id.* at § 239.125.
245. *Id.* at § 239.124.
246. *Id.* at § 239.121, .123.
247. *Id.* at § 239.310.
248. *Id.* at § 239.320.
249. Response from Robert H. van Straten, state records manager, Division of Archives and Records, Nevada State Library and Archives. He included in his reponse the schedule for public libraries.
250. Nev. Admin. Code ch. 239, § 411 (1989).
251. Response from Carol Madsen, secretary, Nevada Library Association.
252. Response from Lew Rogers, controller, Las Vegas-Clark County Library District.
253. Nev. Rev. Stat. Ann. § 239.013 (Michie 1991).
254. N.H. Rev. Stat. Ann. § 5:25 (1988).
255. *Id.* at § 5:25.
256. *Id.* at § 5:29.
257. *Id.* at § 5:38.
258. *Id.* at § 5:33.
259. *Id.* at § 33-A:1.
260. N.H. Rev. Stat. Ann. § 33-A:4-a (1991).
261. N.H. Rev. Stat. Ann. § 33-A:3 (1988).
262. N.H. Rev. Stat. Ann. § 641:7 (1986), 651:2 (1986 & Supp. 1991).
263. Response from Kendall Wiggin, state librarian, New Hampshire State Library.
264. See N.H. Rev. Stat. Ann. § 5:29 (1991).
265. *Id.* at § 91-A:5, 201–D:11.
266. Response from Kendall Wiggin, state librarian, New Hampshire State Library.
267. N.J. Stat. Ann. § 47:3–16 (West 1989).
268. *Id.* at § 47:3–18, –19, –20. Although the statute refers in various places to the Bureau of Records Management, the Bureau was transferred to the Division of Archives and Records Management in 1983.
269. *Id.* at § 47:3–29; N.J. Stat. Ann. § 2C:43–1, –6 (West Supp. 1992).
270. Response from Joseph L. Falca, records analyst 1, Division of Archives & Records Management, Department of State. Mr. Falca included in his response various state publications, including the public library retention schedule, "County & Municipal General Records Retention Schedule," "Instructions for Preparing 'Request and Authorization for Records Disposal,' " and the disposal request and authorization form.
271. Records Retention and Disposition Schedule, Number 901, Public Library (prepared by New Jersey Division of Archives and Records Management, approved 1989).

272. Request and Authorization for Records Disposal, Form No. CR-AA–0005 (2/85) (prepared by New Jersey Division of Archives and Records Management).

273. Response from Bruce E. Ford, assistant director for technical services, Newark Public Library.

274. *Id.*

275. Telephone interview with Bruce E. Ford, assistant director for technical services, Newark Public Library (March 12, 1993).

276. N.J. Stat. Ann. § 18A:73–43.1 (West 1989).

277. N.M. Stat. Ann. § 14–3–2 (Michie 1991).

278. *Id.* at § 14–3–18.

279. N.M. Op. Att'y Gen. 61–36 (1961–62).

280. N.M. Stat. Ann. § 14–3–3, –4, –6 (Michie 1991).

281. *Id.* at § 30–26–1, 31–18–15.

282. Response from Karen Watkins, state librarian, New Mexico State Library.

283. N.Y. Arts & Cult. Aff. § 57.05 (McKinney 1993).

284. *Id.* at § 57.13 (emphasis added).

285. *Id.* at § 57.17.

286. *Id.* at § 57.19.

287. *Id.* at § 57.21.

288. *Id.* at § 57.23, .25.

289. *Id.* at § 57.25.

290. It was not surprising that New York's records management programs are sophisticated, comprehensive, and well-documented. Mr. Bruce W. Dearstyne, director, External Programs Division, State Archives and Records Administration, has considerable expertise in this area. See Bruce W. Dearstyne; The Management of Local Government Records: A Guide for Local Officials (1988).

291. Warren Broderick, Retention and Disposition of Library and Library System Records (Local Records Information Leaflet No. 6, State Archives and Records Administration, undated). Responses to the questionnaire were received from Bruce W. Dearstyne, director, External Programs Division; from Warren Broderick, senior public records analyst, Local Government Records Bureau; and from Thomas D. Norris, principal public records analyst—all three in the State Archives and Records Administration, State Education Department.

292. Warren Broderick, *supra* note 291.

293. Records Retention and Disposition Schedule CO–2 For Use by Counties 47 (1991); Records Retention and Disposition Schedule MU–1 For Use by Municipalities (Cities, Towns, Villages, and Fire Districts) 42 (1991).

294. Response from Thomas D. Norris, principal public records analyst, Bureau of Records Analysis and Disposition, State Archives and Records Administration. Mr. Norris noted that the retention periods vary from agency to agency, because each agency has "customized" schedules.

295. N.C. Gen. Stat. § 132–1 (1992).

296. *Id.*

297. *Id.* at § 121–5, 132–3.

298. *Id.* at § 121–5.

299. *Id.*

300. Response from David J. Olson, state archives and records administrator, Division of Archives and History, Department of Cultural Resources.

301. N.D. Cent. Code § 54–46–04 (1982).
302. N.D. Cent. Code § 54–46–05 (Supp. 1991).
303. N.D. Cent. Code § 54–46–08 (1982).
304. *Id.* at § 54–46–08.1.
305. *Id.* at § 54–46–02.
306. *Id.* at § 54–46–12.
307. Response from Dolores Vyzralik, chief librarian, State Historical Society of North Dakota. The city records manual is published by the Office of Management and Budget, State Records Management Division, and is dated July 1989.
308. North Dakota City Records Management Manual (Office of Management and Budget, State Records Management Division, July 1989).
309. Response from Dolores Vyzralik, chief librarian, State Historical Society of North Dakota.
310. N.D. Cent. Code § 40–38–12 (1982).
311. Ohio Rev. Code Ann. § 149.011 (Anderson 1990).
312. *Id.* at § 149.33, .331.
313. *Id.* at § 149.38.
314. See *id.* at § 149.39, .41, .42.
315. *Id.* at § 149.351.
316. Response from Mona Connolly, assistant to the state librarian, The State Library of Ohio.
317. Russell L. Rouch (deputy state auditor), Management Advisory Service Bulletin 88–28 (Oct. 19, 1988). Mona Connolly, assistant to the state librarian, included a copy of the Bulletin in her response.
318. *Id.*
319. *Id.*
320. Ohio Historical Society Records Retention Schedule, Archives-Library Division, approved 1980.
321. Okla. Stat. Ann. tit. 67, § 203, 305 (West Supp. 1992).
322. *Id.* at § 207.
323. *Id.* at § 204.
324. *Id.* at § 203.
325. *Id.* at § 205.
326. *Id.* at § 206.
327. *Id.* at § 306.
328. *Id.* at § 210.
329. *Id.* at § 306.
330. Response from Robert Clark, director, Oklahoma Department of Libraries, and telephone interview with Mr. Clark, November 13, 1991.
331. Response from Jimmy Welch, director of system operations, Oklahoma Metropolitan Library System, Oklahoma City.
332. Telephone interview with Robert Clark, director, Oklahoma Department of Libraries, November 13, 1991.
333. Or. Rev. Stat. § 192.001 (1991).
334. *Id.* at § 192.005 (emphasis added).
335. *Id.*
336. *Id.* at § 192.015, 357.815.
337. *Id.* at § 192.105.

338. *Id.*

339. Response from Layne Sawyer, deputy state archivist, Archives Division, Secretary of State. Mr. Sawyer indicated that several cities had recently completed their special schedules, including Beaverton, Salem, Tigard, Lake Oswego, Eugene, and Roseburg.

340. Pa. Stat. Ann. tit. 53, § 9002 (1972).

341. *Id.* at § 9003.

342. *Id.* at § 9005.

343. *Id.* at § 9004.

344. *Id.* at § 9006.

345. Pa. Stat. Ann. tit. 16, § 13001 (1972).

346. Pa. Stat. Ann. tit. 16, § 13002 (Supp. 1991).

347. *Id.* at § 13003.

348. *Id.* at § 13004.

349. Response from Diane Smith Wallace, head, Local Government & Public Services Section, Division of Archival and Records Management Services, Pennsylvania Historical and Museum Commission.

350. Subchapter Q, Library Records, submitted by Diana Smith Wallace, head, Local Government & Public Services Section, Division of Archival and Records Management Services, Pennsylvania Historical and Museum Commission.

351. Pennsylvania Historical and Museum Commission, Division of Archives and Manuscripts, Retention and Disposition Schedule for Records of Pennsylvania: Municipalities 21 (May 17, 1982).

352. R.I. Gen. Laws § 38–1–1.1 (1990). See also R.I. Gen. Laws § 38–3–2 (1990) for an identical definition in a related chapter of the same Title 38, governing public records.

353. *Id.*

354. *Id.* at § 38–1–10.

355. R.I. Gen. Laws § 38–3–3, –4 (1991).

356. R.I. Gen. Laws § 38–3–6 (1990).

357. *Id.* at § 38–3–2.

358. R.I. Gen. Laws § 42–8.1–5 (1988).

359. *Id.* at § 42–8.1–10.

360. *Id.* at § 42–8.1–17.

361. *Id.* at § 42–8.1–18.

362. Responses from Beth Perry, chief, Regional Library for the Blind, Rhode Island Department of Library Services; Peter E. Bennett, chief of support services, Providence Public Library.

363. Response from Peter E. Bennett, chief of support services, Providence Public Library.

364. R.I. Gen. Laws § 38–2–2 (1990).

365. R.I. Gen. Laws § 42–8.1–11 (1988).

366. S.C. Code Ann. § 30–1–10(A), 30–4–20(c) (Law. Co-op. 1991).

367. *Id.* at § 30–1–10.

368. *Id.* at § 30–1–80.

369. *Id.* at § 30–1–90.

370. *Id.* at § 30–1–30.

371. Response from John D. Mackintosh, records analyst II, Local Records Analysis Program, South Carolina Department of Archives and History.
372. *Id.*
373. Response from Charles M. Smith, state records program supervisor, State Records Center.
374. *Id.*
375. S.C. Code Ann. § 30–4–20 (Law. Co-op. 1991).
376. S.D. Codified Laws Ann. § 1–27–9 (1988).
377. *Id.* at § 1–27–11.
378. *Id.* at § 1–27–13.
379. *Id.* at § 1–27–18.
380. *Id.* at § 22–11–24, 22–6–1.
381. *Id.* at § 22–11–26.
382. Response from Dr. Jane Kolbe, state librarian.
383. Response from Jim Dertien, city librarian, Sioux Falls Public Library.
384. See S.D. Codified Laws Ann. § 14–2–51 (1992).
385. Tenn. Code Ann. § 10–7–301 (1992).
386. *Id.* at § 10–7–303.
387. *Id.* at § 10–7–401.
388. *Id.* at § 10–7–403.
389. *Id.* at § 10–7–405.
390. *Id.* at § 10–7–411.
391. *Id.*
392. Response from Betty Nance, executive secretary, Tennessee Library Association.
393. Telephone interview with John Thweatt, records program coordinator, State Library & Archives, March 12, 1993.
394. Tenn. Code Ann. § 10–8–102 (1992).
395. *Id.* at § 10–7–504.
396. Tex. Gov't Code Ann. § 441.035 (West 1993).
397. Tex. Gov't Code Ann. § 441.031 (West 1990).
398. *Id.* at § 441.036.
399. *Id.* at § 441.037.
400. *Id.* at § 441.151.
401. *Id.* at § 441.158, .161, .162.
402. Tex Local Gov't Code Ann. § 201.002 (West 1993).
403. *Id.* at § 203.021.
404. *Id.* at § 203.041.
405. *Id.* at § 203.043.
406. *Id.* at § 203.045.
407. Tex. Local Gov't Code Ann. § 202.008 (West Supp. 1993); Tex. Penal Code Ann. § 12.21 (West Supp. 1993).
408. Response from Marilyn von Kohl, director, Local Records Division, Texas State Library.
409. Response from Patricia Smith, executive director, Texas Library Association.
410. See Tex. Local Gov't Code Ann. chapter 205 (West 1993).
411. Utah Code Ann. § 63–2–501, –901 (1992).

412. *Id*. at § 63–2–901.

413. Utah Code Ann. § 63–2–103 (Supp. 1992).

414. *Id*. at § 63–2–103.

415. *Id*. at § 63–2–103(14), 63–2–302.

416. Utah Code Ann. § 63–2–903 (1992).

417. *Id*. at § 63–2–905.

418. Utah Code Ann. § 76–3–204, –301 (1990 & Supp. 1992).

419. Utah Code Ann. § 63–2–87, –88 (1989).

420. Response from Jeffrey O. Johnson, director, Utah State Archives.

421. Response from Eileen B. Longsworth, director, Salt Lake County Library System.

422. Utah Code Ann. § 63–2–302 (1992).

423. *Id*. at § 63–2–103(14), (15).

424. Vt. Stat. Ann. tit. 22, § 454 (1987 & Supp. 1991).

425. *Id*. at § 456.

426. *Id*. at § 453.

427. *Id*. at § 455.

428. Vt. Stat. Ann. tit. 3, § 218 (1985 & Supp. 1991).

429. See Vt. Stat. Ann. tit. 1, § 317 (1991).

430. Va. Code Ann. § 42.1–76 (Michie 1992).

431. *Id*. at § 42.1–77.

432. *Id*. at § 42.1–79.

433. *Id*. at § 42.1–80.

434. *Id*. at § 42.1–81, –82, –85.

435. Va. Code Ann. § 18.2–107, –10 (Michie Supp. 1991).

436. *Id*. at § 18.2–11, –472.

437. *Id*. at § 18.2–472.

438. Response from Louis H. Manarin, state archivist, Virginia State Library & Archives.

439. See Va. Code Ann. § 2.1–342 (Michie 1992).

440. *Id*. at § 42.1–77.

441. Wash. Rev. Code Ann. § 40.14.010 (West 1991).

442. *Id*.

443. *Id*.

444. *Id*. at § 40.14.020.

445. *Id*. at § 40.14.040.

446. *Id*. at § 40.14.050.

447. *Id*. at § 40.14.060.

448. *Id*.

449. *Id*. at § 40.14.070.

450. *Id*.

451. Response from Mary Y. Moore, chief, Library Planning and Development, Washington State Library. Ms. Moore indicated the schedule is too lengthy to provide a copy.

452. Response from Barbara Tolliver, president, Washington Library Association (1992–93).

453. W. Va. Code § 5A–8–4 (1990).

454. *Id*. at § 5A–8–5.

455. *Id.* at § 5A–8–3.

456. *Id.* at § 5A–8–7 (emphasis added).

457. *Id.*

458. *Id.* at § 5A–8–9.

459. *Id.* at § 5A–8–17.

460. *Id.* at § 5A–8–3.

461. *Id.* at § 5A–8–5.

462. *Id.* at § 5A–8–15.

463. W. Va. Code § 61–5–22 (1992).

464. Response from Shirley A. Smith, field services director, West Virginia Library Commission.

465. W. Va. Code § 5A–8–2 (1990).

466. See, e.g., *id.* at § 5A–8–7(c), –9(c).

467. Wis. Stat. Ann. § 19.21 (West 1986 & Supp. 1991). The obsolete records of a city council, village board, or town board may be destroyed only after sixty days' notice to the state historical society with an opportunity for the society to retrieve the records for preservation. Wis. Stat. Ann. § 19.21(4)(a) (West 1986 & Supp. 1991).

468. Wis. Stat. Ann. § 19.21(4)(a), (5)(c) (West 1986). State law provides specific retention periods for certain obsolete county records. See Wis. Stat. Ann. § 59.715, .717 (West Supp. 1992).

469. Wis. Stat. Ann. § 19.21(5)(d) (West 1986).

470. Wis. Stat. Ann. § 16.61 (West 1991).

471. *Id.* at § 16.61(4)(a).

472. *Id.* at § 16.61(4)(b), (c).

473. *Id.* at § 16.61(3)(b), (e).

474. Wis. Stat. Ann. § 946.72, 939.50 (West 1982).

475. Response from Leslyn M. Shires, assistant superintendent, Division for Library Services, Wisconsin Department of Public Instruction.

476. Telephone interview with Michael Stevens, Wisconsin state historian, March 12, 1993.

477. Wyo. Stat. § 9–2–406 (1991).

478. *Id.* at § 9–2–409.

479. *Id.* at § 9–2–411.

480. *Id.* at § 9–2–401.

481. *Id.* at § 9–2–410.

482. *Id.* at § 16–4–201.

483. *Id.* at § 9–2–412.

484. Response from Tony Adams, CRM, records manager, State Archives & Records Management Section, Parks & Cultural Resources Division, Department of Commerce; and Jerry Krois, deputy state librarian, Wyoming State Library. In addition to the retention schedule, Mr. Krois also included state-established instructions for using the Records Management Manual. The State Archives, Records Management and Micrographics Service of the Division of Parks & Cultural Resources, Department of Commerce is the author of the Manual. The retention schedule for libraries is dated September 1990.

485. Wyo. Stat. § 16–4–203(d)(ix) (1992).

3

Recommendations for Change: Record Retention and Destruction

It would be both difficult and unnecessary for the library profession to recommend wholesale changes in the current state record retention laws. Those laws exist in every state and they govern the retention and destruction of a myriad of public records, ranging from state to county to local governmental records. Therefore, the first step for library professionals is to acquaint themselves with laws already in place. As is obvious from the questionnaire responses, the problem with many retention laws is that the profession is either unaware of them or has failed to develop retention schedules required by them. Education and compliance would go a long way toward achieving a systematic program for the proper retention and destruction of library records.

The next step for library professionals is to address the laws themselves and attempt to effect changes in laws that appear inadequate. In doing so, it is helpful to consider a number of issues that have been addressed in other states' laws with varying degrees of success. These are discussed in prior chapters and include which records are included and excluded, procedures for retention or destruction, and penalties for noncompliance.

WHICH RECORDS ARE INCLUDED?

This involves two issues. One has to do with definition of "record." It is important that the law include new technological developments and not restrict itself to written, hard-copy formats. The majority of states have chosen a general definition, such as any record regardless of physical form or characteristic. Some states, such as Indiana, have chosen to elaborate on the general definition by also listing specifically the formats covered by the law, such as paper or paper substitutes and magnetic or machine-readable media. The benefit of specificity may not be significant, since any undeveloped technology will not be included. The general definition appears more comprehensive.[1]

The other issue has to do with what makes a record "public." The definition of most states is very broad and encompasses any library materials that are *created* or *received* in connection with the transaction of library business and that serve as evidence of the organization, function, policies, decisions, procedures, operations, *or other activities* of the library. Clearly, this includes not only accession and shelf lists and minutes of the library board, but also patron registration and circulation records.

Much confusion exists in this area because library professionals assume that, because a record is *confidential*, it is not public. That assumption is mistaken. The term "public record" may be defined in the state law in several different ways. In order to determine its meaning, one must consult the chapter or section of the law at issue. For example, some states exempt library records from the definition of public records in their open records acts or in that portion of the state law that pertains to libraries. However, those same states may include library records in that portion of the law that pertains to records management and retention. Such a determination can be made only by examining the "definitions" section of the records management law. None of these specifically exempt library records, although the laws may apply only to *state* records and not to county and municipal records.

Eight states include only state records[2] and four states include fewer than all county and municipal records.[3] It is incumbent upon library professionals in these states to ensure that comprehensive legislation includes the records of all public libraries. Some library professionals might argue that they do not wish to be included within the statute's coverage, thereby enabling them to determine unilaterally which records should be kept and which discarded. But the profession as a whole must address the long-term implications of such a position, including the possibility of widespread destruction of library records, which will certainly affect the profession as a whole. Although the motives of the current librarian may be benign, those of some future librarian may not be. Ad hoc decision making may be efficient and empowering, but it can also be irresponsible.

WHICH RECORDS ARE EXCLUDED?

Currently, twenty-three states exclude from retention laws library and museum materials that are developed or acquired and preserved solely for reference, historical, or exhibition purposes. Also excluded in those states are stocks of publications. A few states also exempt other miscellaneous materials, as discussed in Chapter 1. Given the very broad definition of public records included in most laws, these exemptions are well-advised.

PROCEDURES FOR RETENTION
AND DESTRUCTION

Here is where most states lack any consensus at all. Chapter 1 discusses the various approaches. The best approach would include careful consideration of *who* administers the procedure and an attempt to make the procedure as efficient as possible. Furthermore, it is important to involve the agency heads in the decision-making process as it relates to that agency's records.

Nearly half the states have designated specialized commissions, boards, committees, or other governmental bodies to administer the records management acts. However, in some states these bodies are organized city by city, or county by county, thereby resulting in a hodgepodge of retention schedules. A preferable approach is to establish a state records management office, whose duty it is to ensure that retention schedules are developed for all state, county, and local agencies.

The state office should initially develop retention schedules for all governmental records common to the agencies, such as personnel, payroll, budget, and similar records. This office is most likely to possess the requisite expertise and knowledge of sound management practices. Retention schedules for records that are unique to each agency, such as library records, must be developed separately with significant involvement of the agency itself.

One efficient method of accomplishing this latter goal is for the state office to solicit proposed retention schedules from each agency. The state office then reviews the schedules to ensure that all interests have been accommodated. The reviewing body should include persons who can represent fiscal, legal, administrative, tax, and historical perspectives. It should include a representative from the state library and state archives and perhaps from the state historical society as well. Once the state reviewing body has determined that the proposed retention schedule meets all the state's objectives and interests, the schedule serves thereafter as authority for the local agency to destroy its records accordingly. Any modifications must receive the approval of the state office.

The federal statute that governs the retention and destruction of federal records follows this recommended procedure. The head of each federal agency must submit to the national archivist lists of records that are "not needed by it in the transaction of its current business and that do not appear to have sufficient administrative, legal, research, or other value to warrant their further preservation."[4] All agency heads must also submit "schedules proposing the disposal after the lapse of specified periods of time of records of a specified form or character" that also do not appear to have "sufficient administrative, legal, research, or other value to warrant their further preservation by the Government."[5] The archivist then examines the lists and schedules and must approve them prior to disposal of the records.[6] The archivist may establish schedules for those "records of a specified form or character common to several or all agencies. . . . " but an individual agency may request changes in these schedules for its own records.[7]

PENALTIES FOR NONCOMPLIANCE

Less than half the states impose penalties for improper destruction of public records. Of those, it is clear that some of the penalties are not designed to punish public officials who are unaware of proper procedures for record destruction, but rather are designed to penalize persons who deliberately destroy public documents in order to hide wrongdoing. But it is also clear that some penalties apply regardless of intent or willfulness. Thus, public library officials who destroy library records in violation of state record retention laws may face severe penalties.

The most effective laws are those in which the penalizing statute appears as a part of the record retention statute, not as a statute buried in a separate section of the law. This serves two goals. First, public officials who read the law relating to record retention have a better chance of learning about the penalty. Second, it is then apparent that the law is designed specifically to punish those who violate record retention laws. Arizona's law represents this approach. In one section of the law,[8] subsections A, B, and C describe the steps that state and local agency heads must follow in developing a records management program. Subsection D states: "A head of a state or local agency who violates this section is guilty of a class 2 misdemeanor."[9] Making the penalty part of the statute itself leaves no doubt as to its intent and, at the same time, notifies anyone who consults the retention statute of the penalty.

The penalty itself should fit the crime. If, for example, the record destruction is inadvertent, the penalty should be minimal. If it is willful, the penalty should be significant. Requiring evidence of willfulness is common in criminal statutes and well-established in the law. Florida's law reflects this approach. It provides that "[a]ny public officer who violates any provision of [the public records chapter] is guilty of a *noncriminal* infraction, punishable by fine not exceeding $500." But "[a]ny person *willfully and knowingly* violating any of the provisions of this chapter is guilty of a misdemeanor of the first degree," punishable by a fine up to $1,000.00 and a prison term up to one year.[10]

A few states provide that in addition to, or in lieu of, criminal penalties, one who has been harmed in some way by the wrongful destruction may bring a civil action against the wrongdoer for damages. This is one option the legislature might consider; however, the difficulty most obvious is in proving "damage." Ordinarily, one will be unable to demonstrate pecuniary damages and any other form of damage will be very difficult to measure. That factor alone does not negate the possibility of damage; after all, tort law commonly measures "pain and suffering" and "emotional damages." But courts and legislatures are often unwilling to create additional intangible damage recoveries. Those states that have allowed civil actions for public records violations of this sort limit them to minimal recoveries or to actions brought by the state, but include attorney fees and costs to make such lawsuits worthwhile.[11]

A few states also provide that public employees who violate the law may lose their jobs.[12] Obviously, employees must be accorded due process prior to termination, and they should not be terminated for an inadvertent destruction.

To ensure that the record retention laws are taken seriously, penalties should be available. But those who might suffer such penalties must be advised of their existence, at the same time as they are advised of the retention law itself. For example, the federal law governing the retention and destruction of federal records includes a "Safeguards" section, which provides that the head of each federal agency must inform agency officials and employees "that records in the custody of the agency are not to be . . . destroyed except in accordance" with the law and also inform them of "the penalties provided by law for the unlawful removal or destruction of records."[13]

ESTABLISHING LIBRARY RECORD RETENTION SCHEDULES

Assuming that the state's law adequately includes library records in its retention law, the next step would be to establish retention schedules for all library records, including patron registration and circulation records. How can libraries determine the kinds of record retention schedules that best serve a variety of interests? Which interests should be accommodated? Certainly the library's business interests must be addressed. The retention schedules in many states already focus on these interests. For example, records relating to budgets, accounting, payroll, personnel, and other administrative matters are common to state and local agencies. A retention schedule for libraries might borrow from these generic schedules. Administrators might seek additional assistance from published sources in the field.[14] Retention schedules for these administrative records will accommodate legal, administrative, and fiscal interests.

What other interests should be accommodated? A survey of state laws reveals various degrees of enlightened lawmaking. For example, some states mandate a consideration of the historical value of records.[15] Even if the state law does not specifically include this factor, it is very significant to public libraries because of the integral role they play in society. Protecting records with historical significance would serve the practical need for policy continuity, but it would also enable future generations to learn how the library operated, what materials it held, and who it served. Involving a local historian or archivist in the process of record evaluation might ensure protection of records with historical value, even though they lack administrative value.

Once the library determines which interests it chooses to include, the next step will be to develop retention schedules for those records that are unique to libraries. These would include such records as accession records, shelf lists, minutes of the library board, patron registration records, and circulation records. An examination of the laws reveals that, in most states, computer-generated records are included in the definition of "public records." The library profession must address the current practice of purchasing a circulation system that automatically erases patron records as soon as library materials are returned. Perhaps libraries will choose to continue this practice by mandating a retention period in conformance with it. For example, New York has adopted a library record retention schedule that requires a retention period of "0 after no longer needed" for circulation records, including interlibrary loans. North Carolina provides that circulation records in manual or electronic form be destroyed when the "transaction is completed." But some libraries might want to rethink the practice if historical considerations play a role. Regardless, the decision should not be made thoughtlessly.

Although it is likely that libraries will value privacy above historical record-keeping in determining retention periods for circulation records, other records lack these privacy concerns. Patron registration records fall somewhere in the middle. Although specific information about a patron's library use should be protected from public disclosure, this does not mean that libraries should engage in wholesale destruction of all information relating to library users. Patron registration records carry significant historical value. In balancing the need for privacy against the need for historical information, the library may decide that historical interests win out. This does not mean, however, that registration records are public; confidentiality laws continue to protect them. What it does mean is that, in determining retention periods for registration records, the library might want to extend the periods for a much longer time than the current brief periods (in those few states that include them at all).

For other records that hold no privacy interest, but hold considerable historical interest, retention schedules should indicate permanent retention. This may necessitate microfilming the records and moving them to off-site storage facilities, but at least they will not be periodically purged.

In developing retention schedules unique to public libraries, the library profession might wish to consult with library organizations representing various interests, such as the Society of American Archivists or the Library History Round Table. The profession might also wish to examine the schedules in those states that have already developed them, including Arizona, Connecticut, Delaware, Florida, Georgia, Kansas, Kentucky, Minnesota, Nevada, New Jersey, New York, North Carolina, North Dakota, Virginia, Washington, and Wyoming.[16]

Despite having well-drafted laws and detailed retention schedules, states will continue to suffer noncompliance unless library professionals are aware of the laws and schedules. Few states have taken measures to remedy the current abysmal compliance rate. Notable exceptions exist.

In Florida, the state periodically offers records management workshops specifically for libraries. They include information about the state's public records laws, basic principles of records management, retention schedules, preservation and disposition of records, and records management in areas of emerging technology. The state also publishes several handbooks pertaining to these issues.

In Minnesota, the record retention schedule is detailed and specific. Both state and local governmental units have developed detailed written guidelines for their agencies. For example, the city of Minneapolis has published a "Guide to Records Management Service," which assists city agencies, including the public library, in establishing records management and retention schedules.

The New York Local Government Records Bureau has published a pamphlet entitled, "Retention and Disposition of Library System Records." It illustrates the kinds of questions likely to be raised in other states and advises library professionals of the state law pertaining to record retention.

CONCLUSION

Improvements in record retention laws will not, in most cases, require a complete legislative overhaul. What is more often required is some fine-tuning, adding provisions for local and county records, clarifying the process, or redrafting confusing statutory language. In many cases, the law is quite adequate, but public awareness of the law is not. In these instances, information and education will accomplish the law's purpose. In either event, the library profession can play a valuable role in educating its public officials and bringing to the fore a subject that demands its attention and thoughtful debate.

NOTES

1. The federal law pertaining to retention and destruction of *federal* records has adopted a general definition of records, which includes

all books, papers, maps, photographs, machine readable materials, or other documentary materials, regardless of physical form or characteristics, made or received by an agency of the United States Government under Federal law or in connection with the transaction of public business and preserved or appropriate for preservation by that agency or its legitimate successor as evidence of the organization, functions, policies, decisions, procedures, operations, or other activities of the Government or because of the informational value of data in them. Library and museum material made or acquired and preserved solely for reference or exhibition purposes, extra copies of documents preserved only for convenience of reference, and stocks of publications and of processed documents are not included.

44 U.S.C. § 3301 (1991). Obviously, many state laws have been patterned after the federal statute. Recently, a judge determined that electronic messages are included in this definition. Armstrong v. Executive Office of the President, 61 U.S.L.W. 2427 (D.C. D.C. Jan. 26, 1993).

2. Those states are Mississippi, Montana, New Mexico, North Dakota, Oklahoma, South Dakota, West Virginia, and Wisconsin.

3. Those states are California (state and county records), Idaho (state and city records), Iowa (state and city records), and Pennsylvania (some county and city records).

4. 44 U.S.C. § 3303 (1991).

5. *Id.*

6. *Id.*

7. *Id.*

8. Ariz. Rev. Stat. Ann. § 41–1346 (1992).

9. *Id.*

10. Fla. Stat. Ann. § 119.10, 775.082, 775.083 (West 1992) (emphasis added).

11. In Kentucky and Utah, damages may be awarded only to the state, not to private parties. See Ky. Rev. Stat. Ann. § 171.990 (Michie/Bobbs-Merrill 1990); Utah Code Ann. § 63–2–88 (1989). In Ohio, one can bring a civil action to enjoin the destruction of records or to recover $1,000.00 for each violation, or both. See Ohio Rev. Code Ann. § 149.351 (Anderson 1990).

12. Kentucky law provides that the employee must *knowingly* violate the law. Ky. Rev. Stat. Ann. § 171.990 (Michie/Bobbs-Merrill 1990). Utah law provides that the employee must *willfully* violate the act and then is subject to suspension without pay or discharge *after a hearing.* Utah Code Ann. § 63–2–87 (1989). Virginia law provides that if a "public officer . . . destroy[s] any record . . . in his keeping and belonging to his office, he shall . . . forfeit his office and be forever incapable of holding any office of honor, profit or trust under the Constitution of Virginia." Va. Code Ann. § 18.2–472 (Michie Supp. 1991).

13. 44 U.S.C. § 3105 (1991).

14. See, for example, Bruce W. Dearstyne, The Management of Local Government Records: A Guide for Local Officials (1988); H. G. Jones, Local Government Records: An Introduction to Their Management, Preservation, and Use (1980); Donald Skupsky, Recordkeeping Requirements (The First Practical Guide

to Help You Control Your Records...What You Need to Keep and What You Can Safely Destroy!) (2d ed. 1989); Donald Skupsky, Legal Requirements for Business Records: Guide to Records Retention and Recordkeeping Requirements: Federal Requirements (1990 & annual updates); Donald Skupsky, Legal Requirements for Business Records: Guide to Records Retention and Recordkeeping Requirements: State Requirements (1990 & annual updates); John M. Fedders & Lauryn H. Guttenplan, *Document Retention and Destruction: Practical, Legal and Ethical Considerations*, The Notre Dame Lawyer, Oct. 1980, at 5.

15. Seventeen states include this consideration. See Chapter 1 for a discussion of this issue.

16. Copies of these retention schedules can be obtained from the sources indicated in notes accompanying the discussion of the schedules in Chapter 2.

PART II

Confidentiality of
Library Records

4

Introduction to Confidentiality Issues

LIBRARY RECORDS AS PUBLIC RECORDS

Part I addressed the retention and destruction of library records, which are generally included within the definition of "public records" for purposes of state retention and destruction laws. Library records may also fall within the definition of "public records" for purposes of state open records acts, or Freedom of Information Acts, which are modeled after the federal open records statute.

Public records have long been considered "open" to various degrees by virtue of their creation by public officials who are paid with public funds.[1] But only recently has the American public begun to expect that records of a public body be made available to them upon request.

The federal Freedom of Information Act[2] was passed in 1966 and was designed to provide public access to government information.[3] One of its Senate sponsors stated: "A government by secrecy benefits no one. It injures the people it seeks to serve; it damages its own integrity and operation. It breeds distrust, dampens the fervor of its citizens, and mocks their loyalty."[4] The statute presumes that all records prepared by a federal governmental agency are open to the public, unless specifically exempt.[5] This means that federal libraries are governed by the Freedom of Information Act and must disclose information unless that information fits within a stated exception.[6]

In the past twenty years or so, state open records statutes have proliferated, often in response to a growing distrust of public officials and an insistence upon open government. These laws generally provide that any records or documents prepared or received by state public officials be made available upon request. Many states include records prepared or received by county and local public officials as well. Now, open records statutes have been passed in all fifty states, leading to some unexpected, and unwelcome, results. One of these results, surely unforeseen when open records laws were passed, is that in some states any member of the public may walk into the local public library and discover who is using the library and for what purposes. Are his or her neighbors reading "pornography" or sexually explicit materials? Has a church member read any self-help books or books dealing with sexual abuse or domestic violence? What about religious cult materials? Has the man next door consulted reference materials to learn more about prostate cancer? Has the schoolteacher requested a computer data search to learn about the latest fertility drugs? Have any of them expressed interest in building a simple but effective bomb?

PROTECTION FROM PUBLIC SCRUTINY

In response to the passage of open records laws and these undesirable results, librarians in many states began to lobby their legislators for passage of new laws to protect library records from the public's prying eyes. They have succeeded in varying degrees.

Before examining these efforts, it is important to understand why librarians (and legislators) have struggled to exempt library records from disclosure. Although the American Library Association today prides itself on its defense of the First Amendment, that defense is a twentieth-century phenomenon.[7] Not until 1929 did the ALA indicate any organized resistance to censorship of library materials; when requested in 1933 to take a stand against book burning by Hitler's troops, the ALA balked.[8] Not until 1938 was any formal statement issued concerning library privacy. In that year, the ALA published its "Code of Ethics for Librarians," which included the provision: "It is the librarian's obligation to treat as confidential any private information obtained through contact with library patrons."[9] The following year, the ALA formally adopted the Library Bill of Rights, which focused on the issue of censorship, and in 1940 the Intellectual Freedom Committee was established.[10] The next thirty years witnessed significant activity by the profession in the area of censorship, but the issue of library record confidentiality lay dormant. Finally, in 1970, the issue received widespread attention when the Internal Revenue Service began to request library circulation records as part of an investigation into the production of homemade explosives and the use of guerrilla warfare. In response, the ALA developed its Policy on Confidentiality of Library Records.[11] In the past twenty years, the policy has often led to legal confrontations between libraries and government officials.

The underlying basis for the profession's defense of intellectual freedom consists of two fundamental principles: the First Amendment guarantee of freedom of expression, and the implied right to privacy. The First Amendment to the United States Constitution states that the government "shall make no law . . . abridging the freedom of speech."[12] Librarians argue that the right to free speech, or "freedom of expression," includes the right to receive information and ideas. In fact, support for this argument can be found in United States Supreme Court opinions. Although the Supreme Court has not ruled directly that library records are protected under the First Amendment, numerous decisions have held that the right to receive information, without public disclosure, is protected.[13] In *Stanley v. Georgia*, the Court declared: "If the First Amendment means anything, it means that a State has no business telling a man, sitting alone in his house, what books he may read or what films he may watch."[14]

In addition to the First Amendment, the right to privacy argument also has support. Although this right is not explicit in the United States Constitution, it has been implied in a number of cases. Librarians argue that such a right extends to protection of library patron information. The argument has met with varying success.[15]

But even as the library profession looks to the country's Constitution for support, it looks at the same time to compromises it believes necessary to function as an effective organization in the local community. In a sense, the profession's bark is worse than its bite. As early as 1939, one author wrote that librarians should keep private information "locked up in our own minds and not report them even to our own families, quite as the good lawyer keeps to himself stories about his clients. . . ."[16] When the library profession began over twenty years ago to focus on protecting patron information, it too asserted that the relationship between a librarian and patron be respected the same way in which the doctor/patient and attorney/client relationships are respected.[17] But at the same time, the profession was quite willing to succumb to court order or subpoena or other governmental pressure, unlike the medical and legal professions. The relationship between lawyers and their clients has far greater protection in the law than that between librarians and patrons. The relationship between the former is *privileged*; the relationship between the latter only *confidential*. The differences are vast and they are not constitutionally based.

Perhaps the two protections should not even be subjected to critical comparison; after all, *public* librarians are bound by the mandate of state open records laws; lawyers, as private actors, are not. Although technically "officers of the court," private lawyers have never been deemed to be state agents. But what about "public" lawyers? Public defenders and state and local prosecutors are surely governmental employees, yet no one would argue that the attorney-client privilege is not available to them. The distinction cannot be explained on this basis.

The lawyer's privilege is based on the important policy of encouraging clients to place their trust in their lawyers and to be completely frank in the relationship. This policy has received recognition in legislatures across the country, resulting in the privilege's widespread acceptance and adoption into the laws of the states. The privilege cannot be breached, even when great physical harm has been committed. For example, in New York, an attorney "shall not disclose, or be allowed to disclose" any communication between the attorney and client, in any action, civil or criminal.[18] In California, the client has a privilege to refuse to disclose, and to prevent another from disclosing, any confidential communication between herself and her lawyer.[19]

In addition to legislation that provides the client with strong protection against disclosure, the legal profession has adopted Rules of Professional Conduct that address the lawyer's duty to his or her client. The lawyer's duty is demonstrated most clearly in the *ABA Model Rules of Professional Conduct*.[20] Rule 1.6 states:

Confidentiality of Information

(a) A lawyer shall not reveal information relating to representation of a client unless the client consents after consultation, except for disclosures that are impliedly authorized in order to carry out the representation, and except as stated in paragraph (b).

(b) A lawyer may reveal such information to the extent the lawyer reasonably believes necessary:

(1) to prevent the client from committing a criminal act that the lawyer believes is likely to result in imminent death or substantial bodily harm; or

(2) [in disputes between the lawyer and client regarding fees or the lawyer's representation of the client].[21]

Failure to comply with an obligation imposed by the Rules may result in disciplinary hearings and, ultimately, in permanent disbarment.

In most states, communications made between husband and wife, attorney and client, clergy and penitent, and doctor and patient are all protected by a statutory privilege. The law embodies the principle that "[t]here are particular relations in which it is the policy of the law to encourage confidence and to preserve it inviolate."[22] Those relations are set forth in state law.

The Federal Rules of Civil Procedure, the body of rules governing trial procedure in all United States federal courts and, by imitation, in most state courts, recognizes the privilege as well. Rule 26 states that a party in a lawsuit may obtain information about "any matter, not privileged, which is relevant."[23] What is "privileged" matter? It is that matter defined by the states[24] in such statutes as those quoted above. Many court cases have discussed the difference between a confidence and a privilege. "A finding of 'privilege'. . . shields the requested information from disclosure despite the need demonstrated by the litigant."[25]

In most cases, the librarian's "privilege" is not a privilege at all; it is merely a "confidence." It can be easily breached with a subpoena or other court order, often without judicial review. In some states, it can be breached simply because the library official decides to produce the requested information. In fact, the protection given to library records is often no protection at all. It certainly does not rise to the level of a privilege.

Librarians cannot have it both ways. If in fact the right to free expression or the right to privacy is constitutionally based, and this right encompasses library confidentiality, as librarians argue, then the right is fundamental and ought not be easily abridged. That is currently not the case; as an examination of state statutes reveals, numerous exceptions exist for breaching the confidentiality of library patron records.

Librarians must decide whether they wish to continue to argue that confidentiality is a constitutional issue. If it is, the laws must be changed to reflect protection of a constitutional magnitude. The library profession must consider legislation adding library patrons to the list of those protected by a "privilege." What are the criteria? Although "[t]he scope of the privilege doctrine is narrow indeed,"[26] it is possible to fashion a library privilege within its boundaries. Basically, any privilege involves balancing the reason for the privilege against the need for information. Four conditions must be met:

1. The communications [between the library and patron] must originate in a *confidence* that they will not be disclosed.
2. This element of *confidentiality must be essential* to the full and satisfactory maintenance of the relation between the parties.
3. The *relation* must be one which in the opinion of the community ought to be sedulously *fostered*.
4. The *injury* that would inure to the relation by the disclosure of the communications must be *greater than the benefit* thereby gained for the correct disposal of litigation.[27]

If the library profession is unable to convince state or federal legislators that library confidentiality deserves protection as a privilege or as a constitutional right, perhaps the approach ought to be couched in terms of satisfying an important societal goal or formulating an important policy. For example, "[t]he manifest purpose of open records statutes is to open government, not the private lives of individuals, to the eyes of the public. Public disclosure of personal reading habits has no relation to this goal."[28]

If libraries are the final, and greatest, repositories of information and ideas, and if as a country we embrace the democratic notion that all persons ought to have free access to information and ideas, then access will not be "free" unless patrons are assured that their requests for library information or materials will remain absolutely protected.

The final chapter of this book explores both a legislative and a policy approach to confidentiality. For now, an examination of the history of confidentiality in the profession will serve as a foundation for future action.

EVOLUTION OF CONFIDENTIALITY LAWS

How did the library profession's attempts to protect library records evolve into a plethora of state laws? As noted above, the first formal statement appeared in 1938. Shortly thereafter, the Intellectual Freedom Committee was created. In 1970, library confidentiality received the profession's widespread attention and, since that time, the profession has continued to issue policies that reflect its ongoing concern with confidentiality.[29]

On July 21, 1970, the American Library Association issued an "emergency advisory statement," warning librarians that the Internal Revenue Service (IRS) had begun to request circulation records in public libraries located in a number of cities, including Atlanta, Cleveland, Milwaukee, and San Francisco. The ALA urged all libraries to adopt policies making circulation records confidential. It also advised that library records be made available to a requesting party pursuant only to "process, order, or subpoena as may be authorized under the authority of, and pursuant to, federal, state, or local law relating to civil, criminal, or administrative discovery procedures or legislative investigatory power." The ALA instructed librarians to resist such orders unless good cause had been shown in court for the disclosure.[30]

The current policy is reflected throughout the *ALA Policy Manual*. The ALA promises to protect "intellectual freedom" by securing First Amendment rights and providing "adequate support" to "[p]ersons whose First Amendment rights are challenged."[31] "The American Library Association opposes any use of government prerogatives that leads to the intimidation of the individual or the citizenry from the exercise of free expression. ALA encourages resistance to such abuse of government power and supports those against whom such governmental power has been employed."[32] And, in a policy entitled "Confidentiality of Library Records," the ALA provides specific guidance:

The American Library Association strongly recommends that the responsible officers of each library, cooperative system, and consortium in the United States:

1. Formally adopt a policy which specifically recognizes its circulation records and other records identifying the names of library users with specific materials[33] to be confidential.

2. Advise all librarians and library employees that such records shall not be made available to any agency of state, federal, or local government except pursuant to such process, order, or subpoena as may be authorized under the authority of, and pursuant to, federal, state, or local law relating to civil, criminal, or administrative discovery procedures or legislative investigatory power.

3. Resist the issuance or enforcement of any such process, order, or subpoena until such time as a proper showing of good cause has been made in a court of competent jurisdiction.[34]

This last point does not mean that libraries should request a judicial hearing, as the wording seems to imply. Rather, as spelled out in an accompanying footnote in the policy, it means merely that librarians should have their legal counsel review the order or subpoena to ensure that it "is in proper form" and that "good cause" for its issuance has been shown on the face of the document.[35]

But no matter how strongly such policies are worded and no matter how specific, they remain only policies of a professional organization that serve as guidelines for the profession's members. They are not mandatory, nor do sanctions exist for their violation. Clearly, they do not withstand assaults by the IRS, the Federal Bureau of Investigation (FBI), the Central Intelligence Agency (CIA), or even the local sheriff. For such assaults, the force of law is necessary.

Prompted in part by the IRS invasion of the libraries in 1970 and in part by other incidents involving government attempts to obtain library records,[36] states began to pass laws protecting such records. These laws usually developed in one of two ways: either as exemptions from open records laws or as a specific section of the state's general library law. A few states adopted both approaches. Some states have no confidentiality statute that protects library records;[37] in fact, until 1992, Mississippi specifically included library records within its definition of open public records.[38]

To date, no federal law applies to nonfederal library records. The Federal Privacy Act[39] governs the disclosure of records held by *federal* agencies. As recently as 1988, a bill was introduced in Congress that would have provided protection for library borrower records and would have applied to all public libraries in the country, but the bill died in committee when members could not resolve questions concerning disclosure to law enforcement officers.[40] Thus, issues of confidentiality must be dealt with state by state.

THE NEED FOR STRONG UNIFORM
CONFIDENTIALITY LAWS

What is wrong with the state-by-state approach? Obviously, lack of uniformity of laws does not in itself present problems. However, it does mean that librarians as professionals lack a consistent body of knowledge that applies to all other library professionals in this vital area; it also requires librarians to equip themselves with knowledge of laws from state to state, recognizing that other librarians may be held to varying standards of conduct. On a more practical level, the lack of uniformity means that library patrons are well protected in some states and not at all protected in others. Some states still have no confidentiality statute. Others have a very weak statute. Still others have ambiguous laws that provide very little guidance to those librarians operating "in the trenches." Some statutes appear to be very strong, yet are purely discretionary, leaving the decision as to disclosure in the hands of whichever library official is currently on duty. Depending upon the request, the employee (or librarian) may find the argument for disclosure too compelling to resist.[41] Many statutes are misunderstood by those operating under them, both librarians and those seeking disclosure. Some federal governmental officials seeking library records have asserted that they are not bound by mere state laws,[42] although this argument has yet to be made formally and stands little chance of success. After all, it is the *librarian* who is bound by law to keep records confidential and librarians are not federal officials.

One problem not so easily resolved is determining which state law applies to a library transaction. For example, assume Patron X visits a public library in State 1, which has a strong, effective confidentiality law. She requests books and other materials the library does not have but is able to obtain through an interlibrary loan from State 2. However, State 2 has no confidentiality law, or has only a weak one. Although State 1 would be prohibited from revealing information about this transaction, State 2 presumably would not. The laws of State 1 would not be binding on the librarian in State 2; thus, a request for records in State 2 relating to this transaction would receive no protection.

Although the problem of confidentiality of library records may appear to some librarians to pale in significance compared to, for example, library budgets, the problem is quite widespread and has taken both a professional and a personal toll on some librarians and their patrons.

Perhaps the most well-known situation involved the FBI's Library Awareness Program, first publicly exposed in *The New York Times* in 1987.[43] Although the FBI continues to remain reticent about discussing the program, it apparently operated in numerous states and involved recruiting library employees for assistance in identifying foreigners using public library materials. The FBI resisted the efforts of the National Security Ar-

chive (NSA) to learn more about the program by means of a Freedom of
Information Act request, prompting the NSA to file a lawsuit in 1988. As
a result of that lawsuit and subsequent events, the wide scope of the program became clear.[44]

The American Library Association learned that the program had been
in operation from 1973 to 1976 and had once again been implemented in
1985. It continued in effect at the time it was exposed. The program focused
primarily on the Soviets obtaining scientific and technical information from
libraries in New York City, but it reached out to include the University of
Maryland (requesting the names of any Soviet nationals who had used the
library and the subject matter of their requests);[45] the University of Wisconsin (agents watched a Soviet national reading *Pravda* and then questioned the librarian about his conduct);[46] the universities of Michigan,
Utah, Houston, California at Los Angeles; and public libraries in New
Jersey and Florida.[47]

In some of these cases, library employees were asked to violate state
confidentiality laws.[48] Often coercion, intimidation, or appeals to patri-
otism were employed,[49] demonstrating clearly the need for laws that provide no discretion to the library employee. Where a law absolutely prohibits
the employee from disclosing information, the law provides the employee
with a logical shield from intimidation.[50]

During the Library Awareness Program, the FBI sought information
concerning not only written materials used by suspected foreign spies, but
also information relating to computerized data searches,[51] demonstrating
a flaw in state laws that protect only materials *borrowed* by library patrons,
or only circulation records. The agency often bypassed library supervisors,
targeting instead lower-ranking employees,[52] demonstrating the need for
libraries to implement strong, specific policies that are then considered an
integral part of training for every library employee.

In short, the Library Awareness Program was a government-sponsored
attempt to recruit librarians in the spy business. As one agent asserted,
librarians, working in collusion with FBI agents,

> would be able to see what kind of person you are. They could check out your
> handwriting, see whether you're a research student or whether you're crazy or
> whether you're a threat. There is a chance that a librarian would see some suspicious
> activity and call us, and we would investigate and catch someone.[53]

One well-known successful attempt to obtain library records involved
the records of John Hinckley, the man who shot then-President Reagan.
Hinckley carried a Jefferson County (Colorado) Public Library card when
he was arrested. William A. Knott, director of the library, was "directed
by the County Attorney ... within hours of the shooting, to examine"
library records to see if any pertained to Hinckley. Then, the director was

approached by a reporter, seeking the same information. The director reports, "I was frankly powerless to deny him access." The county attorney had recently determined that the library's confidentiality policy was contrary to state law. After the reporter gave up the search, the FBI descended, spending several weeks searching library files. The director was then subpoenaed to bring to the United States attorney the books and magazines that Hinckley checked out. Finally, the FBI wanted to search "meeting rooms bookings records." The director had no legal protection against this onslaught and therefore complied.[54]

During Congressional hearings about the Library Awareness Program, Judith Krug, chair of the ALA's Intellectual Freedom Committee, and C. James Schmidt, Research Libraries Group, testified about numerous instances of attempts by third persons to obtain library records. They included attempts:

1. by New Mexico police to obtain circulation records during an investigation into the "Chicano guerrilla movement" (1976);

2. by a divorced father in Illinois to obtain his daughter's library records to determine if she was using his last name or the name of his ex-wife's new husband (1978);

3. by Florida religious groups to obtain names of those reading certain books so they could be recruited into religious organizations (1978);

4. by New York detectives to obtain names of persons reading books about lie detector tests because they suspected someone was trying to cheat on such tests (1979);

5. by a husband in Virginia to obtain his wife's circulation records to show she had been contemplating divorce for some time (1979);

6. by a hospital staff member to obtain the hospital library records to determine who was viewing sex therapy films (1980);

7. by police to obtain circulation records of an Albany, New York, college student from her college library to see if she had checked out books about infant care, after she reported finding a newborn infant in an alley (1980);

8. by the Moral Majority to obtain names of public school employees who had borrowed the film, *Achieving Sexual Maturity* (1981);

9. by Indiana law enforcement officers to obtain circulation records on books about satanism (1985);

10. by both the Baton Rouge, Louisiana, sheriff's office and the Whitestown, New York, police to obtain the names of persons who had borrowed books about the occult (1988).[55]

In addition to these and other examples of attempts to obtain library records, a recent questionnaire to librarians throughout the country revealed the pervasiveness of the problem. In 1988 a man was observed outside of the public library in Wrangell, Alaska, a town of about 2,600 persons. He was engaging in behavior that an observer alleged constituted child abuse. The local social service agency received the report and attempted to identify the man by asking the library for his identity and address. He was believed to have used the library prior to the alleged conduct. The library director refused to provide the information pursuant to the state's law, which protects "the names, addresses, or other personal identifying information of people who have used materials" in the library.[56] The social service agency filed a complaint with the city manager, accusing the library of failing to cooperate. However, both the city manager and the city attorney supported the library's position and the complaint was retracted. No further attempts were made.[57]

In May 1991 in the Boynton Beach, Florida, City Library, the library director was presented with a subpoena asking for the names of all persons who had checked out a particular book. The subpoena arose within the context of a criminal case and was presented by the public defender's office. The director sought the advice of the city attorney, expressing her concerns about the subpoena, in light of its generality. The city attorney agreed and asked the public defender to make a more specific request. There was no reply and no further attempts were made.[58] The library director reports that, in addition to this attempt, "[o]ther lawyers have tried intimidation without success."[59]

In Idaho, the Boise Public Library reported "several, casual, low pressure instances, where . . . staff members were asked for circulation information by law enforcement agencies."[60] Fortunately, when advised of the state confidentiality law, the officers backed down.

Library officials in Lebanon, Indiana, were not so protective of patron privacy. In 1986 and 1987, in a series of bizarre incidents designed to shame borrowers into returning overdue books, Lebanon Public Library personnel disregarded privacy concerns altogether. In actions supported by the library board, the library published in the local newspaper a list of borrowers with overdue books, along with the names of materials borrowed. The list included the names of persons who had checked out: *Two Guys Noticed Me . . . and Other Miracles*, *What About Teenage Marriage*, *What Only a Mother Can Tell You About Having a Baby*, *The Myth of Senility*, and *I Should Have Seen It Coming When the Rabbit Died*.[61] The list created "a buzz in the community of 12,000."[62] "It's affording the town a great deal of entertainment," said one former library board member.[63] Furthermore, the local newspaper reported that the ALA's Office for Intellectual Freedom supported the action, asserting that privacy protection does not apply when a patron fails to return a book on time. Besides, naming names "does what they want it to do . . . it brings the books back."[64] Nothing in Indiana's current confidentiality law prevents the librarian from continuing to employ this very "effective" tactic.[65]

In many states, such information is not protected. Louisiana reported two instances in the past several years involving subpoenaed records; one subpoena was successfully resisted and one led to compliance. Maryland reported that "[m]any incidences have occurred. It is usually the police wanting a circulation record or a parent wanting their child's records."[66] A number of states specifically exempt the records of a minor from protection, allowing library officials to turn over such information to a parent or guardian. Another incident in Maryland involved the Anne Arundel County Public Library. A woman was murdered shortly after she had visited the library; her body was found nearby. Police wanted to know when she had returned which books, but the retrieval system was too complicated to allow easy access to this information. The police instead captured the murderer by relying on other evidence.[67]

The Minneapolis Public Library was involved in a locally publicized case in 1985, when a restaurant patron fled the restaurant without paying his $55.83 tab. He left behind a library book. In an effort to track him down, the police understandably looked to the library for help. When the library refused to provide his name under the state's confidentiality law, the police simply obtained a court order and the library complied.[68]

The Omaha Public Library reported that it is "asked [for protected information] and we refuse on a regular basis."[69] In North Carolina, within the past few years, at least two requests were made from public libraries for patron information. A local Friends of the Library group requested the names and addresses of currently registered library borrowers from the Rowan County Public Library in Salisbury, but the request was refused under the state's confidentiality law. In Kenansville, local police sought the names of those who had borrowed a book that dealt with hallucinogenic plants. Two local youths had borrowed the book, experimented with some plants, and consequently became ill. The police apparently wanted to warn others, but the request was refused and the police did not pursue the matter.[70]

A recent survey in Oregon, conducted by the Oregon Library Association Intellectual Freedom Committee, revealed that five of the fourteen responding academic libraries and fifteen of the fifty-eight public libraries had received a request in the past five years for information protected by the state's confidentiality laws.[71]

In Pennsylvania, a well-publicized case involved a murderer who was a frequent patron of the public library. She had been in the library at 2:00 one afternoon, and at 3:30 she went on a shooting spree at a local shopping mall, leaving three dead and seven seriously wounded. The police wanted to know everything they could about her, including her reading habits and her behavior while at the library.[72] Although the librarian at first refused, citing the state's confidentiality law, the police eventually obtained a court order, forcing the librarian to testify in court against her library patron.

She came face to face with the grim reality that the confidentiality law does not provide much protection in the face of a court order. Commenting on the grueling experience she was forced to undergo, she lamented, "I wished for something like 'librarian/patron privilege.' "[73]

In Texas, a local district attorney subpoenaed library records of those who had checked out childbirthing books at the Decatur Public Library for the past nine months, as part of his investigation into the abandonment of an infant. The library resisted and a local judge finally quashed the subpoena, citing a "constitutional" privilege (Texas has no confidentiality statute). Although the judge refused to support the district attorney's generalized request for library records, he indicated he might do so in a specific case involving a specific suspect. He noted in his opinion:

In the event the State discovers an unexploded bomb, the wiring and details of which was [sic] identical or similar to illustrations contained in library books of recent publication, the State might well be within its rights in a specifically worded subpoena duces tecum, to require identity of patrons who had recently checked out those specific books as reasonable bounds of the State's police powers. However, the inquiry would have to be carried out on a case by case basis in compliance with due process.[74]

Additional responses to the author's questionnaire revealed the following information. In Utah, both law enforcement and fire department officials have requested patron information from the Salt Lake County Library System library. In Washington, law enforcement officials make similar requests "from time to time," although the library complies only after the officials produce a court order. In Wisconsin, a common loophole in the confidentiality law enabled two town boards in Eau Claire County to obtain the names and addresses of library users and the number of items checked out by each. The law, as in many other states, protected only the names of the items checked out. The library director was forced to comply, but he noted, "Users had expressed concern because it's seen as a private matter. Furthermore it could have a chilling effect on library use by people who fear how officials may use that information."[75] As a result, Wisconsin's confidentiality law was amended in 1992 to close the loophole. It now protects library records that indicate the identity of anyone "who borrows or uses the library's . . . materials, resources, or services."[76]

The ALA's Office of Intellectual Freedom has received a number of recent reports of attempts to breach library confidentiality:

1. Indiana (relating to a crime committed locally), June 1992.
2. Maryland (inquiry about who was using the history of labor library, related to a labor dispute), February 1992.
3. Texas (summons from U.S. Customs Service to produce records about who checked out a video cassette), November 1991.

4. Washington, D.C. (seeking evidence to show a patron involved in litigation was unstable), October 1991.

5. New Jersey (prosecutors inquire about patron who sought library information concerning child abuse laws), October 1990.

6. New York (New York City detectives subpoena public library circulation records of all patrons reading poetry of Scottish poet Aleister Crowley in connection with a gunman calling himself "the Zodiac." As a result of this search, a library patron was questioned and fingerprinted, although he did not match the description of the assailant and was not even of the same race. He was later cleared.), July 1990.[77]

The possibility of obtaining incriminating information from libraries is so well-known that a National Association of Chiefs of Police textbook recommended in 1990 that police officers investigating satanism

[c]heck with school and public librarians to see which books [about the occult] are missing or overdue. Get the name of the last person who checked out the book. Also, many libraries still use cards that every borrower has to sign. A quick glance at this card . . . will tell you who has checked out the book. . . .[78]

Obviously, the problem of access to library records is not diminishing. In fact, an ALA staff member recently remarked that telephone calls about attempts to breach library confidentiality occur with such frequency that the ALA cannot document all of them.[79]

A problem that has not yet captured widespread public attention involves the use of ever-widening computer networks. As libraries increasingly load patron data into their computer banks, the risk of security breaches increases as well. As early as 1981, one author warned that "the public release of library records may affect eligibility for credit, insurance, employment, and other necessities of modern life."[80] Although the actual risk of such breaches may be minimal, the public *perception* of the risk may influence user choices.[81] For example, one who believes he has engaged in sexual conduct that places him at risk of contracting the AIDS virus may be discouraged from seeking AIDS information out of fear that his insurance company or employer will have access to such information. Anything less than the strongest of confidentiality laws will only exacerbate the problem.

Various solutions have been proposed. Librarians are often advised to strengthen their internal library policies concerning confidentiality.[82] Although doing so is certainly advisable, particularly in those states that make disclosure discretionary rather than mandatory, policies will have little effect when law enforcement officials or members of the media seek access. Open records laws easily trump internal library policies.

Another facile solution, one increasingly employed by libraries across the country, is to destroy the library records as soon as the materials are returned.[83] But destruction of these public records may violate record retention laws and result in fines or imprisonment or both. In fact, libraries across the country are currently in violation of record retention laws in their attempts to protect the confidentiality of patron records. This remedy is too drastic. Not only does it result in a violation of state law, but it also destroys irremediably all traces of what may ultimately constitute valuable historical information. Alternative solutions abound and will be examined in Chapter 7.

For now, an examination of the current confidentiality statutes will suffice to demonstrate various approaches that states are taking to the problem.

NOTES

1. Gary E. Brown, *The Right to Inspect Public Records in Ohio*, 37 Ohio State L.J. 518, 518–19 (1976).

2. 5 U.S.C. § 552 (1977 & Supp. 1992).

3. Thomas M. Susman, *The Privacy Act and the Freedom of Information Act: Conflict and Resolution*, 21 J. Marshall L. Rev. 703, 704 (1988).

4. 110 Cong. Rec. 17,087 (daily ed. July 28, 1964) (statement of Sen. E. Long).

5. Susman, *supra* note 3. *See* 5 U.S.C. § 552 (1977 & Supp. 1992).

6. See Mark K. Wilson, Comment, *Surveillance of Individual Reading Habits: Constitutional Limitations on Disclosure of Library Borrower Lists*, 30 Amer. U.L. Rev. 275, 298 (1981).

7. Judith F. Krug & James A. Harvey, *ALA and Intellectual Freedom: A Historical Overview*, in American Library Association Office for Intellectual Freedom, Intellectual Freedom Manual xiii–xiv (3d ed. 1989) [hereinafter Krug & Harvey]. See also Bruce S. Johnson, *"A More Cooperative Clerk": The Confidentiality of Library Records*, 81 L. Libr. J. 769, 772–73 (1989).

8. Krug & Harvey, *id.* at xiv. "[T]he profession's stance on intellectual freedom has sometimes lagged behind society at large. . . . " The ALA's "position has fluctuated, being influenced by such factors as taste, quality, responsibility, morality, legality, and purpose." *Id.* at xiii. See also Evelyn Geller, Forbidden Books in American Public Libraries, 1876–1939: A Study in Cultural Change, 143, 156 (1984).

9. *Midwinter Council Minutes*, 33 Am. Libr. Ass'n Bull. 127, 129 (1939); *see also* Johnson, *supra* note 7, at 773.

10. Krug & Harvey, *supra* note 7, at xiv.

11. *Id.* at xix.

12. U.S. Const. amend. 1. Although this amendment refers only to the *federal* government, it applies to *state* government as well, through the due process clause of the Fourteenth Amendment. Murdock v. Commonwealth of Pennsylvania, 319 U.S. 105 (1943). The amendment has been interpreted to include the actions of state and local government officials.

13. See, e.g., Martin v. City of Struthers, 319 U.S. 141, 143 (1943) (the First Amendment "necessarily protects the right to receive" information); Gibson v. Florida Legislative Investigation Committee, 372 U.S. 539 (1963); NAACP v. Alabama, 357 U.S. 449 (1958) (First Amendment protects anonymity of members

of organizations); Thomas v. Collins, 323 U.S. 516 (1945) (First Amendment protects the right to recruit workers for labor unions without registering to do so).

14. 394 U.S. 557, 565 (1969).

15. See Chapter 6 for a discussion of cases resolved by state courts or state attorneys general.

16. Louis F. Ranlett, *The Librarians Have a Word for It: Ethics*, 64 Libr. J. 738, 740 (1939).

17. Krug & Harvey, *supra* note 7, at xix.

18. N.Y. Civ. Prac. L. & R. § 4503 (McKinney 1992).

19. Cal. Evid. Code § 954 (West Supp. 1993).

20. These Rules are promulgated by the American Bar Association. Individual states then adopt their own rules for professional ethics, usually based on these model rules.

21. This rule has been very controversial in the legal profession and many states have modified it to permit disclosure in other circumstances. See, e.g., Oklahoma Rule 1.6, which allows a lawyer to reveal information relating to a client's intent to commit *any* crime, and also requires a lawyer to reveal information "when required by law or court order."

22. Utah Code Ann. § 78–24–8 (1992).

23. Fed. R. Civ. P. 26.

24. Fed. R. Evid. 501.

25. Baldridge v. Shapiro, 455 U.S. 345, 362 (1982). See also Luey v. Sterling Drug, Inc., 240 F. Supp. 632 (D.C. Mich. 1965); Rosenblatt v. Northwest Airlines, Inc., 54 F.R.D. 21 (D.C.N.Y. 1921) ("There is no banker-client privilege. The scope of the privilege doctrine is narrow indeed.").

26. Rosenblatt v. Northwest Airlines, Inc., 54 F.R.D. 21 (D.C.N.Y. 1921).

27. Wigmore on Evidence, § 2285, at 527 (1961). *Accord* Int'l Tel. & Tel. Co. v. United Tel. Co. of Fla., 60 F.R.D. 177 (D.C. Fla. 1973).

28. Wilson, *supra* note 6, at 302.

29. For a brief history of the ALA Codes of Ethics and Policy Statements, see Johnson, *supra* note 7, at 772–81.

30. *Advisory Statement to U.S. Libraries from the American Library Association*, 19 Newsl. on Intell. Freedom 65, 65 (1970). See also Intellectual Freedom Manual, *supra* note 7, at 103.

31. ALA Policy Manual (1991–92), at 137.

32. *Id.* at 153.

33. The words, "with specific materials," were officially deleted from the Policy in 1975. *See* Intellectual Freedom Manual, *supra* note 7, at 105. Although they appear as printed above in the ALA Policy Manual, they do not appear in the Policy distributed by the ALA Intellectual Freedom Committee office.

34. ALA Policy Manual (1991–92), at 152.

35. Policy on Confidentiality of Library Records (as revised July 2, 1986, issued by the ALA in 1992).

36. For example, Zoia Horn was the head of the Reference Department at Bucknell University in Lewisburg, Pennsylvania. Father Philip Berrigan and the "Harrisburg Seven" were imprisoned nearby, awaiting trial for antiwar activities. The FBI recruited a convict, positioned him in a cell next to Father Berrigan, and arranged for him to work part-time in the Bucknell University library to report on

Berrigan's contacts with the library. Ms. Horn realized that she had an FBI "plant" working in the library, when she was subpoenaed to testify before a grand jury. H. N. Foerstel, Surveillance in the Stacks: The FBI's Library Awareness Program, at 7–10 (1991).

37. Neither Hawaii, Kentucky, Ohio, nor Texas have confidentiality statutes, although formal Attorney General Opinions in Kentucky and Texas offer some protection of library records from disclosure. See Ky. OAG 81–159 (Apr. 21, 1981) & Ky. OAG 82–149 (Mar. 12, 1982), which together protect from disclosure the circulation records of any library that is tax supported or receives "as much as 25 percent of their funds from state or local authority." Ky. OAG 82–149. However, although libraries in Kentucky are not mandated to disclose circulation records, they may do so if they choose. The decision is discretionary. Ky. OAG 82–149. Furthermore, although attorney general opinions carry some weight, they do not have the force of law; a court might disagree with the opinion if the issue comes before it.

See also Texas Open Records Decision No. 100 (July 10, 1975), which opines that "we believe that the courts, if squarely faced with the issue, would hold that the First Amendment . . . makes confidential that information in library circulation records which would disclose the identity of library patrons in connection with the material they have obtained from the library." In 1990 one local trial court judge agreed that library records are protected. See The Decatur Public Library v. The District Attorney's Office of Wise County, No. 90–05–192 (Texas 271st Judicial District Court, May 9, 1990). The case is discussed in *Judge Quashes Subpoena of Decatur Library Records*, Wise County Messenger, May 13, 1990, p. 1. However, this decision is not binding on other courts.

In Ohio during the 1991 legislative session, a bill was introduced to protect library records from the open records law, but it died in committee. Response to author's questionnaire from John Stewart, assistant state archivist, Ohio Historical Society, November 22, 1991.

38. Mississippi OAG May 10, 1985: "There is no specific exception to the Public Records Act of 1983 which would cover the list of borrowers from a public LI-BRARY; nor would such a list be protected by the Federal Privacy Act of 1974. . . . such a list would be a public record." In 1992, Mississippi adopted a library record confidentiality law. See Miss. Code Ann. § 39–3–365 (1993).

39. 5 U.S.C. § 552a.

40. S. Rep. 100–599, 100th Congs., 2d Sess. 1988 (Oct. 5, 1988). For a discussion of the legislative history of the bill, see Foerstel, *supra* note 36, at 125–33.

41. For example, William A. McGalliard, vice-chair of the board of the Oklahoma Department of Libraries, while asserting privacy of library records, also favored cooperation with law enforcement officials to prevent subversion and sabotage. Stephen Harter & Charles Busha, *Libraries and Privacy Legislation*, 1976 Libr. J. 475, 478, citing William A. McGalliard, *Cooperation Needed to Preserve Freedom*, Okla Libr., Oct. 1970, at 22.

42. Foerstel, *supra* note 36, at 149–50.

43. See Foerstel, *supra* note 36, for a discussion of the events surrounding this program.

44. *Id.* at 13.

45. *Id.* at 62.

46. *Id.* at 68. "Alexander Rolich, the library's Soviet and East European bibliographer, told of teams of agents who would watch a Soviet national while he read *Pravda.* 'They wanted to know if the newspaper he was reading looked funny, or like it had been marked up.' "

47. *Id.* at 68–69, 75.

48. *Id.* at 54.

49. *Id.* at 69.

50. At the University of Maryland, library personnel sought the advice of the University attorney, who advised that Maryland law at that time did not *prohibit* the disclosure; thus, the library had discretion to determine whether or not to disclose. See *id.* at 62.

51. *Id.* at 69.

52. *Id.* at 77.

53. *FBI Asks Librarians to Help in the Search for Spies*, Philadelphia Inquirer, Feb. 23, 1988, p. 17A.

54. William A. Knott, *Confidentiality of Records*, 106 Libr. J. 2162 (1981).

55. Video and Library Privacy Protection Act of 1988, Joint Hearing before the Subcommittee on Courts, Civil Liberties, and the Administration of Justice, House Committee on the Judiciary, and the Subcommittee on Technology and the Law, Senate Committee on the Judiciary, 100 Cong., 2d Sess., Aug. 3, 1988, pp. 42–44. See also Foerstel, *supra* note 36, at 123–24.

56. See Alaska Stat. § 09.25.140 (1992).

57. Telephone Interview with Kay Jabusch, Public Library, Wrangell, Alaska (July 6, 1992).

58. Response to author's questionnaire by Virginia K. Farace, director, Boynton Beach City Library (1992).

59. *Id.*

60. Response to author's questionnaire by Marilyn Poertner, assistant director, Boise Public Library (1992).

61. Reported in the Lebanon Reporter, March 1 & 5, 1986.

62. Reported in The Arizona Daily Star, April 13, 1986.

63. Reported in The Indianapolis Star, March 8, 1986.

64. *Id.*, quoting Judith F. Krug, director of the ALA's Office for Intellectual Freedom.

65. Indiana's confidentiality law provides that library records are exempt from public disclosure "at the discretion of" the library. Ind. Code Ann. § 5–14–3–4 (West 1989).

66. Response to author's questionnaire by J. Maurice Travillian, assistant state superintendent, State Department of Education (1991–92).

67. Telephone interview with JoAnn Pinder, a former employee there, August 1992. She also recounted requests for confidential records received by other libraries where she has been employed.

68. The library record, however, was of no assistance. The culprit had checked out the book, *From Where I Sit*, by Merv Griffin and Peter Barsochini, under an assumed name. "The address was for a room at the Continental Hotel in Minneapolis . . . [b]ut the room registered [sic] to a little old lady who had lived there for a very long time." *Police Are Forced to Play by Book to Check Out Clue, But Find Only a Blank Page*, Minneapolis Star and Tribune, Oct. 1, 1985, p. 3B.

69. Response to author's questionnaire by Michael Phipps, director, Omaha Public Library (1992).

70. Response to author's questionnaire by John Welch, assistant state librarian, Division of State Libraries (1992).

71. Survey attached to letter from Mary Ginnane, library development administrator, Oregon State Library, July 24, 1992.

72. Janis M. Lee, *Confidentiality: From the Stacks to the Witness Stand*, Am. Libraries 444 (June 1988).

73. *Id.* at 448.

74. The Decatur Public Library v. The District Attorney's Office of Wise County, No. 90–05–192 (Texas 271st Judicial District Court, May 9, 1990).

75. *Library Director Warns of Invasion of Privacy*, The Capital Times, December 27, 1990, p. 3D.

76. Wis. Stat. Ann. § 43.30 (West 1992).

77. All of these incidents are reported in the files of the ALA Office of Intellectual Freedom.

78. *Witch-Hunting in High School*, Harper's Magazine, December 1990, at 20, 22.

79. Interview with Anne Levinson Penway, ALA Office of Intellectual Freedom, Chicago (July 27, 1992).

80. Wilson, *supra* note 6, at 275, 289.

81. Consider, for example, the publication of library users' names, *along with the names of the borrowed materials*, in the local newspaper in Lebanon, Indiana, in 1986 and 1987. See *supra* text accompanying notes 61–65.

82. Bruce M. Kennedy, *Confidentiality of Library Records: A Survey of Problems, Policies, and Laws*, 81 L. Libr. J. 733, 745 (1989).

83. Foerstel, *supra* note 36, at 134.

5

Current Status of State Confidentiality Statutes

The development of state confidentiality statutes is fairly modern, with the passage of the earliest statutes occurring in 1980.[1] As is typical of any new body of law, only time can demonstrate the flaws and loopholes of a particular statute, and, in this case, time has done so. Over the past fourteen years, it has become apparent that some confidentiality laws are stronger than others, and the gradual evolution toward stronger laws has demonstrated that not all confidentiality laws are created equal. In fact, the disparities are striking.

One common feature of the laws is their framework. Generally, they provide a definition of the kinds of libraries whose records will receive protection, a description of the material and information that are protected, a list of exceptions for which protection will not be provided, and, in some states, procedures to ensure due process when a dispute arises, or penalties for violation of the confidentiality laws.

In some states, the confidentiality law appears as a part of the open records act. In these cases, library records are generally classified as public records, but exempt from the open records laws,[2] or are classified as records that are not public.[3] The classification scheme may prove significant. If the records are public, albeit confidential, they are governed by laws that apply generally to public records. These might include record retention laws or laws that make all public records available after a period of years.

In some states, the library confidentiality law is not part of the open records law at all, but rather appears as a separate statute, generally within the state's "library code" or "library law."[4] Although such a design ensures a greater likelihood that library professionals will be aware of it, it also ensures that others will be less aware of it as an exception to open records laws. Thus, a few states have incorporated the library confidentiality law into both the open records act and the library act.[5] This is the better approach.

An analysis of the various laws can provide the foundation for drafting new, stronger confidentiality laws. Surely a dozen or so years of dealing with the problem can direct the profession toward better legislation in the future. The analysis will include the following issues:

1. Which libraries are included?
2. What information and materials are protected?
3. Are the laws discretionary or mandatory?
4. Are there exceptions to the law?
5. What process is due?
6. Can penalties be imposed for violation of the law?

Appendix D consists of a state-by-state analysis of confidentiality statutes.

WHICH LIBRARIES ARE INCLUDED WITHIN CONFIDENTIALITY LAWS?

The most obvious inclusion is "public" libraries, because they are funded with public money, either state or local or both, and because their records generally constitute public records. But does this include school or university libraries? Special libraries? Libraries only partially funded by public monies? In fact, the range of definitions for libraries included within the confidentiality laws is much greater than one would suppose.[6]

For example, the definitions for publicly funded libraries whose records are protected by confidentiality laws include the following:

• public, public school, or college and university libraries[7]
• any library which is in whole or in part supported by public funds[8]
• any library which is in whole or in part supported by public funds, including the records of a public library system[9]
• any library which is in whole or in part supported by public funds, including the records of public, academic, school, and special libraries and the State Library[10]
• State Library or any local library which is established or maintained under any law of the Commonwealth or the library of any university, college or educational institution chartered by the Commonwealth or the library of any public school

or branch reading room, deposit station or agency operated in connection therewith[11]

- all public libraries[12]
- library or library system supported by public monies[13]
- public, school, academic, and special libraries and library systems supported in whole or in part by public funds[14]
- public, free association, school, college, and university libraries[15]
- any public municipal library, including the State Library[16]
- library operated by any state agency, political subdivision, or statewide system[17]
- publicly funded library[18]
- any library receiving public funds, any library that is a state agency and any library established by the state, an instrumentality of the state, a local government, district or authority, whether or not that library is regularly open to the public[19]
- public, private, school, college, technical college, university, and state institutional libraries and library systems, supported in whole or in part by public funds or expending public funds[20]

Obviously, the focus of these definitions is that a library that receives public funding falls within the protection of the confidentiality law. This makes sense when one realizes that most of the confidentiality laws serve as exceptions to open records laws, which themselves allow inspection of records that are prepared by public officials with public monies. In fact, one state has specifically stated that protection from disclosure "applies to any library which is subject to the Open Records Law."[21]

It is important to note that some statutes specifically include the State Library. This takes on special significance in those states that include library records within the definition of public records under the state's record retention laws. The retention law may mandate that records in the State Library be retained for many years. If, under state law, any library records must be preserved by transfer to the State Library or archives, the confidentiality given to those records should be preserved by the caretakers of their new home. Most laws do not address such potentiality.

Also, although state public schools and universities are publicly funded, some states have seen fit to specifically include those libraries within the definition, most likely to avoid the argument that "public libraries" refers only to those libraries the citizenry generally refers to as the town or city or county library. Indeed, when the FBI sought the library circulation records of the University of Maryland at College Park in 1986, the campus attorney advised the library staff member that Maryland law protected public library records, but that the university library was not a public library.[22]

Some states have not defined the kinds of libraries covered by the statute, instead referring generally to "library" records.[23] These statutes clearly leave themselves open to varying interpretations, resulting in the potential for disputes and abuse. Although the public has long complained about the complexity and technical nature of legal documents, such complexity can be viewed as an attempt to ward off future disputes about the meaning of the law. After all, if a library director, in attempting to protect his or her library records, can point directly to a law that accurately and specifically describes the library at issue, the director has a more powerful shield than if he or she can point to a law that states only that "library records" are protected. The advantage of a detailed statute, if well drafted, is that it demonstrates that the legislature considered and intentionally included the type of library appearing in the statute. A general statute may indicate that the legislature had not even considered that a nontraditional library might fall within its scope.

Only one state has chosen an intentionally restrictive definition of libraries protected by the confidentiality law. The State of West Virginia protects libraries "maintained wholly or in part by any governing authority from funds derived by taxation and the services of which are free to the public," but does not include "special libraries, such as law, medical or other professional libraries, or school libraries which are maintained primarily for school purposes."[24]

Some states make it clear in their statutes that confidentiality is not just a *public* library issue. The broadest definitions are those that protect the records of "any library"[25] or "a person . . . engaged in the business of . . . lending books or other written materials, sound recordings, or video recordings. . . ."[26] But other statutes focus on whether or not the public has access to the library. They include:

• library which is established by the state; a county, city, township, village, school district, or other local unit of government or authority or combination of local units of governments and authorities; a community college district; a college or university; or any private library open to the public[27]

• library which makes materials available to the public including libraries operated by the state, a municipality, or a public school, including the state university[28]

One state includes public libraries and libraries "of an educational, historical or eleemosynary institution, organization or society."[29] And another includes a

• library maintained by any State or local governmental agency, school, college or industrial, commercial or other special group, association or agency, whether public or private.[30]

Approaches to coverage appear to take two quite different directions, one very general (all libraries) and the other very specific. In the law, generalized coverage may at first appear to be the more inclusive and therefore the better approach; however, generalities often leave room for varying interpretations, particularly for those intent on breaching the confidence. Furthermore, in those states that make protection merely discretionary, generalized definitions may provide those seeking information with the weaponry needed to break down a library employee's resistance.

WHAT INFORMATION AND MATERIALS ARE PROTECTED?

Here again one finds numerous attempts to include within the statutory protection as much library patron information as possible. Again, because this type of confidentiality law is fairly modern, one can see an evolution in the law's definition, beginning with attempts to protect circulation records and eventually including more and more information in reaction to advancing technology or to third-party attempts to bypass confidentiality.

One approach defines protected materials as "registration and circulation records." A registration record is "information which a library requires a patron to provide to become eligible to borrow books and other materials," and a circulation record is "information which identifies patrons borrowing particular books and other material."[31] Although simplicity has its virtue, these definitions may not include other uses a patron makes of a library, such as reference assistance or a request for a data base search. The definition appears to apply only to those instances when a patron *borrows* material from a library—that is, removes it from the library. One statute anticipates this problem and defines material protected as "[c]irculation records showing *use* of specific library materials by named persons."[32]

Because of the limitations of this kind of definition, the majority of states have focused instead on protecting information that personally identifies a patron and associates him or her with the use of specific library materials. These statutes protect:

- all library records containing personally identifiable information, meaning any information that would identify a patron[33]
- personally identifiable information contained in the circulation records[34]
- circulation and similar records of a library which identify the user of library materials[35]
- library or archival records which can be used to identify any library patron[36]
- records that when examined alone or with other records identify a patron[37]
- records related to the circulation of library materials which contain the names or other personally identifying details regarding the users[38]
- records which contain information relating to the identity of a library patron relative to the patron's use of books or other materials at the library[39]

- records relating to the identity of library patrons or the identity of library patrons in regard to the circulation of library materials.[40]

Note that even these seemingly simple definitions leave room for interpretation and, ultimately, more disclosure than most librarians desire. For example, statutes that refer only to circulation of materials or registration-identifying information necessarily limit the law's protection. It makes little sense to protect the library patron when he or she checks out a book, but to afford no protection when the patron requests assistance from the reference librarian or requests a computerized data base search.

Some states specifically define library "materials" as a "book, document, film, record, art work or other library property."[41] A couple of statutes are even more detailed; there, library materials requested, used, or obtained may include: "circulation of library books, materials, computer data base searches, interlibrary loan transactions, reference queries, patent searches, requests for photocopies of library materials, title reserve requests, or the use of audiovisual materials, films, or records."[42]

Another area of weakness addressed by some statutes is the connection of a patron's name with other library records. For example, if a library wants to protect patrons' privacy, it may require them to record their social security numbers or other identifying numbers for checkout purposes. If the law protects only the names of borrowers, it will not protect the numbers that, when combined with other cross-referenced records, will easily identify the name of the borrower. Therefore, some states have passed laws that protect "records . . . which, when examined alone, or when examined with other public records, would reveal the identity of the library patron checking out, requesting, or using an item from a library."[43] This wording is also intended to cover more than the borrowing of materials from the library.

In fact, a number of states focus on the *use* a patron makes of a library, to ensure that confidentiality protection is not limited to the circulation of materials. These states protect from disclosure:

- information of people who have used materials made available to the public by a library[44]
- information which identifies a user of *library services* as requesting or obtaining specific materials *or services* or as otherwise using the library[45]
- information that identifies a person as having requested or obtained specific information, materials, or services, or as otherwise having used the library[46]
- information that identifies . . . a person as a patron of the library or that indicates use or request of materials from the library[47]
- information that identifies the use a patron makes of that library's materials, services, or facilities[48]

This last definition is unusual in that it includes protection of information concerning the patron's use of the library *facilities*. This would appear to protect information concerning meeting rooms a patron reserves for his or her use, information that the FBI sought about John Hinckley after he shot then-President Reagan.[49] The law also appears to protect information about the patron's conduct in the library generally. The usefulness of such a provision can be seen in considering the case of Janis M. Lee, formerly director of the Swarthmore, Pennsylvania, Public Library. When a library patron went on a killing spree, Ms. Lee was subpoenaed to testify against the patron. She recounts that although the state confidentiality law protected books the patron had borrowed, the law did not address testimony in response to such questions as "how did she act, what kinds of reference questions did she ask, what materials did she photocopy." Ms. Lee says, "[The defendant] was my patron, and I felt like a traitor."[50]

A question prompted by statutes that protect against disclosure of those using a library is how to define a "patron." An argument can be made that a group, or organization, is a library patron. Some state laws specifically protect information pertaining to a "group of individuals."[51] Thus, information about a group using a library meeting room would be protected under such a law.

In addition to the focus on how a patron uses the library, some statutes focus on the format of the materials, to emphasize that written records, as they are traditionally envisioned, are not the only records protected. These statutes protect new technologically innovative record-keeping devices. Thus, the following materials are protected:

- any record or other information[52]
- document, record, or other method of storing information retained by a library[53]
- records [that] include, but are not limited to, library, information system, and archival records related to the circulation and use of library materials or services[54]
- documents or information in any format retained in a library[55]
- circulation record or other item, collection, or grouping of information about an individual that is maintained by a library[56]
- that portion of *data* maintained by a library.[57]

Some states have gone beyond traditional bounds of protection. An opinion of the Tennessee attorney general asserts that procedures in which patrons sign a library card that is reinserted into the book after return to the library constitutes a violation of the patron's rights, both under the state's confidentiality law and perhaps even under the First and Fourteenth Amendments of the United States Constitution.[58] Opinions of the attorneys general of several other states are in agreement.[59]

Arkansas law specifically directs that "[p]ublic libraries shall use an au-

tomated or Gaylord-type circulation system that does not identify a patron
with circulated materials after materials are returned."[60] The problem with
this statute is that it envisions automatic purging of circulation records,
but destruction of circulation records, deemed by law to be public records,
constitutes a crime in some states. In Arkansas, for example, as in other
states, records of the state and of the various cities, towns, school districts,
and counties are "property of the people of this state."[61] "Public records"
include all papers or

> other documents, regardless of physical form, including records produced by or
> for use with electronic or mechanical data processing devices, and which have been
> or shall be created or received by any agency . . . or official thereof in the exercise
> of his office, or in the conduct, transaction, or performance of any business, duty,
> or function pursued in accordance with law.[62]

Destruction of such records may be made only in accordance with the state
Public Records Management and Archives Act of 1973.[63] Thus, before any
library decides that destruction of records is the best way to preserve
confidentiality, it is well advised to check its public record retention statute
first.

   A couple of states, although without specific library confidentiality provisions, do offer some protection by means of general statutory language.
Kentucky law protects "[p]ublic records containing information of a personal nature where the public disclosure thereof would constitute a clearly
unwarranted invasion of personal privacy."[64] A Kentucky attorney general
opinion interprets this law to mandate a "weighing of an individual's right
of privacy against the public interest."[65] In so doing, "the individual's
privacy rights as to what he borrows from a public library . . . is [sic] overwhelming" and would therefore be protected.[66]

   Hawaii has no library confidentiality law, either, but a general exemption
to its Freedom of Information Act protects "[g]overnment records which,
if disclosed, would constitute a clearly unwarranted invasion of personal
privacy."[67] Although this language mirrors the language of the Kentucky
statute, it has not yet been interpreted in the context of library records,
and there is no guarantee that it would be interpreted similarly. The language requires a balancing act by someone, presumably a state court judge.

   Nor does Texas have a library confidentiality law, although a Texas
attorney general opinion finds that the First Amendment protects library
records.[68] One lower court judge has concurred with this opinion, finding
a constitutional privilege in one case involving a general request for the
names of any library patrons who had borrowed childbirthing books.[69] The
opinion is not binding on any other court, however, and, as mentioned
earlier, attorney general opinions may influence other courts but they are
not binding.

One final category of protected information is one quite common in state laws: the information having to do with material donated to libraries under the terms set forth by the donor. As stated in various laws, the following materials are not subject to open records laws:

- library and museum material [and, in some states, archival material] contributed by private persons, to the extent of any limitations placed thereon as conditions of the contribution[70]
- library or archival records deposited with, or acquired by, a library upon a condition that the records be disclosed only to qualified researchers or after the passing of a specified period of years or after the death of specified persons[71]
- any records or documents . . . through or concerning any gift, grant, conveyance, bequest, or devise, the terms of which restrict or regulate public access to such records or documents[72]
- materials of a historical or educational value upon which the donor or seller has imposed restrictions with respect to access to and inspection of the materials for a definite period of time as specified by the donor or seller.[73] And in Rhode Island, the "identity of the contributor of a bona fide and lawful charitable contribution whenever public anonymity has been requested" is protected.[74]

HOW PROTECTED IS THE INFORMATION?
MANDATORY VERSUS DISCRETIONARY LAWS

Most states have confidentiality laws. Librarians properly pride themselves on their successes in the past twenty years, and without librarians most of these laws would not exist. But the strength of these laws has been severely undermined in many states because they are discretionary only. They depend for their success entirely on the discretion of the library employee from whom information is requested.

Subtle wording in the statutes may mask their weaknesses. Strong, mandated confidentiality can be stated either affirmatively—that library records "shall remain" or "shall be kept" confidential—or negatively—that libraries "shall not allow disclosure" of their records or that records "shall not be disclosed." However, only thirty-one states include such language.[75]

The rest of the states have statutes that are clearly discretionary or at least arguably so. Virginia's law is the most obvious example of a legislative decision to grant discretion to the record custodian; it states that library records are exempted from the state's freedom of information act, "but may be disclosed by the custodian in his discretion."[76] Indiana law states that library records are exempt from the open records law "at the discretion of" the library.[77] Iowa law protects library records "unless otherwise ordered . . . by the lawful custodian."[78] Four states merely provide that library records shall not be deemed public records.[79] Although this means that the librarian is not obligated under the state's freedom of information act to disclose the records, the law does not prohibit him or her from doing so. Four states in fact provide that the library is "not required" to disclose records,[80] and six provide that library records are exempt from disclosure under the state's open records law.[81] Finally, one state, Utah, provides that the library must disclose records under certain conditions, but further states: "Nothing . . . prohibits a governmental entity from disclosing a record . . . if the governmental entity determines that disclosure is in the public interest."[82]

Obviously, in the face of discretionary confidentiality laws, a strong library policy is essential. Suggestions for such a policy can be found in Chapter 7.

EXCEPTIONS TO CONFIDENTIALITY LAWS

Every state has exceptions to its library records confidentiality laws, in part a testament to the nature of legislative compromise. In some states, the exceptions easily consume the rule itself.

Patron Consent and Library Administration

Two common exceptions that pose no significant threat to patron privacy are patron consent to disclosure of his or her records, and library personnel requirements of the records for the library's day-to-day operation. Even in these areas, however, some laws allow abuse.

Although many states require *written* consent by the library patron,[83] some do not.[84] Some states do not mention consent at all; presumably, however, since the law is designed to protect the patron's privacy right, the patron is entitled to waive that right.

The notion of "informed" consent appears in a couple of state statutes. Arkansas law provides that patron information may be disclosed with the patron's informed, written consent.[85] Minnesota law goes even further, defining informed consent as a "statement in plain language, dated, specific in designating the person or agency authorized to disclose and the person or agency to whom the data shall be disclosed, specific as to the purpose of disclosure and as to the expiration date, ordinarily less than one year."[86] Utah law requires that when the requesting party is not the patron, the requester must produce a power of attorney from the patron or a notarized release from the patron "or his legal representative [e.g., attorney] dated no more than 30 days before the date of the request."[87] Such safeguards avoid the possibility of a library including a general waiver in the library registration application. General waivers in advance of a specific request for patron records do not provide adequate privacy protection, because the patron ordinarily cannot foresee that any third person might be interested in his or her library records. The patron may not even be aware that records are kept or that they might be made available to others. Thus, the waiver is not "informed."

Although it might be taken for granted that *someone* at the library would have access to the patron's records, the question of whom and for what purpose has been addressed in a number of state laws as exceptions to confidentiality requirements. If the patron's privacy is of utmost significance, then it becomes important to shield patron information as much as possible, in effect, to build a wall around the information, allowing invasion only when necessary. Some laws reflect this policy. They approach the problem from two perspectives: *who* should have access and *for what purpose*.

Obviously the better approach is to address both issues. Some, however, address only one, as, for example, providing disclosure of records to "the library itself,"[88] or for the purpose of assessing fines,[89] or for "ordinary business and only for the purposes for which the record was created,"[90] or for "inter-library cooperation and coordination,"[91] or for library administration.[92]

The most common two-pronged approach to this problem allows disclosure to the "library itself if necessary for the reasonable operation of the library."[93] Many states allow disclosure by members of the library staff or persons acting within the scope of their duties within the library administration in the ordinary course of business or in the performance of their duties.[94] Alabama law includes the state education department or state public library service when necessary for the library's proper operation.[95] And four states permit disclosure to persons outside the library, presumably collection agencies, for fine collection purposes.[96] Depending upon the wording of the state's confidentiality law, records in the hands of collection agencies remain library records and, if the law protects such records generally, the custodian is irrelevant. For example, most confidentiality laws protect public library records; they remain public library records no matter who holds them. But if the law prohibits a *library* from disclosing records, it may have no effect on a collection agency. Although it will be a rare instance when this might pose a problem, a well-drafted, comprehensive confidentiality law should take it into account.

Statistical Compilations

Another very common exception to confidentiality laws is really no exception at all. It applies to statistical compilations prepared by library administrators that do not identify individual patrons.[97] Because many laws apply only to personally identifiable information, the compilation of statistics would not violate the law, even without this exception. In those states that protect registration or circulation records or "library records," the patron's privacy is not violated by the compilation of statistics that do not identify individual patrons. Thus, such an exception would not pose a threat to patron privacy. Libraries no doubt find such statistical compilations helpful and often necessary, and a comprehensive statute should include such an exception.

Court Orders and Subpoenas

What most distinguishes the protection of confidentiality from the protection of privilege is that a court order or even a subpoena can eviscerate confidentiality. A privilege is unaffected by a subpoena and will often withstand court orders. From the very earliest attempts to protect library records, the library profession has been willing to carve out an exception for court orders. Although the ALA includes in its official policy the recommendation that libraries "[r]esist the issuance or enforcement of any such process, order, or subpoena until such time as a proper showing of good cause has been made in a court of competent jurisdiction,"[98] most states ignore such advice when drafting confidentiality laws.

Many states provide that library records lose their protection upon the presentation of a court order,[99] although several of these require additional due process protection.[100] Some of them give way to either a court order or a subpoena.[101] A subpoena is a "command to appear at a certain time and place to give testimony upon a certain matter. A subpoena duces tecum requires production of books, papers and other things."[102] Neither type of subpoena requires a hearing or any judicial involvement prior to issuance and service. In fact, an attorney can type and sign a subpoena in his or her office with no court involvement at all.[103] Subpoenas are, in reality, fairly easy to obtain and may be issued in bulk from the court clerk. A court order, however, is an order issued and signed by a judge, generally after a hearing or after due consideration of the written arguments of all parties concerned, although an order might be signed by a judge perfunctorily.

Some states have attempted to protect library records from the pro forma subpoena or court order. Thus, they might require disclosure only with a court order upon a specific finding that the disclosure is necessary to protect public safety or to prosecute a crime[104] or because the merits of disclosure "clearly exceed the demand for individual privacy."[105] How one proves necessity is questionable. For example, can a local sheriff or even an ordinary citizen obtain such an order simply by his or her statement of necessity? Would requiring an affidavit offer more safeguards against abuse? In fact, confidentiality laws rarely address such issues. If the library profession is at all willing to allow a court order to overcome library confidentiality, the law should at least include requirements for a hearing and judicial review.

Another requirement of a strong law would allow disclosure only in *criminal* cases where law enforcement officials have a specific suspect targeted. Criminal cases involve public safety; civil cases, such as divorce, tort, and contract cases, do not. Therefore, if the patron's privacy is to be breached at all, it should be the rare instance and then only for criminal investigations. A couple of states have recognized the distinction. South Carolina allows disclosure when "necessary to protect public safety" or to "prosecute a crime," but requires that, in a civil matter, one requesting disclosure must show "good cause before the presiding Judge. . . ."[106] Pennsylvania allows disclosure only in a criminal proceeding pursuant to a court order.[107]

The requirement that officials have a specific suspect targeted is also necessary to prevent "fishing expeditions" by local prosecutors and to ensure that exceptions to privacy protection are as narrow as possible. This prevents law enforcement officials from scouring library records to find suspicious activity. It is consistent with other criminal due process requirements, such as the requirement of probable cause before persons can be subjected to searches; police cannot simply stop persons in the street without at least some articulable reason for doing so. Nor should they be allowed to search one's reading interests without some specific suspicion of wrongdoing.

A couple of states have addressed the court order exception in very specific ways. In Iowa, library records can be released "to a criminal justice agency only pursuant to an investigation of a particular person or organization suspected of committing a known crime," where a "connection exists between the requested release of information, and a legitimate end," and where "the need for information is cogent and compelling."[108] The specificity of Iowa's law was a result of a case in 1983, in which the Des Moines Public Library was forced to produce a list of patrons who had checked out books dealing with witchcraft and related matters. At the time, library records in Iowa were confidential, "unless . . . ordered by a court." A law enforcement officer produced a subpoena, issued by the court clerk.[109] The records were ordered to be produced.

In Utah, patron privacy may be breached by court order, but only if it is signed by a state or federal judge (not a justice of the peace, a lower level official), involves a matter already in controversy, and the court has considered the merits of the record request.[110] Washington allows disclosure but only if the court, "after a hearing with notice . . . to every person in interest and the agency," finds that protection of records is "clearly unnecessary to protect any individual's right of privacy or any vital governmental function."[111]

These laws clearly protect patron records more carefully than a general requirement of a "court order." They do not go far enough, however. If, as most librarians believe, library records should be as protected as the records between doctors and patients or lawyers and clients, they have a long way to go toward that protection.

Records of a Minor Child

Apparently, in some states, the privacy of children does not deserve the protection of adult privacy. Confidentiality laws in these states carve out exceptions for the library records of minor children. These laws generally provide disclosure of library records to parents or custodians of a minor child,[112] or to the custodial parent or guardian of a minor child,[113] or to the parent of a child under 18,[114] or to the parent or legal guardian of an unemancipated minor or legal guardian of a legally incapacitated individual.[115] Some statutes focus on school libraries, providing that the "parent of a minor child shall have the right to inspect the registration and circulation records of any school or public library that pertain to his or her child."[116] Obviously, in these states, parents can turn over the records to anyone else interested in the minor's reading interests. Two states facilitate the process by allowing disclosure of a minor's library records upon the written consent of the child's parents (or the guardian if the patron is a ward).[117]

Most likely the statutes that strip minors of library confidentiality are the result of legislative compromise. But that does not make them acceptable. Imagine a sixteen-year-old child who has suffered sexual abuse by her father, or who is pregnant and needs to learn where to seek help. If she cannot afford to visit the local bookstore, the public or school library may be her only source of information. The policy behind patron confidentiality for adults may be even stronger for minors in these circumstances.

Limitation of Years

Library confidentiality acts do not specifically place time limitations on protection of library records. In fact, the trend is to destroy circulation records as soon as possible after the materials have been returned to the library. However, as has been noted in Part I of this book, such destruction may violate public record retention laws. If those laws include library records, as they generally do, such records are to be treated as any other public record for purposes of retention and destruction. Similarly, when library confidentiality laws appear as exceptions to the state's open records laws, rather than as free-standing library confidentiality laws, they may be bound by the same restrictions as other public records.

As mentioned earlier, under the wording of some open records acts, library patron records have been classified as records that are *not* public; they will not be subject to any time limitations placed on public records.

However, in the states in which library patron records *are* public, albeit confidential, their protection lasts only so long as the law allows. Laws vary, providing protection against public access for twenty-five years,[118] for ten years after death of the individual or thirty years from the date the record was created,[119] or up to seventy,[120] seventy-five,[121], eighty,[122] or one hundred years.[123] An argument could certainly be made that one's right of privacy ends upon his or her death; therefore, library records should be released thereafter. In many states, under the law of tort, which includes defamation and the right of privacy, one's privacy interest lapses upon death and any violation thereafter is not actionable. The assumption is that after death one has no further privacy interest whose violation results in damage. For the library profession, the issue becomes a complicated matter, requiring a balancing of the privacy interest against the interest in historical events. Would it not be helpful to know (albeit after his or her death, or fifty years after the event) what an American president was reading when he decided to launch an attack on a neighboring country, or the kinds of literature that may have influenced a Pulitzer Prize winner? Perhaps some library professionals, perhaps the overwhelming majority, are not willing to sacrifice privacy for the sake of such information. But the decision should be made thoughtfully and carefully. Consideration of time limitations on privacy protection should play a role in any library confidentiality law.

WHAT PROCESS IS DUE?

Although it is clear that the library profession desires confidentiality of library records, it is just as clear that few states have been able to legislate legal procedures to ensure due process for both the library and the patron. Too often, due process concerns arise only *after* one is presented with a subpoena or court order. It is also clear that procedural protection is most needed when the law is substantively weak. If the law is drafted to allow for disclosure only in extreme circumstances, detailed procedures may be unnecessary.

Perhaps the most detailed law establishing proper procedure is that of the District of Columbia. Because it is set forth in a statute, rather than merely in a library policy, it is binding upon library personnel as well as upon those who request library records. It provides as follows:

A person whose records are requested . . . may file a motion in the Superior Court . . . requesting that the records be kept confidential. The motion shall be accompanied by the reasons for the request. . . .

Within 2 working days after receiving a subpoena issued by the court for public library records, the public library shall send a copy of the subpoena and the following notice, by certified mail, to all affected library patrons:

"Records or information concerning your borrowing records in the public library . . . are being sought pursuant to the enclosed subpoena.

"In accordance with the . . . Confidentiality of Library Records Act of 1984, these records will not be released until 10 days from the date this notice was mailed.

"If you desire that these records or information not be released, you must file a motion in the Superior Court . . . requesting that the records be kept confidential, and state your reasons for the request. A sample motion is enclosed.

"You may wish to contact a lawyer. If you do not have a lawyer, you may call the District of Columbia Bar Lawyer Referral Service."

The public library shall not make available any subpoenaed materials until 10 days after the above notice has been mailed.[124]

The statute allows the notice to be waived, but only if the government applies to the court for a waiver and the judge finds that:

(A) The investigation being conducted is within the lawful jurisdiction of the government authority seeking the records.

(B) There is reason to believe that the records being sought are relevant to a legitimate law enforcement inquiry.

(C) There is reason to believe that the notice will result in:

    (i) Endangering the life or physical safety of any person;

    (ii) Flight from prosecution;

    (iii) Destruction of or tampering with evidence;

    (iv) Intimidation of potential witnesses; or

    (v) Otherwise seriously jeopardizing an investigation or official proceeding.[125]

The significance of this law is that there is a presumption of notice. To overcome that presumption requires judicial involvement. In addition to a fine of up to $300.00 against any library employee who violates this law, the patron also has the right to file a civil action against the wrongdoer for actual damages or $250.00, whichever is greater, plus attorney fees and court costs.[126]

Other states provide some process, but none as detailed as the District of Columbia. For example, Michigan requires notice, an opportunity to be heard at a court hearing, and the right to be represented by a lawyer, but only for the *library*, not for the *patron*.[127] In Minnesota, the party denied access may bring the issue to the judge; the judge then decides if the benefit to the requesting party outweighs the harm to the library or patron. The judge may also decide whether notice is warranted.[128] However, this "process" is no more than is implied by any confidentiality statute. In reality, *either* party may seek a court order, either to gain access to library records or to prevent such access, pursuant to the terms of the state's law. Of course, in most states, the patron would not even be aware that access to his records is being sought.

New Mexico law gives the library the right to be represented by counsel at any court hearing,[129] again not a concession at all, since parties to litigation can always hire their own lawyer. The "due process" provided in the State of Washington actually may work against library record confidentiality. There, although library records are exempt from the open records laws, a judge may find that inspection will be permitted if exemption "is clearly unnecessary to protect any individual's right of privacy or any vital governmental function." Fortunately, such a finding may issue only "after a hearing with notice thereof to every person in interest" and the library.[130] In Wyoming, the law provides that if the library denies access, the requesting party can ask for a written statement of the reasons for the denial and may ask the court for an order requiring disclosure. If the library "believes that disclosure would do substantial injury to the public interest, notwithstanding that the record might otherwise be available to inspection," the library may seek court protection.[131]

Most of the state statutes do not set forth any process at all. There, the state rules of civil or criminal procedure would govern. This may entail a request for an emergency court hearing after a librarian has been handed a subpoena or court order. No matter what process the state procedural rules provide, it is certain that the experience will be confusing and stressful for a librarian facing the situation for the first time.

The advantages of a detailed procedure for handling library record requests are obvious. In contrast to an internal library procedure for handling such requests, a procedure set forth in state statutes informs and binds all interested parties. It strips the stressful confrontation of much of its uncertainty, guiding all participants in the same direction and providing them with a clear roadmap toward resolution. No matter what the substantive result, a detailed state procedure will eliminate the chance that someone will err procedurally and affect the outcome thereby. More significantly, it ensures that all participants are provided due process—that is, the protection they need and deserve.

PENALTIES

Penalties for violation of confidentiality laws currently range from none to unlimited civil damages to criminal sanctions, including fines and prison sentences. Penalties ought to be available to all parties involved—the requesting party, the library, and the patron. The most common penalty laws involve sanctions for violation of the state's open records laws, usually directed at government agencies that wrongfully *refuse* to allow inspection of their public records. The rarer case is a penalty for wrongfully *disclosing* protected records.

Penalties for wrongful disclosure include the following: "Any public employee who knowingly releases" protected public records in Utah has committed an infraction, less serious than a misdemeanor or felony, and "may be subject to disciplinary action."[132] In Wyoming, such conduct constitutes a misdemeanor subject to a fine up to $100.00.[133] In Maryland, the person injured may seek actual and punitive damages in a civil suit, in addition to a criminal fine up to $1,000.00;[134] and in Minnesota, he or she is entitled to actual damages, plus costs and attorney fees, unless the violation is willful, in which case exemplary damages of $100.00 to $10,000.00 are permitted.[135] In Louisiana, any person violating the confidentiality law for the first time will be fined $100.00 to $1,000.00 or imprisoned for one to six months. Any subsequent conviction will bring a fine of $250.00 to $2,000.00 or imprisonment of two to six months, or both.[136]

Eight states and the District of Columbia provide penalties specifically fashioned for violation of *library* confidentiality laws.[137] In some, the laws penalize "any person" who violates the law;[138] in others, only the library employee or official is penalized.[139] In some states, the penalties are criminal; in others, civil. Criminal penalties for violation of the library confidentiality law include a fine up to $300.00;[140] a fine up to $200.00 or thirty days in jail or both, or "appropriate public service or education" or both;[141] or a fine up to $500.00 or thirty days for a first offense, up to $1,000.00 or sixty days for a second offense, and up to $2,000.00 or ninety days for a third and subsequent offenses.[142] Civil penalties allow library patrons to bring a lawsuit for actual damages or $250.00, whichever is greater, plus attorney fees and costs;[143] or for actual damages or $100.00, whichever is greater, plus fees and costs;[144] or for damages (with no limit) and costs (but not attorney fees).[145]

NOTES

1. Bruce M. Kennedy, *Confidentiality of Library Records: A Survey of Problems, Policies, and Laws*, 81 L. Libr. J. 733, 756 (1989).
2. See, e.g., Cal. Gov't Code § 6254(j) (West Supp. 1991); Colo. Rev. Stat. Ann. § 24–72–204(3)(a) (1990); Idaho Code § 9–340(9) (1992); La. Rev. Stat. Ann. § 44:13 (West 1992); Md. State Gov't Code Ann. § 10–616 (1992); S.C. Code Ann. § 30–4–20 (Law. Co-op. 1991). Of those states that include the confidentiality law within open records acts, most of them imply that library records are public records, but exempt from disclosure under the open records act.
3. See, e.g., Ga. Code Ann. § 24–9–46 (Michie 1992) ("Circulation and similar records of a library . . . shall not be public records"); Mass. Gen. Laws Ann. ch. 78, § 7 (West 1982) ("That part of the records of a public library which reveals the identity and intellectual pursuits of a person using such library shall not be a public record."); Minn. Stat. Ann. § 13.02(12) (Supp. 1991), 13.40 (Supp. 1992);

Nev. Rev. Stat. Ann. § 239.013 (Michie 1991) ("Any records of a public library or other library which contain the identity of a user and the books . . . or other property of the library which he used are confidential and not public books or records."); R.I. Gen. Laws § 38–2–2 (1990) ("[T]he following records shall not be deemed public"); Utah Code Ann. § 63–2–103(11) & (14), 63–2–302 (1992); Vt. Stat. Ann. tit. 1, § 317(b)(19) (1991) ("public record . . . means all papers . . . or any other written or recorded matters . . . except . . . records relating to the identity of library patrons or the identity of library patrons in regard to the circulation of library materials."); W. Va. Code § 10–1–22 (1992) ("Circulation and similar records of any public library . . . are not public records.").

This statutory design that classifies library records as records that are not public is less common than the design that implies library records are public records, but exempted from open records laws.

4. See, e.g., Conn. Gen. Stat. Ann. § 11–25 (West 1986); Mich. Comp. Laws Ann. § 397.601 (West 1988) ("This act shall be known . . . as 'the library privacy act.' "); Mo. Ann. Stat. § 182.815, .817 (Vernon 1991); Mont. Code Ann. § 22–1–1101 (1991) ("This part may be cited as the 'Montana Library Records Confidentiality Act.' "); N.M. Stat. Ann. § 14–3A–1 (Michie 1992) ("Confidential Materials Act"); Wis. Stat. Ann. § 43.30 (West 1992).

5. See, e.g., Ala. Code § 41–8–10 & 36–12–40 (1992); Colo. Rev. Stat. Ann. § 24–72–204 & 24–90–119 (West 1990); Ill. Ann. Stat. ch. 81, para. 1201, 1202 & ch. 116, para. 207 (Smith-Hurd 1992); Md. State Gov't Code Ann. § 10–616 & Educ. § 23–107 (1992); N.H. Rev. Stat. Ann. § 91–A:5(IV) & 201–D:11 (1991); S.C. Code Ann. § 30–4–20(c) & 60–4–10 (Law. Co-op. 1991).

6. In some instances, the definition of "library" is not included in the confidentiality statute. There, the researcher will have to draw upon other provisions that may be found in the statute pertaining to libraries generally.

7. Ala. Code § 36–12–40 & 41–8–10 (1992).

8. Cal. Gov't Code § 6267 (West 1991); Fla. Stat. Ann. § 257.261 (West 1991); Miss. Code Ann. § 39–3–365 (1993); N.D. Cent. Code § 40–38–12 (1985).

9. Wis. Stat. Ann. § 43.30 (West 1987).

10. La. Rev. Stat. Ann. § 44:13 (West 1992).

11. Pa. Stat. Ann. tit. 24, § 4428 (1992).

12. Conn. Gen. Stat. Ann. § 11–25 (West 1986); Mass. Gen. Laws Ann. ch. 78, § 7 (West 1992). An attorney general opinion in Connecticut has interpreted this to include the state library. 81 Conn. Op. Att'y Gen. (December 15, 1981).

13. Ariz. Rev. Stat. Ann. § 41–1354 (1992).

14. Ark. Code Ann. § 13–2–701 (Michie 1987).

15. N.Y. Civ. Prac. L. & R. § 4509 (McKinney 1992). A public library is a library other than a professional, technical, or public school library, which is established for the public's free use. A free association library is one "established and controlled, in whole or in part, by a group of private individuals operating as an association, close corporation or as trustees under the provisions of a will or deed of trust" and "maintained for the benefit and free use on equal terms of all the people of the community." N.Y. Educ. § 253 (McKinney 1992). As with many other statutory schemes, the researcher is often forced to bounce back and forth between statutes to see the whole scheme. For example, although "public library" may not be defined further in the confidentiality law, one can often refer to statutes

dealing with "libraries" to find a more detailed definition. See also Md. Educ. Code Ann. § 23–107 (1988).

16. Me. Rev. Stat. Ann. tit. 27, § 121 (West 1988).

17. Minn. Stat. Ann. § 13.40 (West 1987).

18. Neb. Rev. Stat. § 84–712.05(10) (1991); Utah Code Ann. § 63–2–302 (1992).

19. N.M. Stat. Ann. § 18–9–3 (Michie 1992).

20. S.C. Code Ann. § 30–4–20 (Law. Co-op. 1991).

21. 82 Ky. Op. Att'y Gen. 149 (Mar. 12, 1982). In Kentucky, this includes "all tax supported libraries and all private libraries which receive as much as 25 percent of their funds from state or local authority"—school, public, academic, special, or private. *Id.*

22. H. N. Foerstel, Surveillance in the Stacks: The FBI's Library Awareness Program (1991), at 62. In 1988, Maryland passed a new library confidentiality law, which explicitly applies to "a free association, school, college or university library." Md. Code Ann., Educ. § 23–107 (1988).

23. See, e.g., Ga. Code Ann. § 24–9–46 (Michie 1992); Idaho Code § 9–340 (1992); Ind. Code Ann. § 5–14–3–4 (West 1989); Iowa Code Ann. § 22.7 (West 1989); Kan. Stat. Ann. § 45–221 (1986); R.I. Gen. Laws § 38–2–2 (1990). By falling within Title 38, "Public Records," it can be assumed the Rhode Island law applies to records of those libraries which are public in nature.

24. W. Va. Code § 10–1–1 (1992).

25. La. Rev. Stat. Ann. § 44:13 (West 1992); Nev. Rev. Stat. Ann. § 239.013 (1991); N.H. Rev. Stat. Ann. § 201–D:11 (1991); Vt. Stat. Ann. tit. 1, § 317(19) (1991); Va. Code Ann. § 2.1–342 (Michie Supp. 1992); Wash. Rev. Code Ann. § 42.17.310 (West 1991); Wyo. Stat. § 16–4–203(d)(vi, ix) (1992).

26. Mich. Stat. Ann. § 445.1712 (Callaghan Supp. 1992). This is a fairly new law (1989), which appears designed primarily for protection of the purchase or renting of books and videotapes, but the definitions are broad enough to include library records.

27. Mich. Comp. Laws Ann. § 397.602 (West 1988); Mo. Ann. Stat. § 182.815 (Vernon 1991); Mont. Code Ann. § 22–1–1102 (1991); N.C. Gen. Stat. § 125–18 (1991). See also Tenn. Code Ann. § 10–8–101 (1992).

28. Alaska Stat. § 09.25.140 (Supp. 1992).

29. Ill. Ann. Stat. ch. 81, para. 1201 (Smith-Hurd 1987).

30. N.J. Stat. Ann. § 18A:73–43.1 (West 1989).

31. Ala. Code § 36–12–40 & 41–8–9, 41–8–10 (1992); Cal. Gov't Code § 6267 (West 1991); Fla. Stat. Ann. § 257.261 (West 1991); Ill. Ann. Stat. ch. 81, para. 1201 (Smith-Hurd 1992); S.C. Code Ann. § 60–4–20 (Law. Co-op. 1991).

32. Or. Rev. Stat. § 192.501(1) (1991) (emphasis added). However, the strength of this definition is substantially diluted by additional language, which allows disclosure when "the public interest requires disclosure in the particular instance." *Id.*

33. S.D. Codified Laws Ann. § 14–2–51 (1992).

34. Conn. Gen. Stat. Ann. § 11–25 (West 1986). The weakness in this statute is that only circulation records are protected, not registration records or reference requests.

35. Ga. Code Ann. § 24–9–46 (Michie 1992); Ill. Ann. Stat. ch. 116, para. 207

(Smith-Hurd 1992); Kan. Stat. Ann. § 45–221 (1986); W. Va. Code § 10–1–22 (1992).

36. Ind. Code Ann. § 5–14–3–4 (West 1989).

37. Utah Code Ann. § 63–2–302 (1992).

38. Pa. Stat. Ann. tit. 24, § 4428 (1992).

39. Me. Rev. Stat. Ann. tit. 27, § 121 (West 1988); Miss. Code Ann. § 39–3–365 (1993); Nev. Rev. Stat. Ann. § 239.013 (Michie 1991). For similar language, see Del. Code Ann. tit. 29, § 10002(d)(12) (1992).

40. Vt. Stat. Ann. tit. 1, § 317(19) (1991).

41. Mo. Ann. Stat. § 182.815 (Vernon 1991); Mont. Code Ann. § 22–1–1102 (1991).

42. Ark. Code Ann. § 13–2–703(b) (Michie 1987); N.Y. Civ. Prac. L. & R. § 4509 (McKinney 1992).

43. Idaho Code § 9–340 (1992); Iowa Code Ann. § 22.7 (West 1989); Neb. Rev. Stat. § 84–712.05(10) (1991); R.I. Gen. Laws § 38–2–2(21) (1990). See also Md. Stat Gov't Code Ann. § 10–616, 23–107 (1992) (records that contain "an identifying particular assigned to the individual and identifies the use a patron makes of that library's materials, services, or facilities").

44. Alaska Stat. § 09.25.140 (1991); N.J. Stat. Ann. § 18A:73–43.2 (West 1989).

45. Ariz. Rev. Stat. Ann. § 41–1354 (1992); Colo. Rev. Stat. Ann. § 24–90–119 (West 1990); Tenn. Code Ann. § 10–8–102 (1992) (emphasis added). By specifically referring to library services, reference requests and computerized searches would be included.

46. N.C. Gen. Stat. § 125–18, 125–19 (1992).

47. N.M. Stat. Ann. § 18–9–3 (Michie 1992). Under this law, the fact that an individual even uses the library is protected.

48. Md. State Gov't Code Ann. § 10–616, 23–107 (1992).

49. William A. Knott, *Confidentiality of Records*, 106 Libr. J. 2162 (1981).

50. Janis M. Lee, *Confidentiality: From the Stacks to the Witness Stand*, Am. Libr., 444, 448 (June 1988).

51. La. Rev. Stat. Ann. § 44:13 (West 1992); Okla. Stat. Ann. tit. 65, § 1–105 (West 1993).

52. Ariz. Rev. Stat. Ann. § 41–1354 (1992); Colo. Rev. Stat. Ann. § 24–90–119 (West 1990); Tenn. Code Ann. § 10–8–102 (1992).

53. Mich. Comp. Laws Ann. § 397.602 (West 1988); Mo. Ann. Stat. § 182.815 (Vernon 1991) (includes information not only retained, but also received or generated); Mont. Code Ann. § 22–1–1102 (1991) (includes information retained, received, or generated); N.M. Stat. Ann. § 18–9–3 (Michie 1992); N.C. Gen. Stat. § 125–18, 125–19 (1992).

54. N.H. Rev. Stat. Ann. § 201–D:11 (1991).

55. Ark. Code Ann. § 13–2–703(b) (Michie 1987); N.Y. Civ. Prac. L. & R. § 4509 (McKinney 1992). Similar language ("regardless of format") can be found in La. Rev. Stat. Ann. § 44:13 (West 1992); Okla. Stat. Ann. Tit. 65, § 1–105 (West 1993).

56. Md. State Gov't Code Ann. § 10–616, 23–107 (1992).

57. Minn. Stat. Ann. § 13.40 (West Supp. 1992) (amended from "records" to "data" in 1991).

58. 88 Tenn. Op. Att'y Gen. 203 (Dec. 6, 1988). Although attorney general

opinions are not binding, they are given some weight, at least until a court rules on the issue.

59. 81 Conn. Op. Att'y Gen. (Dec. 15, 1981) (library "is prohibited from disclosing to the public all personally identifiable information contained in its circulation records"); see also 80 Nev. Op. Att'y Gen. 6 (Mar. 10, 1980); 41 Or. Op. Att'y Gen. 435 (April 13, 1981).

60. Ark. Code Ann. § 13–2–703 (Michie 1987).

61. *Id.* at § 13–4–104.

62. *Id.* at § 13–4–103(3). The statute exempts "library and museum material made or acquired and preserved solely for reference purposes, extra copies of documents . . . and stock of publications and reproduced documents." *Id.*

63. *Id.* at § 13–4–101.

64. Ky. Rev. Stat. Ann. § 61.878 (Michie 1992).

65. 81 Ky. Op. Att'y Gen. 159 (Apr. 21, 1981).

66. *Id.*

67. Haw. Rev. Stat. § 92F–13 (1992).

68. Tex. Open Records Decision No. 100 (July 10, 1975).

69. The Decatur Public Library v. The District Attorney's Office of Wise County, No. 90–05–192, Texas 271st Judicial District Court, May 9, 1990, John R. Lindsey, Judge. See also Bruce Cummings, *Judge Quashes Subpoena of Decatur Library Records*, Wise County Messenger, May 13, 1990, p. 1.

70. Colo. Rev. Stat. Ann. § 24–72–204 (West 1990). For the same language, but with the addition of archival material, see Idaho Code § 9–340 (1992); Kan. Stat. Ann. § 45–221 (1986); Md. State Gov't Code Ann. § 10–616 (1992); Minn. Stat. Ann. § 138.17(5) (West 1993); Okla. Stat. Ann. tit. 51, § 24A.11 (West 1988); Wyo. Stat. § 16–4–203(d) (vi) (1992).

71. Ind. Code Ann. § 5–14–3–4 (West 1989).

72. Wash. Rev. Code Ann. § 42.17.315 (West 1991).

73. N.M. Stat. Ann. § 14–3A–2 (Michie 1992).

74. R.I. Gen. Laws § 38–2–2 (1990).

75. Ala. Code. § 41–8–10 (1992); Alaska Stat. § 09–25–140 (1992); Ariz. Rev. Stat. Ann. § 41–1354 (1992); Ark. Code Ann. § 13–2–703 (Michie 1987); Cal. Gov't Code § 6267 (West Supp. 1991); Colo. Rev. Stat. Ann. § 24–72–204 (West 1990); Conn. Gen. Stat. Ann. § 11–25 (West 1986); Fla. Stat. Ann. § 257.261 (West 1991); Ga. Code Ann. § 24–9–46 (Michie 1992); Ill. Ann. Stat. ch. 81, para. 1201 (Smith-Hurd 1992); La. Rev. Stat. Ann. § 44:13 (West 1992); Me. Rev. Stat. Ann. tit. 27, § 121 (West 1988); Md. State Gov't Code Ann. § 10–616 (1992); Mich. Comp. Laws Ann. § 397.603 (West 1988); Minn. Stat. Ann. § 13.40 (West 1987); Miss. Code Ann. § 39–3–365 (1993) (records may be released only under specifically defined conditions); Mont. Code Ann. § 22–1–1103 (1991); Nev. Rev. Stat. Ann. § 239.013 (Michie 1991); N.H. Rev. Stat. Ann. § 201–D:11 (1991); N.J. Stat. Ann. § 18A:73–43.2 (West 1989); N.M. Stat. Ann. § 18–9–4 (Michie 1992); N.Y. Civ. Prac. L. & R. § 4509 (McKinney 1992); N.C. Gen. Stat. § 125–19 (1992); Okla. Stat. Ann. tit. 65, § 1–105 (West 1993); Pa. Stat. Ann. tit. 24, § 4428 (1992); S.C. Code Ann. § 60–4–10 (Law. Co-op. 1991); S.D. Codified Laws Ann. § 14–2–51 (1992); Tenn. Code Ann. § 10–8–102 (1992); W. Va. Code § 10–1–22 (1992); Wis. Stat. Ann. § 43.30 (West 1987); Wyo. Stat. § 16–4–203 (1992). The District of

Columbia also has a statute that mandates that library records "shall be kept confidential." D.C. Code Ann. § 37–106.2 (1981).

76. Va. Code Ann. § 2.1–342 (Michie 1992).

77. Ind. Code Ann. § 5–14–3–4(b) (West 1987).

78. Iowa Code Ann. § 22.7 (West 1989). But Iowa law also provides that library records "shall be released to a criminal justice agency *only pursuant to*" a specific criminal investigation under specified circumstances. *Id.* The effect of this wording is that the director may have complete discretion to disclose records in noncriminal matters but less discretion in criminal cases.

79. Del. Code Ann. tit. 29, § 10002(d) (1992); Mass. Gen. Laws Ann. ch. 78, § 7 (West 1992); R.I. Gen. Laws § 38–2–2 (1990); Vt. Stat. Ann. tit. 1, § 317 (1991). The Massachusetts law also provides that the library may disclose library records for specific purposes, implying that it may disclose only for those purposes. However, any law that must be read by implication is a weak law, dependent upon the whim of the court and its statutory interpretation.

80. Cal. Gov't Code § 6254 (West Supp. 1991); Haw. Rev. Stat. § 92F–13 (1992) (this is not a library records confidentiality law, but rather protects records that "would constitute a clearly unwarranted invasion of personal privacy"); Kan. Stat. Ann. § 45–221 (1986); Mo. Ann. Stat. § 182.817 (Vernon 1991).

81. Idaho Code § 9–340 (1992); Ill. Ann. Stat. ch. 116, para. 207 (Smith-Hurd 1992); Neb. Rev. Stat. § 84–712.05 (1991) (library records "may be withheld"); N.D. Cent. Code § 40–38–12 (1985) (statute also provides that records may be released pursuant to court order or subpoena; the implication is that they may not be released without such order, but the statute is ambiguous, therefore weak); Or. Rev. Stat. § 192.501 (1991); Wash. Rev. Code Ann. § 42.17.310 (West 1992) (but Wash. Rev. Code Ann. § 42.17.310(3) (West 1992) also provides that a court can determine, after a hearing, that the exemption "is clearly unnecessary to protect any individual's right of privacy or any vital governmental function" and inspection may then be permitted).

82. Utah Code Ann. § 63–2–202 (Supp. 1991).

83. Ariz. Rev. Stat. Ann. § 41–1354 (1992); Cal. Gov't Code § 6267 (West Supp. 1991); Colo. Rev. Stat. Ann. § 24–90–119 (1990); D.C. Code Ann. § 37–106.2 (1981); Ga. Code Ann. § 24–9–46 (Michie 1992); La. Rev. Stat. Ann. § 44:13 (West 1992); Me. Rev. Stat. Ann. tit. 27, § 121 (West 1988); Mich. Comp. Laws Ann. § 397.603 (West 1988); Miss. Code Ann. § 39–3–365 (1993); Mo. Ann. Stat. § 182.817 (Vernon 1991); Mont. Code Ann. § 22–1–1103 (1991); N.M. Stat. Ann. § 18–9–4 (Michie 1992); N.C. Gen. Stat. § 125–19 (1992); Okla. Stat. Ann. tit. 65, § 1–105 (West 1993); Tenn. Code Ann. § 10–8–102 (1992); W. Va. Code § 10–1–22 (1992).

84. N.H. Rev. Stat. Ann. § 201–D:11 (1991); N.Y. Civ. Prac. L. & R. § 4509 (McKinney 1992); S.C. Code Ann. § 60–4–10 (Law. Co-op. 1991).

85. Ark. Code Ann. § 13–2–704 (Michie 1987).

86. Minn. Stat. Ann. § 13.05(4)(d) (West 1988).

87. Utah Code Ann. § 63–2–202 (1992).

88. Ala. Code § 41–8–10 (1992).

89. Cal. Gov't Code § 6254 (West Supp. 1991).

90. Md. State Gov't Code Ann. § 10–616, 23–107 (1992).

91. Mass. Gen. Laws Ann. ch. 78, § 7 (West 1992).

92. Wyo. Stat. § 16–4–203(d) (1992).

93. Ariz. Rev. Stat. § 41–1354 (1992); Colo. Rev. Stat. Ann. § 24–90–119 (1988); D.C. Code Ann. § 37–106.2 (1981); N.H. Rev. Stat. Ann. § 201–D:11 (1991); N.J. Stat. Ann. § 18A:73–43.2 (West 1989); N.Y. Civ. Prac. L. & R. § 4509 (McKinney 1992); N.C. Gen. Stat. § 125–19 (1992).

94. Cal. Gov't Code § 6267 (West 1991); Ga. Code Ann. § 24–9–46 (Michie 1992); La. Rev. Stat. Ann. § 44:13 (West 1992); N.M. Stat. Ann. § 18–9–4, 18–9–5 (Michie 1992); Okla. Stat. Ann. tit. 65, § 1–105 (West 1993); S.C. Code Ann. § 60–4–10 (Law. Co-op. 1991); S.D. Codified Laws Ann. § 14–2–51 (1992) (acts by library officers or employees in maintaining a checkout system); W. Va. Code § 10–1–22 (1992); Wis. Stat. Ann. § 43.30 (West 1987) (includes administration of library system).

95. Ala. Code § 41–8–10 (1992).

96. Ark. Code Ann. § 13–2–705 (Michie 1987); La. Rev. Stat. Ann. § 44:13 (West 1992); Mont. Code Ann. § 22–1–1103 (1991); Tenn. Code Ann. § 10–8–102 (1992).

97. Ala. Code § 41–8–10 (1992); Ark. Code Ann. § 13–2–705 (Michie 1987); Cal. Gov't Code § 6267 (West 1991); Fla. Stat. Ann. § 257.261 (West 1991); Ill. Ann. Stat. ch. 81, para. 1201 (Smith-Hurd 1992); Minn. Stat. Ann. § 13.05 (West 1987); Miss. Code Ann. § 39–3–365 (1993); Mo. Ann. Stat. § 182.815 (Vernon 1991); Mont. Code Ann. § 22–1–1103 (1991); N.H. Rev. Stat. Ann. § 201–D:11 (1991); N.C. Gen Stat. § 125–18 (1992); Tenn. Code Ann. § 10–8–101 (1992); Wash. Rev. Code Ann. § 42.17.310(2) (West 1992).

98. ALA Policy Manual, at 52.4(3) (1991–92).

99. Ariz. Rev. Stat. Ann. § 41–1354 (1992); Cal. Gov't Code § 6267 (West 1991); Fla. Stat. Ann. § 257.261 (West 1991) ("proper" judicial order); Haw. Rev. Stat. § 92F–28 (Supp. 1992); Ill. Ann. Stat. ch. 81, para. 1201 (Smith-Hurd 1992); Ind. Code Ann. § 5–14–3–4 (West 1989); Iowa Code Ann. § 22.7 (West 1989); La. Rev. Stat. Ann. § 44:13 (West 1992); Me. Rev. Stat. Ann. tit. 27, § 121 (West 1988); Minn. Stat. Ann. § 13.40 (West 1987); Miss. Code Ann. § 39–3–365 (1993); N.M. Stat. Ann. § 18–9–4 (Michie 1992); Okla. Stat. Ann. tit. 65, § 1–105 (West 1993); S.D. Codified Laws Ann. § 14–2–51 (1992); Tenn. Code Ann. § 10–8–102 (1992); Wis. Stat. Ann. § 43.30 (West 1987).

100. See, e.g., D.C. Code Ann. § 37–106.2 (1992); Mich. Comp. Laws Ann. § 397.603 (West 1988); Minn. Stat. Ann. § 13.03(6) (West 1987).

101. Colo. Rev. Stat. Ann. § 24–90–119 (West 1988); Ga. Code Ann. § 24–9–46 (Michie 1992); N.J. Stat. Ann. § 18A:73–43.2 (West 1989); N.H. Rev. Stat. Ann. § 201–D:11 (1991); N.Y. Civ. Prac. L. & R. § 4509 (McKinney 1992); N.C. Gen. Stat. § 125–19 (1992); N.D. Cent. Code § 40–38–12 (1985); W. Va. Code § 10–1–22 (1992).

102. Black's Law Dictionary 1426 (6th ed. 1990).

103. See Fed. R. Civ. P. 45.

104. Mo. Ann. Stat. § 182.817 (Vernon 1991); Nev. Rev. Stat. Ann. § 239.013 (Michie 1991).

105. Mont. Code Ann. § 22–1–1103 (1991).

106. S.C. Code Ann. § 60–4–10 (Law. Co-op. 1991).

107. Pa. Stat. Ann. tit. 24, § 4428 (1992).

108. Iowa Code Ann. § 22.7(13) (West 1989).

109. Brown v. Johnston, 328 N.W. 2d 510 (Iowa 1983). Although Iowa's rules called for court approval before a subpoena issued, it was "not clear in this case whether the application was 'approved' by the court," nor was it apparently relevant. *Id.* at 512.

110. Utah Code Ann. § 63–2–202 (Supp. 1991).

111. Wash. Rev. Code Ann. § 42.17.310(3) (West 1992).

112. La. Rev. Stat. Ann. § 44:13 (West 1992).

113. Wyo. Stat. Ann. § 16–4–203(d) (ix) (1992).

114. S.D. Codified Laws Ann. § 14–2–51 (1992).

115. Utah Code Ann. § 63–2–202 (Supp. 1991).

116. Ala. Code § 36–12–40, 41–8–10 (1992). See also Alaska Stat. § 09.25.140 (1992) (records of a public elementary or secondary school library identifying a minor child may be disclosed to the parent or guardian of that child); N.M. Stat. Ann. § 18–9–5 (Michie 1992) (records of school libraries may be disclosed to legal guardian of unemancipated minors or legally incapacitated persons).

117. Ga. Code Ann. § 24–9–46 (Michie 1992); W. Va. Code Ann. § 10–1–22 (1992).

118. Or. Rev. Stat. § 192.495 (1991).

119. Minn. Stat. Ann. § 13.10 (West 1993).

120. Tenn. Code Ann. § 10–7–504(c) (1992).

121. Ga. Code Ann. § 50–18–100 (1992); Ind. Code Ann. § 5–14–3–4 (West 1989). Georgia also provides that the record can be released as early as twenty years after its creation upon the unanimous approval in writing of the State Records Committee. Ga. Code Ann. § 50–18–100 (1992). How this might apply to library records is purely conjectural, but one might imagine an American president assassinated during his or her presidency and the scramble for information about any part of his or her personal life. Even twenty years in that case might seem too long to wait.

122. Haw. Rev. Stat. § 94–7 (1992).

123. Va. Code Ann. § 42.1–78 (Michie 1992).

124. D.C. Code Ann. § 37–106.2 (1981).

125. *Id.*

126. *Id.*

127. Mich. Comp. Laws § 397.603 (West 1988).

128. Minn. Stat. Ann. § 13.03(6) (West 1988).

129. N.M. Stat. Ann. § 18–9–4 (Michie 1992).

130. Wash. Rev. Code Ann. § 42.17.310(3) (West 1992).

131. Wyo. Stat. § 16–4–203(e), (f) (1992).

132. Utah Code Ann. § 63–2–801 (1992).

133. Wyo. Stat. § 16–4–205 (1992).

134. Md. Code Ann., State Gov't § 10–626, 10–627 (1988).

135. Minn. Stat. Ann. § 13.08 (1988).

136. La. Rev. Stat. Ann. § 44:37 (West 1982).

137. Arizona, Arkansas, Colorado, Florida, Michigan, Montana, New Mexico, and South Carolina.

138. Ariz. Rev. Stat. Ann. § 41–1354 (1992); Ark. Code Ann. § 13–2–702 (Michie 1987); Fla. Stat. Ann. § 257.261 (West 1991); Mont. Code Ann. § 22–1–1111 (1991);

N.M. Stat. Ann. § 18–9–6 (Michie 1978); S.C. Code Ann. § 60–4–30 (Law. Co-op. 1991).

139. Colo. Rev. Stat. Ann. § 24–90–119 (West 1988); D.C. Code Ann. § 37–106.2 (1981); Mich. Comp. Laws Ann. § 397.604 (West 1988).

140. Colo. Rev. Stat. Ann. § 24–90–119 (West 1988); D.C. Code Ann. § 37–106.2 (1981).

141. Ark. Code Ann. § 13–2–702 (Michie 1987).

142. S.C. Code Ann. § 60–4–30 (Law. Co-op. 1991). Arizona law provides for a fine up to $500.00 and 30 days in jail. Ariz. Rev. Stat. Ann. § 13–707, –802 (1989). Florida law provides for a fine up to $500.00 and 60 days in jail. Fla. Stat. Ann. § 257.261, 775.082, 775.083 (West 1991).

143. D.C. Code Ann. § 37–106.2 (1981); Mich. Comp. Laws Ann. § 397.604 (West 1988).

144. Mont. Code Ann. § 22–1–1111 (1991).

145. N.M. Stat. Ann. § 18–9–6 (Michie 1978).

6

Resolving the Conflict Through Litigation, Attorney General Opinion, and Informal Methods

Given the library profession's ongoing debate and interest in the issue of library confidentiality, surprisingly few cases have involved review by the states' appellate courts. In a few cases, the state attorney general has been asked to resolve a question concerning the extent of the protection. But by far the majority of requests for disclosure have been handled at the lowest levels of court involvement, usually requiring no court hearing at all. This may indicate that those seeking disclosure defer to the library's denial, but it may also signal that compliance is too easily attained or that confidentiality laws are too weak. In some cases, the protection that librarians value so highly serves merely as an inconvenient hurdle for the requesting party to jump.

LITIGATION

Only two cases involving disclosure of library records have been reported in the national law reporter system. This does not mean that others have not occurred; but it does mean that they have most likely occurred at the trial court level, resolved there rather than at the appellate level. In some instances, appellate cases are not published either, although those cases that the courts deem to be important are generally published. It would appear that an issue of public interest, like library patron privacy, would be reported if it had risen to the appellate level.

It is important to recognize that a state case involving interpretation of that state's laws is not binding on another state. However, a court is likely to consider how other states have interpreted statutes similar to its own, when deciding a novel issue. Thus, in determining whether any case will carry weight in one's state court, it is necessary to first examine the two statutes being interpreted to find similarity. If the other state's statute varies significantly, an interpretation of it will be of little value.

Brown v. Johnston[1] arose when an Iowa state law enforcement agency launched an investigation of cattle mutilations in several counties. An agent asked the Des Moines Public Library for circulation records but "was told that as a matter of library policy, such records were confidential." The county attorney, on the request of the state agent, obtained a subpoena duces tecum.[2] This was not difficult. The attorney simply handed a brief form to the court clerk and the clerk handed back a subpoena. As in most courts, subpoenas are issued routinely without judicial involvement, notice, or hearing.[3] The subpoena here requested the names of persons who had checked out a long list of books, most of them concerning witchcraft and similar topics. Shortly after the subpoena was served on the library, a library patron filed a lawsuit against the library board and the state agency chief to block the disclosure. The library thereafter filed its own lawsuit against the chief and the county attorney. Eventually, the two suits were joined together, with both the library patron and the library board as plaintiffs.[4]

The law that the court applied in this case provided:

The following public records shall be kept confidential, unless otherwise ordered by a court, by the lawful custodian of the records, or by another person duly authorized to release the information: . . .

13. The records of a library which, by themselves or when examined with other records, would reveal the identity of the library patron checking out or requesting an item from the library.[5]

The library argued both statutory and constitutional protection of the records. Both arguments failed.

Concerning the statutory argument, the court held that, although a "general citizen" might not have access to the records, the county attorney has broad investigative authority, which includes the right of access to library records. Additionally, the court pointed out that the statute permits a court order to override confidentiality. In this case, the county attorney had obtained a subpoena, albeit without judicial involvement.

Concerning the constitutional argument, the court held that neither the First nor the Fourth Amendment (which protects against unreasonable searches) protects library records in this case. The court weighed the "societal need for the information and the availability of it from other sources" against the "effect of forced disclosure of these records."[6] Societal need won out.

The other reported case arose in Alaska in 1990 and did not involve law enforcement officials. *Municipality of Anchorage v. Daily News*[7] arose when an Anchorage newspaper sought the performance report of the head librarian at Anchorage Public Library. The "confidential" report had been drafted by the Anchorage Library Advisory Board to the city's mayor. When both the Board and the mayor refused to turn over the report, the newspaper filed suit. The court ordered the report released.

On appeal, the city argued, among other things, that the *librarian* should have been given notice and an opportunity to be heard and to be joined as a party (only the municipality was sued) and also that the report was confidential. Both arguments failed. The court found that allowing the librarian to intervene as a party would have done no more to protect his interest than allowing the city to represent his interest. Although the court agreed "that it may have been desirable for [the librarian] to have been given notice of the pending release and an opportunity to present argument to the court, . . . we cannot conclude on this record that failure to notify [him] of the pending release constituted a reversible denial of due process of law."[8] In other words, he should have been given notice and an opportunity to be heard, but the error was not so egregious as to result in a reversal of the decision.

The court easily disposed of the argument that the record was confidential. Citing the state open records law, the court found that the library record was a public record subject to disclosure.[9] Although exceptions to the law might have protected library circulation records, there was no exception for this kind of library record. The court noted that "[e]xceptions to these disclosure requirements are construed narrowly in furtherance of the legislature's expressed bias in favor of broad public access."[10] The court made it clear that any law that exempts public records from disclosure had better be explicit. In the absence of an explicit exemption, the court will weigh "the public interest in disclosure on the one hand, and the privacy and reputational interests of the affected individuals together with the government's interest in confidentiality, on the other."[11] Here, because the report did not deal with the personal, intimate details of the librarian's life, the balance fell in favor of disclosure. This case, like the Iowa case, demonstrates the strong state policy in favor of disclosure. In fact, the court stated in the Alaska case that the burden is on the record custodian to explain why the records should not be disclosed. It is presumed that all public records should be disclosed, even when the person seeking them is not a law enforcement official and when the public safety is not at stake. Courts in other states have stated similar propositions.[12]

ATTORNEY GENERAL OPINIONS

Attorney general opinions have less precedential value than cases decided by state courts, even in the states where they are rendered. They are advisory opinions written by an attorney in the state's attorney general office in response to inquiry by an individual or other entity in the state, rather than in the context of legal questions raised in a lawsuit. They answer the inquiry, but they are not binding. They serve as a temporary answer to a problem only until such time as the state court has an opportunity to resolve the issue in a real case. Nevertheless, they provide guidance in an area unresolved by the courts.

A number of queries to attorneys general have involved the question of library circulation records. In two states that lack confidentiality laws, the attorney general opinions serve as the only protection against disclosure.

In Texas, a 1975 attorney general opinion addressed the question as to whether the identity of library patrons was protected under Texas law.[13] The opinion states:

No Texas statute makes library circulation records or the identity of library patrons confidential, and no judicial decision in this state . . . has declared it confidential. However, we believe that the courts, if squarely faced with the issue, would hold that the First Amendment of the United States Constitution . . . makes confidential that information in library circulation records which would disclose the identity of library patrons in connection with the material they have obtained from the library.

Although this opinion does not have the full force of law, it found support when, fifteen years later, a Texas district judge (trial court judge) quashed a district attorney's subpoena for library circulation records in the Decatur Public Library. The judge ruled that, although "the State through its legitimate police powers can and does impinge on the individual's privilege of privacy . . . the State's right must be done with due process and only when the government can demonstrate that such an intrusion is reasonable."[14] In this case, a newborn baby was abandoned and the district attorney attempted to subpoena circulation records indicating who had checked out childbirthing books during the past nine months. One factor the judge cited in denying the subpoena was that there was no specific suspect; he indicated he might be inclined to allow disclosure in other circumstances as, for instance, when an unexploded bomb was discovered and library materials contained information that suggested a specific patron had built the bomb based on that information.[15]

The other state protected by attorney general opinion rather than a specific library confidentiality law is Kentucky. There, the state librarian sought guidance concerning the interpretation of a law that protects "public records containing information of a personal nature where the public disclosure thereof would constitute a clearly unwarranted invasion of personal privacy."[16] He asked whether public library registration and circulation records would be included in such a definition. The attorney general answered affirmatively, noting that "the individual's privacy rights as to what he borrows from a public library . . . is [sic] overwhelming" and that there is "no public interest at all to put in the scales opposite the privacy rights of the individual."[17] The attorney general cautioned, however, that although the library could not be *forced* to disclose a record, it could do so if it wished to.[18]

Other attorney general opinions that address the issue of library record confidentiality generally served as stopgap measures in the early 1980s until legislation could be passed to give the records strong protection. This includes opinions in Iowa,[19] Nevada,[20] and Oregon.[21] At least one attorney general opinion sets forth what is commonly understood among librarians today—that having patrons sign the back of a library book or a card inserted in the book violates library confidentiality laws,[22] as a matter of both statutory and constitutional law.

By requiring that the patron sign the check out card, thereby making a record of the patron's reading habits for all the world to see, the library conditions the receipt of a government benefit (use of the library) on the patron's willingness to waive the privacy interest in the right to receive information which is protected by the First and Fourteenth Amendments.[23]

In fact, a number of librarians now use a variety of techniques to protect library confidentiality. These range from such simple methods as obliterating each borrower's name with a black marker, to having borrowers sign a slip of paper that is discarded after the book's return, or using more sophisticated (and more expensive) automated systems that automatically erase borrower information upon the book's return. Furthermore, library employees are often instructed that when a requested book is available, the employee should inform the requesting patron only, rather than another member of the patron's household, or at least leave a message that "the material requested" has now come in.

The final attorney general opinion that bears mentioning is a 1985 Mississippi opinion. In it, the attorney general succinctly determined that a list of public library borrowers is a "public record" and hence subject to disclosure. He noted that the state then had no specific exception to the open records act that would protect such records. Thus, in Mississippi, such records were open to the public. In 1992, however, Mississippi finally passed a library confidentiality law.[24]

INFORMAL METHODS OF RESOLUTION

Most conflicts in the area of library record confidentiality are resolved informally. Because of this, it is difficult to determine the degree to which librarians are subjected to requests for records, both quantitatively and qualitatively (in what frequency and to what degree). Anecdotal evidence abounds. Library conferences are favorite venues for such "war stories," and some of these incidents make their way into the literature. But one thing is certain. The tales that are told represent just a fraction of the total cases in which librarians are put on the spot, are subjected to subtle and not-so-subtle pressure, or are threatened.

These tales, some of which were told in Chapter 4, demonstrate that many informal requests are resolved when the library employee advises the requesting party that the records are confidential. When the records are sought by subpoena or court order, the response may be compliance; but in a number of instances these have been successfully resisted, either by requesting that the inquiry be more specific or by seeking a court hearing before the judge. What is important is that the library be prepared to deal with the requests when they are made and that all library employees be made aware of the proper library procedure. Insisting that all requests be directed immediately to the library director minimizes the chances that coercion or intimidation or ignorance will result in disclosure.

If questions exist about the interpretation of state law governing library records, librarians might want to consider seeking an attorney general's opinion in advance of a confrontation. Litigation is always a last resort, because of the expense, time, and emotional toll it entails. But there are times when the toll is worthwhile, and those times are likely to occur in defense of the library patron's right to privacy.

NOTES

1. 328 N.W. 2d 510, 511 (Iowa 1983).
2. A subpoena duces tecum is an order to appear and produce those documents specified in the subpoena.
3. For example, New York law provides that a subpoena

may be issued without a court order by the clerk of the court . . . an attorney of record for a party . . . or any member of a board, commission or committee authorized by law to hear, try or determine a matter or to do any other act, in an official capacity, in relation to which proof may be taken or the attendance of a person as a witness may be required.

N.Y. Civ. Prac. L. & R. § 2302 (McKinney 1991). See Chapter 5 section entitled "Exceptions to Confidentiality Laws" for a discussion of the ease with which subpoenas can be obtained.

4. 328 N.W. 2d at 511. Obviously, there was some confusion as to the proper procedure to follow when faced with a subpoena. A confidentiality law that contains a detailed procedural scheme would be of assistance.

5. 328 N.W. 2d at 511, quoting Iowa Code § 68A.7 then in effect. After the decision in this case, Iowa librarians apparently contacted their state legislators. Today, Iowa law includes an additional sentence:

The records shall be released to a criminal justice agency only pursuant to an investigation of a particular person or organization suspected of committing a known crime, the connection exists between the requested release of information, and a legitimate end and that the need for the information is cogent and compelling.

Iowa Code Ann. § 22.7(13) (West 1989).

6. 328 N.W. 2d at 512.

7. 794 P. 2d 584 (Alaska 1990).

8. *Id.* at 592.

9. Alaska Stat. § 9.25.110, cited in the case, provides that "Unless specifically provided otherwise the books, records . . . writings and transactions of all agencies and departments are public records. . . . " Obviously, the law protecting circulation records did not apply to the performance report.

10. 794 P. 2d at 589.

11. *Id.* at 590.

12. See, e.g., Chambers v. Birmingham News Co., 552 So. 2d 854 (Ala. 1989) (resumes and employment applications to county personnel department are public records subject to disclosure; burden is on the party refusing disclosure).

13. Open Records Decision No. 100 (July 10, 1975).

14. The Decatur Public Library v. The District Attorney's Office of Wise County, No. 90–05–192, Texas 271st Judicial District Court, May 9, 1990, John R. Lindsey, Judge. The case is discussed in Bruce Cummings, *Judge Quashes Subpoena of Decatur Library Records*, Wise Co. Messenger, Decatur, Texas, May 13, 1990, at 1.

15. *Id.*

16. Ky. Rev. Stat. Ann. § 61.878(1)(a). That law remains in effect today.

17. 81 Ky. Op. Att'y Gen. 159 (April 21, 1981).

18. *Id.* In a later opinion, the attorney general defined "public library" as including "all tax supported libraries and all private libraries which receive as much as 25 percent of their funds from state or local authority," i.e., the same libraries that are bound by the state open records law. 82 Ky. Op. Att'y Gen. 149 (March 12, 1982).

19. 79 Iowa Op. Att'y Gen. 79–8–25 (August 24, 1979). This opinion noted that library records are public records and subject to disclosure. However, subsequent legislation was enacted to specifically protect library records. See Iowa Code Ann. § 22.7(13) (West 1989).

20. 80 Nev. Op. Att'y Gen. 6 (March 10, 1980). This opinion protects library records as a matter of United States constitutional law. The attorney general cites the First Amendment as a basis for his opinion and the Texas Open Records Decision No. 100 (July 10, 1975) for support. Nevada library records are now protected under Nev. Rev. Stat. Ann. § 239.013 (Michie 1991).

21. Or. Op. Att'y Gen. 435 (April 13, 1981) (The disclosure of circulation records would ordinarily be an unreasonable invasion of privacy, although disclosure of

patrons' names and addresses would not constitute an invasion of privacy.). Oregon library records are now protected under Or. Rev. Stat. § 192.501 (1991).

22. See 88 Tenn. Op. Att'y Gen. 203 (December 6, 1988).

23. *Id.*

24. Miss. Code Ann. § 39–3–365 (1993).

7

Recommendations for Change: Confidentiality of Library Records

Although the library profession declares its solid commitment to patron privacy, the current state of affairs must be significantly improved before that commitment is satisfied. Changes must be made in both library policy and state laws. The former, of course, is within the reach of every library professional; the latter will prove more difficult, albeit necessary.

Uniformity in library confidentiality policies and state laws is also a worthy goal. In this world of mobility, career changes, and interstate library cooperation, uniformity would serve those library professionals whose career changes take them to another state and would also serve those who reach across state lines to better serve their own patrons. In a profession that shares so many structural and functional similarities, vast differences in policies and laws make little sense and add yet another layer of confusion to a rapidly changing professional world.

LIBRARY CONFIDENTIALITY POLICIES

As a first step toward protection of patron policy, all libraries, both public and private, should adopt a strong, clear, well-publicized confidentiality policy. The American Library Association "Policy on Confidentiality of Library Records"[1] is a good place to start. It recommends that libraries:

1. Formally adopt a policy which specifically recognizes its circulation records and other records identifying the names of library users to be confidential in nature.

2. Advise all librarians and library employees that such records shall not be made available to any agency of state, federal, or local government except pursuant to such process, order, or subpoena as may be authorized under the authority of, and pursuant to, federal, state, or local law relating to civil, criminal, or administrative discovery procedures or legislative investigative power.

3. Resist the issuance or enforcement of any such process, order, or subpoena until such time as a proper showing of good cause has been made in a court of competent jurisdiction.*

*Note: Point 3, above, means that upon receipt of such process, order, or subpoena, the library's officers will consult with their legal counsel to determine if such process, order, or subpoena is in proper form and if there is a showing of good cause for its issuance; if the process, order, or subpoena is not in proper form or if good cause has not been shown, they will insist that such defects be cured.[2]

The ALA has also formulated "Suggested Procedures" for implementing the policy. Any library staff member who is approached with a request for protected information should immediately refer the requesting party to "the responsible officer of the institution, who shall explain the confidentiality policy."[3] The officer is to consult with the library's attorney "to determine if such process, order, or subpoena is in good form and if there is a showing of good cause for its issuance."[4] If the order is not in proper form, the library should insist that the requesting party correct the defect. "Any threats or unauthorized demands (i.e., those not supported by a process, order, or subpoena)" should be reported to the library's attorney, and any other related problems should be reported to the library's responsible officer.[5]

Placing the burden of responding to disclosure requests on the library's chief officer accomplishes several things. It ensures, as much as possible, that the policy will be followed consistently. More significantly, it protects lower-level employees from the pressure of having to say no. As became obvious during the Library Awareness Program in the 1980s, those seeking information often intentionally target lower level employees with coercive and intimidating methods of reaching their goals.[6]

In an additional "Policy Concerning Confidentiality of Personally Identifiable Information About Library Users,"[7] the ALA asserts that confidentiality extends to " 'information sought or received, and materials consulted, borrowed or acquired,' and includes database search records, reference interviews, circulation records, interlibrary loan records and other personally identifiable uses of library materials, facilities, or services."

Not all libraries have adopted similar policies. In a state where the confidentiality law is weak, adopting a strong policy may compensate. For example, Indiana's law protects library records "at the discretion" of the library.[8] The State Library director has suggested that, in order to protect patron records "the Library Board must have officially adopted a policy excluding such records from public access."[9] The recommended policy parrots that of the ALA, including the suggested procedures for implementing the policy.

The Minneapolis Public Library exemplifies a commitment to patron privacy in line with the state's strong privacy law.[10] The library's policy mirrors that of the ALA. In addition, the library has addressed specific problems that may arise under the policy. For example, in a policy statement entitled "Telling Patrons What Books or Materials Are Outstanding or on Reserve," the library cautions that when patrons request information about materials charged to them, they must make their request in person and provide identification; requests by telephone will not be honored. When the persons to whom the materials are charged are minors, the minors' parents should not be given the information unless the minors accompany their parents into the library and request the information themselves. The information must be given to the minors who may then give the information to their parents. In the alternative, the information may be mailed to the minors at their addresses.

The Minneapolis Public Library has also formulated a policy concerning its homebound patrons: "Any community library that is maintaining a card file which lists a homebound client and titles of books which have circulated to that client is in violation of" the state law. The library instead recommends that homebound patrons provide a letter of consent to the library to keep such a list or otherwise to have the homebound volunteer, rather than the library, keep the list. Obviously, this public library is not willing to take the expedient route if doing so infringes on its patrons' privacy.

Other libraries drafting strong confidentiality policies should ensure that book cards are no longer used or that patrons need not sign a register attached to the book cover.[11] When the library telephones a patron's home or office to inform the patron that requested material is in, it is important not to reveal the material itself. The library should either have the patron return its call or advise the person at the other end of the line that "the materials requested" are in.

The ALA recommended policy itself could be strengthened. Its weakest link is the recommended response to a subpoena. The ALA urges libraries to "resist" the subpoena and defines resistance as consulting the library's legal counsel to ensure if the subpoena is "in proper form and if there is a showing of good cause for its issuance." The ALA provides no guidance as to what "proper form" might look like and what might constitute "good cause." Although a number of librarians report that those seeking information quickly back down when a library resists the subpoena, others report the opposite. It would behoove the ALA to elaborate, setting guidelines for its constituency. Every library's policy should also include a strong,

clear statement that breach of the policy constitutes misconduct, serious
enough for dismissal of the employee, including the library director who
breaches it.

But even with a strong library policy that takes the decision out of the
hands of lower level employees and that dictates the standards by which
the librarian should be guided, the policy does not have the effect of law.
Furthermore, many library boards may not want to dictate specific policies
that govern the conduct of the library director. They may view their interference as indicating a lack of confidence in the library professional.
Librarians themselves may so view it. However, experience indicates that
such policies are advantageous for the library director. In the face of pressure by the FBI, local police, the local city council, or a parish priest, the
director need only point to his or her library policy to refuse the request
for information and thereby escape the responsibility of making the
"wrong" or unpopular decision.

Obviously, a state *law* mandating library record confidentiality is an even
better alternative. Although the local city council or parish priest might
respect library policy, others might give it little deference. A well-drafted
state law, however, allows for no discretion; it must be obeyed. Such a
law removes from the library board the burden of enacting library policy.
A state law applies to all library employees, regardless of their judgment;
although today's library director may lead the battle in defense of the First
Amendment, tomorrow's director may not be so diligent. A state law would
force his or her protection of library records.

Library Confidentiality Laws

A strong confidentiality law addresses several questions. Chapter 5 addresses these questions in the context of current laws. This chapter examines them again to determine how to strengthen existing law:

1. Which libraries should be included?
2. What information or materials should be protected?
3. Should the laws be discretionary or mandatory?
4. What exceptions should be allowed?
5. What process should be due?
6. Should penalties be imposed for violating the law?

This section will examine possible answers to these questions so that the
library profession may choose those options that best comprise the strongest confidentiality law.

In addition to focusing on the law's coverage, it is also important to
focus on the law's accessibility within the state's statutes. Locating the

confidentiality law within the general library code as an independent library confidentiality statute makes it more likely that those within the profession will read it and incorporate it into their general body of knowledge. If well drafted, it will also provide focused, clear guidance to those who consult it. But it has the disadvantage of being buried in a code that few besides librarians will ever consult. Locating it within the state's open records act will more likely alert those who seek public information under the act, but it is less likely to be read and integrated by those within the profession. Furthermore, the open records acts often exempt numerous records from their coverage, and including a library provision among so many others may create confusion or ambiguity. For example, some courts have interpreted open records laws to apply to private citizen access only, not to government agency access.[12] This may mean that the records exempt from public disclosure, such as library records, might in fact be available to government agencies. The better alternative would be to follow the example of the handful of states that include the confidentiality provisions in both the open records act and the library code.[13]

Which Libraries Should Be Included?

As was apparent in Chapter 5, states that protect library records define "library" in various ways. Including all "public libraries" does little to clarify the law's coverage. Does that term include only those libraries open to the public? Only those wholly funded with public money? Those partially funded with public money? Does it include public university libraries? Does it include the State Library or state archives? Most confidentiality provisions apply only to those libraries traditionally considered "public." Certainly it is important to determine which libraries would be considered "public" under the open records acts and then draft a confidentiality law that protects at least those records from public scrutiny. After all, confidentiality laws are in part a response to the openness created under the open records acts. States following this approach would have confidentiality laws that apply, not only to public libraries in the traditional sense, but also to the State Library; to the library of a university, college, technical or vocational school, or other educational institution; library systems; and special libraries funded in whole or in part by public money. Although it might be a simple matter to state in the statute that confidentiality applies to whatever library records are included in the state's open records law, that definition would entail the interpretation of a more cumbersome law. Simplicity and directness have advantages.

Furthermore, even if a library's records are not deemed "public" under the open records laws, a statute should make it clear that they too are protected. Following this approach, several state confidentiality laws apply to all libraries, with no restrictions. Perhaps the best advice is to choose as broad a definition as possible and draft the law in such a way that it is clear that the legislature intends the definition to be broad:

Any library or archives or special library, whether public or private, whether supported, established, or operated in part or in whole by any public funding or by private funding, including but not limited to a library maintained by a state, county, and local governmental unit; or by an agency, school, school district, college, university, industry, commercial or other group, association, organization, or society.

What Information or Materials Should Be Protected?

As was apparent in Chapter 5, states have also approached this question in a variety of ways. Obviously, the library profession desires to protect all information about its patrons' use of the library. Therefore, a strong confidentiality law must be as inclusive as possible. Certainly more than registration and circulation records should be protected. But the danger of listing individually the type of library materials or services protected is that something will be overlooked or unanticipated. A better approach is to protect "records and other information" about a patron, not just in terms of the materials borrowed or used, but in terms of any use the patron or group of patrons make of the library. Imagining the library as a bubble into which a patron enters, the entirety of which has been declared a zone of privacy, describes the kind of coverage a law should seek. Thus, the law might protect "records and other information that identify a person or persons as having requested or obtained specific information, materials, or services, or as otherwise having used the library."

A confidentiality law should also protect material donated to libraries under the terms set forth by the donor. A number of states already include such provisions. Simply stated, a law should protect any records or materials made through or concerning any gift, grant, conveyance, bequest, or devise, to the extent of any limitations placed thereon as conditions for the gift, grant, conveyance, bequest, or devise.

The ideal law would also extend to interlibrary transactions to protect a library patron from the less-protective law of another state. Wisconsin has recently enacted a law that may provide some protection in this area.[14] In that state, the confidentiality law extends to those libraries supported in whole or in part by public funds and includes a library system. Section 2 of the new law provides that such a library can disclose patron information to another library only if the other library meets one of the following requirements:

(a) The library is supported in whole or in part by public funds.
(b) The library has a written policy prohibiting the disclosure of the identity of the individual except as authorized under [Section 3 below].

(c) The library agrees not to disclose the identity of the individual except as authorized under [Section 3 below].

Section 3 provides:

A library to which an individual's identity is disclosed under sub. (2) and that is not supported in whole or in part by public funds may disclose that individual's identity to another library for the purpose of borrowing materials for that individual only if the library to which the identity is being disclosed meets at least one of the requirements specified under sub. (2)(a) to (c).[15]

This novel statute works well if the interlibrary transaction takes place within the state boundaries. For example, if one public library seeks to borrow materials for its patron from another public library, it may disclose the patron's name because the second library is publicly funded and will therefore be bound as well by the state confidentiality law. But if the patron's library must borrow the materials from a private library (one not included in the confidentiality law), it may disclose the patron's name only if the second library has a written policy prohibiting disclosure or if it promises not to disclose the patron's identity.

This structure operates toward better patron protection within the state. But what might happen if a patron at the University of Wisconsin requests through interlibrary loan a book that can only be found in a state that has a weak confidentiality law or none at all? The second library may in fact be publicly funded yet have no duty to protect the patron's identity. One solution might be to prohibit an interstate library transaction that jeopardizes patron privacy, thus forcing libraries to rely only on those states with strong confidentiality laws. This places a severe burden on librarians, requiring them to learn the confidentiality laws of all fifty states; additionally, it may limit the library's ability to serve its patrons by eliminating some states' libraries as possible sources of necessary materials. A better solution is to follow the lead of some libraries, which simply avoid disclosing a patron's name when requesting materials from another library. The patron's identity is not relevant in an interlibrary loan transaction. Obviously, a strong uniform confidentiality law would eliminate many problems. Currently, the law in both Arkansas and New York protects patron identity in interlibrary loan transactions.

Should the Law Be Discretionary or Mandatory?

To ask the question is to answer it. Any law that places the decision and burden of whether or not to divulge library records upon the shoulders of the librarian or library staff is too weak. Currently, only thirty-one states have strong, mandatory laws.

What Exceptions Should Be Allowed?

As discussed in Chapter 5, confidentiality laws often allow disclosure of patron records when the patron consents to such disclosure and when administratively necessary to the library's proper operation. Consent, however, may be obtained in various ways. One could argue that a patron who signs a generalized form upon registration for a library card has "consented" to all the terms therein, even if those terms include language that allows disclosure to all who request it. But a strong law would provide that the consent be "informed"—that is, that the patron consent in writing to the disclosure of specific records that have been requested by a third party.

Minnesota's law, for example, defines informed consent as a "statement in plain language, dated, specific in designating the person or agency authorized to disclose and the person or agency to whom the data shall be disclosed, specific as to the purpose of disclosure and as to the expiration date, ordinarily less than one year."[16] This language prevents widespread disclosure on the basis of boilerplate language in a registration form.

The administrative exception to confidentiality laws also makes sense, if delineated in narrow terms. The law should allow disclosure only to members of the library staff acting within the scope of their duties within the library administration and then only as necessary for the reasonable operation of the library. Those libraries that depend on outside agencies for the collection of overdue materials or fines must ensure that patron information remains confidential. If the law protects "library records and other information," it will also protect that information in the hands of the library's representatives. It would, however, be helpful to have the outside agency sign a contract to that effect.

Statistical compilations of library data are frequently deemed exceptions to confidentiality laws. However, because they do not reveal information about particular library patrons, they do not represent a threat and, in fact, are necessary to the proper functioning of libraries.

Another common exception to confidentiality laws is the "court order" or "subpoena" exception. But this exception reflects too much deference to the legal system and is rarely accompanied by a definition or by any restrictions. It makes little sense to allow broad-ranging fishing expeditions into the reading habits of all library patrons, simply on the whim of a district attorney in a criminal case or of another attorney in a civil lawsuit. Any inspection of library records should be allowed only in narrow circumstances when the public safety is at stake, and never in a noncriminal case.

A strong law would allow some disclosure in a criminal case, but not the free-ranging disclosure available in most states. Iowa amended its law after suffering the effects of a weak law. Its current law now allows disclosure of library records "to a criminal justice agency only pursuant to an investigation of a particular person or organization suspected of committing a known crime" and only where a "connection exists between the requested release of information, and a legitimate end," and where "the need for information is cogent and compelling."[17] Additional safeguards will include specific due process protection as discussed below.

A final exception to confidentiality laws that has been widely accepted is that concerning minors. Obviously, the strongest law would not allow such disclosures. One can easily imagine circumstances that demonstrate both sides of this argument. On one side is the six-year-old child who checks out a book and loses it. The parents must pay the library for the book. It seems unreasonable to ask parents to pay for a book whose title and contents remain a mystery. On the other side is a sixteen-year-old girl who checks out a book about incest after suffering sexual abuse from her father. Her privacy must be protected. No state has yet managed to resolve this dilemma. Perhaps the best approach is to provide confidentiality for the records of all library patrons, including minors and incapacitated adults. By signing library registration forms for their children that impose financial responsibility upon a parent, the parent agrees to pick up the tab regardless of the material borrowed. Very young children are unable to borrow materials on their own and must have the assistance of their parents. As they grow older, they become more capable of checking out materials on their own and may also become more financially responsible. If not, and their parents are called upon to pay the bills, the issue of the specific materials borrowed should be settled between the child and his or her parents. A law that allows a parent or guardian to routinely review a minor's reading list paints with too broad a brush.

Other exceptions to confidentiality laws are uncommon, although they warrant consideration. Although no library confidentiality law specifically places a time restriction on protection, some open records laws provide that access to public records is available after a period of years. This, of course, assumes that the records will be available for disclosure at the end of that period. Assuming that libraries begin to appreciate the value of library records, including circulation records, and begin to accommodate that appreciation in retention laws, a provision that patron records be available after the death of the patron, or seventy-five years after the record is made, would greatly facilitate the work of historians.

Another approach to research interests is to provide for a "researcher" exemption. Georgia has a law that provides that confidential records

may be used for research purposes by private researchers providing that:

(1) The researcher is qualified to perform the research;

(2) The research topic is designed to produce a study that would be of potential benefit to the state or its citizens;

(3) The researcher will agree in writing to protect the confidentiality of the

information contained in the records (Researcher cannot use named persons in notes or finished study).[18]

The law also provides that "[t]he use of such confidential records for research shall be considered a privilege and the agreement signed by the researcher shall be binding on him."[19] A recent Canadian law also demonstrates a commitment to research interests, allowing the disclosure of confidential information for research purposes under specified restrictions.[20]

The National Archives allows disclosure of confidential information for research purposes as well. Researchers who seek access to personal information held by the Archives must submit a proposal, describing their project, their institution, a list of their publications, and references.[21] Such a provision should extend confidentiality protection to this information when it is placed in the hands of researchers.[22] Penalties should be severe for researchers who violate their agreements.

What Process Should Be Due?

Most states do not provide for any process at all. A few, however, have developed elaborate due process mechanisms that serve as a roadmap for librarians faced with a demand for library records. The District of Columbia has the most detailed procedure, but others have provided for at least minimal process. The advantage of a detailed, specific procedure is that it ensures the same process for all record requests and gives much-needed guidance to the librarian who is not routinely faced with this dilemma. The disadvantage is that it may provide too much process when all that is needed is a simple "no." Furthermore, an elaborate procedure may be unnecessary if, given a choice, the patron chooses to disclose.

If the confidentiality law is drafted narrowly to include only those cases that involve the violation of criminal law and that focus on a specific suspect, then much of the process provided in some states becomes unnecessary. At a minimum, the library should be given the opportunity for a hearing before a judge. Unless the law enforcement agency can demonstrate why a criminal suspect should not be given notice of the attempt to examine his or her records (for example, that he or she might flee the jurisdiction or inflict harm), he or she too should be given adequate notice and an opportunity to be heard before a judge prior to the disclosure. The burden of proof in this instance should be on the law enforcement agency, with the presumption in favor of nondisclosure. In some cases, the identity of the patron must be protected. There the library should be allowed to object in the patron's behalf or notify him without revealing his identity to others.

Those states that allow broad disclosure of records in response to a generalized "court order" or "subpoena" must ensure that due process mechanisms are more detailed and comprehensive. What kind of process should be provided? Even the most basic conception of due process entitles affected parties to notice and an opportunity to be heard, at a meaningful time and in a meaningful manner.[23] This means that a judicial hearing ought to be provided before a record is disclosed. It also means that all parties should be given time to prepare their cases, including the time to hire an attorney, if desired. A period of at least several days should elapse between the time of notice and the hearing. Notice should be of a type reasonably calculated to inform the affected parties[24] of the proceedings involving them, preferably personal hand-to-hand service, but at least by certified mail. The notice should include specific directions as to the steps the recipients must take in order to protect their rights. The steps should be inexpensive and simple.

Other considerations include placing the burden of proof upon the party requesting the record, giving the presumption of nondisclosure to the library, and providing the court with statutory guidance in making its decision. This might include a statement that citizens place a high value upon library patron privacy and that it is the rare case in which this privacy may be breached. The statute might also require that the court find an emergency exists, such as one involving death or serious bodily injury, before allowing disclosure. Obviously, the more specific the confidentiality law, the less discretion the court will have to allow its breach. The process outlined in the District of Columbia statute may prove illustrative.

Should Penalties Be Imposed for Violating the Law?

The confidentiality law is only as strong as its enforcement. If no penalties exist for the law's violation, the law is weak. On the other hand, if penalties exist but are buried in the morass of open records laws or criminal laws, they offer little deterrent value. The most effective location for a penalty provision related to a library confidentiality law is within the law itself. A few states have adopted this approach.

Another issue relates to the kind of penalty imposed. The two broad categories are civil and criminal liability. Civil liability means that the person wronged by violation of the law, in this case the library patron whose records have been wrongfully disclosed, may sue the wrongdoer— either the library or the requesting party, or both—for an amount of damages or for an injunction against disclosure, if it has not yet occurred. Full compensation would include attorney fees and the costs of litigation, if the patron wins the lawsuit. If the disclosure is reckless or wanton or willful, punitive damages may also be appropriate.

Criminal liability means that the wrongdoer is punished, either by paying a fine to the state or by serving time in jail. The patron who has been wronged, however, receives no monetary compensation. The advantage of criminal liability is that it may serve as a strong deterrent. Nothing prohibits a state from enacting both civil and criminal penalties. This may be the better approach.

Against whom will the civil and/or criminal penalty be assessed? Much will depend on the circumstances. If the library has done its job adequately, through proper training and education of its employees, then the individual employee who nevertheless violates both library policy and state law should be penalized. If the library supervisor has not adequately trained and educated his or her employees, liability may rest there. General legal principles of governmental employer/employee liability will determine the ultimate responsibility.

Additional penalties might include termination of the employee who wrongfully discloses patron information. However, such a penalty is most likely addressed in the employee's employment contract. Certainly, an employee who violates library policies may be subject to termination.

The library is forced to walk a fine line between disclosure and nondisclosure. On the one hand, the policy behind *open records law* favors disclosure. On the other hand, the policy behind *library confidentiality laws* favors nondisclosure. In either event, violation should be penalized. But, if the library professional values patron privacy as it seems to assert, then the penalty for wrongful disclosure should be at least as severe as the penalty for wrongful nondisclosure.

RELATED FEDERAL LAWS

Several attempts have been made to enact a national law governing privacy, some of them successful, others not. The Privacy Act of 1974 is "designed to protect the privacy of individuals by providing them with more control over the gathering, dissemination, and accuracy of information about themselves contained in government files."[25] The law provides that no federal agency "shall disclose any record which is contained in a system of records... to any person, or to another agency" without the written consent of the record's subject, except pursuant to specified exceptions.[26] The problem with this law is (1) it applies only to *federal* libraries and (2) it is general in nature, does not apply to library records specifically, and is therefore overly complex. A law pertaining specifically to library records is preferable.

The same problems can be seen in the Uniform Information Practices Code,[27] a proposed uniform law approved by the National Conference of Commissioners on Uniform State Laws in 1980. It is designed to "provide a uniform state law on privacy and freedom of information"[28] and relates to information collected and maintained by state and local governments, thus by definition applying to most public libraries. However, only one state, Hawaii, has so far adopted the law and then with some modifications.[29] Because the proposed uniform law is not drafted with library records in mind, it is unduly complex and ambiguous for that purpose. In addition, the law is discretionary, giving agencies authority to withhold exempt materials, but not compelling them to do so.[30] The law permits disclosure where doing so would not be "a clearly unwarranted invasion of personal privacy"[31] or if the disclosure is made to "another agency . . . if disclosure is . . . for the purpose of a civil or criminal law enforcement investigation. . . ."[32] Other exceptions exist in the law. The value of a specific library record confidentiality law is obvious.

The Province of Ontario has recently adopted a Freedom of Information and Protection of Privacy Act, which serves as a combination open records and privacy act.[33] As with similar acts in this country, it is long and fairly complex, primarily because of its comprehensiveness. It protects personal information and prohibits an agency head from disclosing such information, except with the prior written consent of the information's subject or "in compelling circumstances affecting the health or safety of an individual" or if another statute provides for disclosure or "if the disclosure does not constitute an unjustified invasion of personal privacy" or "for a research purpose" under specific conditions. The conditions are:

(i) the disclosure is consistent with the conditions or reasonable expectations of disclosure under which the personal information was provided, collected or obtained,

(ii) the research purpose . . . cannot be reasonably accomplished unless the information is provided in individually identifiable form, and

(iii) terms and conditions relating to,

(A) security and confidentiality,

(B) the removal or destruction of the individual identifier . . . at the earliest time at which removal or destruction can be accomplished consistent with the purpose of the research . . . , and

(C) the prohibition of any subsequent use or disclosure of the record in individually identifiable form without the express authorization of the institution,

have been approved by the responsible minister and the person obtaining the record has filed . . . a written statement indicating that the person understands and will abide by the terms and conditions.[34]

The law also provides guidelines for determining whether a disclosure constitutes an unjustified invasion of privacy, with a *presumption* against disclosure under certain conditions, including the revelation of one's "racial or ethnic origin, sexual orientation or religious or political beliefs or associations."[35]

The Ontario law also provides for notice to the subject before disclosure of information relating to him or her, if the agency head believes that disclosure "might constitute an unjustified invasion of personal privacy."[36]

The subject is given twenty days to provide reasons why the disclosure should not be allowed, with opportunity for an appeal should the agency head decide to allow disclosure.[37] Anyone who willfully and wrongfully discloses information is subject to criminal liability and a fine up to $5,000.00.[38]

Although the Canadian law is thorough and well-drafted, it represents a broad approach to the issue of privacy. Substantial discretion is given over to the agency head and the definition of an "unjustified" invasion of privacy leaves much to be desired. For the purposes of library records, a narrower, more specific law would be helpful.

Recently, Congress addressed such a law geared specifically toward library records. The law failed. It was originally proposed as a Library and Video Privacy Protection Act, but when law enforcement officials became involved, the library portion dropped out. No adequate compromise could be reached on the exceptions to confidentiality. The bill instead passed as a Video Privacy Protection Act, protecting those who borrow videotapes from disclosure of their viewing habits.[39] It is certain that such legislation will be attempted again, but until such time as it succeeds, each state is left to its own devices.

PROPOSED UNIFORM CONFIDENTIALITY LAW

This section proposes language for a strong library confidentiality law. It does not address open records laws generally, although as mentioned above it is very helpful to include the library confidentiality provisions in such laws. However, rather than attempt to amend current open records laws by including the entire library portion within them, it is suggested that the open records law make specific reference to the library confidentiality law, by name and code number. That accomplishes the goal of alerting those who consult the open records law to the library exception, while requiring only minimal amendment to the open records law.

A strong confidentiality law would include the suggestions made in this chapter. The following proposed law reflects these suggestions, but it is by no means the only approach to this issue. Within each state, passage of a new confidentiality law must take into account the context of existing legislation and the political feasibility of passing new legislation. The following is an example of a strong confidentiality law.

THE LIBRARY RECORD CONFIDENTIALITY ACT

A. For purposes of this section, "library" means any library or archives or special library, whether public or private, whether supported, established, or operated in part or in whole by any public funding or by private funding, including but not limited to a library maintained by a state, county, and local governmental unit; or by an agency, school, school district, college, university, industry, commercial or other group, association, organization, or society.

B. Library records and other information that identify a person or persons as having requested or obtained specific information, materials, or services, or as otherwise having used the library, including but not limited to records related to the circulation or use of library materials; or to computer data base searches, interlibrary loan materials, and title reserve requests; or to the use of audio-visual materials, films, records, or meeting rooms, shall be confidential and shall not be disclosed except as stated in (D) below.

C. Library records and other materials made through or concerning any gift, grant, conveyance, bequest, or devise to the library shall be confidential and shall not be disclosed to the extent of any limitations placed thereon as conditions for the gift, grant, conveyance, bequest, or devise.

D. Library records may be disclosed in the following circumstances:

1. When the patron consents in writing in a statement in plain language, dated, specific in designating the person or agency authorized to disclose and the person or agency to whom the data shall be disclosed, specific as to the purpose of disclosure and as to the expiration date, ordinarily less than one year;

2. To the library staff acting within the scope of their duties within the library administration as necessary for the reasonable operation of the library; or to a collection agency acting jointly with the library only to the extent necessary for the return of overdue or stolen library materials or to collect fines;

3. Statistical compilations prepared by library administrators which do not identify individual patrons;

4. To a criminal justice agency pursuant to a court order signed by a state or federal judge in a criminal proceeding as part of an investigation of a particular person or organization:

i. when the person or organization is suspected of committing a known crime; and

ii. where a connection exists between the requested release of information and a legitimate end; and

iii. where the public safety is at stake; and

iv. where the need for information is cogent and compelling;

5. When the request for record disclosure does not name a specific library patron and the records were created seventy-five or more years earlier;

6. When the request for record disclosure concerns a specific library patron and the patron is no longer alive.

E. Within two working days after receiving a court order as set forth in (D)(4) above, the library may file a motion in the court in which the criminal action is pending, requesting either that the order be rescinded or that it be held in abeyance until the subject of the records be given written notice, served upon him or her by certified mail or personal service, notifying him or her that the records are being sought, and an opportunity be provided for the subject to respond to the order. If the court refuses to rescind the order, the court shall hold the order in abeyance and order service upon the subject of the records unless it finds that there is reason to believe that the notice will result in:

   i. Endangering the life or physical safety of any person;

   ii. Flight from prosecution;

   iii. Destruction of or tampering with evidence;

   iv. Intimidation of potential witnesses; or

   v. Otherwise seriously jeopardizing an investigation or official proceeding.

F. Any person who violates this Act commits a [misdemeanor or felony, in the designated class] and shall be punished by a fine of not more than $———, plus ——— days in jail, or both. In addition, the aggrieved library patron may also bring a civil action against the individual violator for actual damages or $1,000.00, whichever is greater, punitive damages, reasonable attorneys' fees, court costs, and such other relief, legal and equitable, to which the patron may be entitled.

EXPLANATION OF THE ACT

This proposed act provides broad coverage of the kinds of libraries and library records that are included. It makes clear that the format of the records is irrelevant, and that information about any use that a patron makes of a library is protected. The law is mandatory and thus does not place the decision of disclosure upon the shoulders of the library director or staff.

Exceptions to the act are narrowly tailored. Patron consent must be written, informed, and specific. Court orders must fit within the statute's narrow definition, and then the library is provided with additional safeguards that are designed to protect the due process rights of both the library and the library patron. The interest of researchers and scholars is accommodated by means of time limitations on record confidentiality. When the request is generalized—for example, a request for all patron records from 1900 to 1905—the seventy-five-year limitation governs. When the request is specific—for example, a request for the patron records of "John Smith"—the age of the records is irrelevant; all that matters in that instance is that the patron no longer be alive. An alternative to the "term of years" limitation would be the "researcher's" exemption, as discussed in this chapter.

Whether violation of the statute constitutes a misdemeanor or felony will depend upon the designation of criminal offenses in each state. For example, a first-degree misdemeanor in one state may carry the same penalty as a second-degree felony in another state. Similarly, the precise amount of a criminal fine and length of jail sentence depends upon how the violation is characterized. Each state should determine how best to characterize violation of library confidentiality laws.

If a law similar to the one proposed above is enacted in all states, much of the uncertainty surrounding library confidentiality will be eliminated.

Such a scheme offers substantial protection to library patrons (and to the First Amendment), while at the same time adequately accommodating the interests of libraries, law enforcement officials, and researchers. Because the law is narrowly tailored to accommodate these interests, it offers detailed, specific guidance to all who consult it. Such a law would demonstrate the library profession's commitment to the First Amendment principles it has long espoused.

NOTES

1. Adopted January 20, 1971; revised July 4, 1975 & July 2, 1986, by the ALA Council.

2. *Id.*

3. "Suggested Procedures for Implementing 'Policy on Confidentiality of Library Records,' " adopted by the ALA Intellectual Freedom Committee, January 9, 1983; revised January 11, 1988.

4. *Id.*

5. *Id.*

6. See H. N. Foerstel, Surveillance in the Stacks: The FBI's Library Awareness Program (1991), at 69, 77 ("the FBI has usually bypassed library supervisors in pursuing the Library Awareness Program").

7. Adopted July 2, 1991, by the ALA Council.

8. Ind. Code Ann. § 5–14–3–4 (West 1989).

9. Notice from Indiana State Library dated May 26, 1988, and mailed to the author in response to her questionnaire by Sandi Thompson, public library consultant, Indiana State Library (1992).

10. The state law protects from disclosure "[t]hat portion of data maintained by a library which links a library patron's name with materials requested or borrowed by the patron or which links a patron's name with a specific subject about which the patron has requested information or materials." Such information can be obtained only by court order. Minn. Stat. Ann. § 13.40 (Supp. 1992).

11. In checking out the latest edition of the ALA Office for Intellectual Freedom's *Intellectual Freedom Manual* recently at the library of a university's library school, the author was surprised to find in a pocket attached to the back cover a slip of paper with the names of prior borrowers.

12. Bruce M. Kennedy, *Confidentiality of Library Records: A Survey of Problems, Policies, and Laws*, 81 L. Libr. J. 733, 758 (1989).

13. See, e.g., Alabama, Colorado, Illinois, Maryland, New Hampshire, and South Carolina. Bruce M. Kennedy argues that "[a]n independent statute is easier to understand. The scope of the privacy right is spelled out in the four corners of a single, short statute." He also states that such a statute does not carry the legislative baggage of an integrated statute, i.e., one which is included as part of the state's open records law. For example, it may be necessary to consult the legislative intent and judicial interpretation of a law to determine its meaning. In doing so, it is easier to consult an independent law, rather than having to wrestle with the usually more cumbersome open records law. Kennedy also worries that a confidentiality law is more likely to be discretionary if buried within an open

records act. See Kennedy, *supra* note 12, at 733, 755. He is right in some respects. However, including such a law in both the open records act and the library code, and utilizing careful language, might alleviate some of these flaws.

14. See Wis. Stat. Ann. § 43.30 (West. Supp. 1992).

15. *Id.*

16. Minn. Stat. Ann. § 13.05(4)(d) (West 1988).

17. Iowa Code Ann. § 22.7(13) (West 1989). But Iowa's law is weakened by its discretionary nature and ambiguity. The law provides that library records are confidential, "unless otherwise ordered by a court" or "by the lawful custodian of the records. . . . " One interpretation of the law would place conditions upon release to a "criminal justice agency," but place no such conditions upon release of records relevant to a *civil* action. See *id.*

18. Ga. Code Ann. § 50–18–101 (1992).

19. *Id.*

20. Ontario Freedom of Information and Protection of Privacy Act of 1987 (1987 S.O. 1987, chap. 25). For a discussion of this Act, see Heather MacNeil, Without Consent: The Ethics of Disclosing Personal Information in Public Archives (1992).

21. MacNeil, *id.* at 138.

22. MacNeil reports in her recent book that three scholars were subpoenaed regarding the publication of the "Pentagon papers." Although they had promised confidentiality to their sources, the court forced them to disclose. *Id.* at 146.

23. Fuentes v. Shevin, 407 U.S. 67, 80 (1972).

24. Mullane v. Central Hanover Bank & Trust Co., 339 U.S. 306 (1950).

25. Thomas M. Susman, *The Privacy Act and the Freedom of Information Act: Conflict and Resolution*, 21 J. Marshall L. Rev. 703, 705 (1988).

26. 5 U.S.C. § 552a.

27. 13 U.L.A. 277 (1986).

28. *Id.*

29. See Haw. Rev. Stat. § 92F–1 to 92F–42 (Supp. 1992).

30. Uniform Information Practices Code § 2–103 & Comment, 13 U.L.A. 290 (1986).

31. *Id.* at § 3–101, 13 U.L.A. 296 (1986).

32. *Id.* at § 3–103, 13 U.L.A. 300 (1986).

33. See 1987 O.S. 1987 chap. 25, adopted in 1987.

34. *Id.* at § 21.

35. *Id.*

36. *Id.* at § 28.

37. *Id.*

38. *Id.* at § 61.

39. S. Rep. No. 599, 100th Cong., 2d Sess., *reprinted in* 1988 U.S. Code Cong. & Admin. News 4342–1.

Appendixes

Appendix A
Survey of State Officers Responsible for Public Records

PLEASE ANSWER THE FOLLOWING QUESTIONS. IF YOU REQUIRE ADDITIONAL SPACE, PLEASE USE THE BACK OF THIS SURVEY OR ATTACH ADDITIONAL SHEETS OF PAPER. THANK YOU FOR YOUR ASSISTANCE.

1.   Has your office established a written records retention/ disposition schedule which sets forth the length of time public library records must be retained? (*Public library records include circulation and registration records, correspondence, papers, and documents prepared or received by the library relating to the conduct of its public business.*)

Yes_____   No_____

a.   If you answered Yes to Question Number 1, please attach copies of the schedule.

b.   If you answered Yes to Question Number 1, please state the manner in which libraries in your state receive information about the schedule.

2.   If you answered No to Question Number 1, please state the following:

a.   Who determines when public library records may be destroyed?

b.   What procedures, if any, are required prior to destruction of public library records?

c   Who must approve the destruction of public library records?

d.   How long are public library records retained?

e.   Are penalties imposed for improper destruction of library records, and, if so, what are they?

3.   Are you aware of any local ordinances in your state which govern the retention or disposition of public library records or which govern the confidentiality of public library records? (*Local ordinances are laws enacted by cities, towns, villages, or other municipalities, but do not include state laws.*)

Yes_____   No_____

If your answer to Question Number 3 is Yes, please attach copies of such ordinances or provide identifying information about such ordinances so that copies might be obtained.

Appendix A (continued)

4.   Are you aware of any instances in your state in which
public librarians were asked to reveal to a third party either
circulation or registration records of library users?

     Yes_____   No_____

     If your answer to Question Number 4 is Yes, please state
your knowledge of such instances or identify the libraries
involved so that more information might be obtained.

5.   Please add any comments or questions you have concerning
records retention schedules and confidentiality issues as they
relate to public libraries in your state.

Name, address, telephone number, and title of person answering
this Survey:

_____
Name

_____
Address

_____
Telephone number (including area code)

_____
Title

Appendix B
Survey of Librarians for Major U.S. Public Libraries

PLEASE ANSWER THE FOLLOWING QUESTIONS. IF YOU REQUIRE ADDITIONAL SPACE, PLEASE COMPLETE YOUR ANSWER ON THE BACK OF THIS SURVEY OR ATTACH ADDITIONAL SHEETS OF PAPER. THANK YOU FOR YOUR ASSISTANCE.

1. Has your library established its own written records retention/disposition schedule which sets forth the length of time library records must be retained? (Public library records include circulation and registration records, correspondence, papers, and documents prepared or received by the library relating to the conduct of its public business.)

Yes _____   No _____

If you answered Yes to Question Number 1, please attach copies of the schedule.

2. If you answered No to Question Number 1, please state the following:

a. How do you determine when your library records may be destroyed?

b. What procedures, if any, are required prior to destruction of library records?

c. Who must approve the destruction of library records?

d. How long are library records retained?

3. Have you been made aware of any local ordinances in your state which govern the retention or disposition of public library records or which govern the confidentiality of public library records? (Local ordinances are laws enacted by cities, towns, villages, or other municipalities, but do not include state laws.)

If your answer to Question Number 3 is Yes, please attach copies of such ordinances or provide identifying information about such ordinances so that copies might be obtained.

4. Do you know whether smaller public libraries in your state follow the same records retention/disposition schedule or procedure as you do?

Yes, they do _____ No, they do not _____ I don't know _____

If they do not, can you briefly explain the method they follow in determining how long to retain library records?

Appendix B (continued)

5.   Are you aware of any instances in your state in which public librarians were asked to reveal to a third party either circulation or registration records of library users?

        Yes _____   No _____

        If your answer to Question Number 5 is Yes, please state your knowledge of such instances or identify the libraries involved so that more information might be obtained.

6.   Please add any comments or questions you have concerning records retention schedules and confidentiality issues as they relate to public libraries in your state.

Name, address, telephone number, and title of person answering this Survey:

_____
Name

_____
Address

_____
Telephone Number (including area code)

_____
Title

Thank you for your time!

Appendix C
Survey of ALA State Chapter Executives

PLEASE ANSWER THE FOLLOWING QUESTIONS. IF YOU NEED ADDITIONAL SPACE,
PLEASE USE THE BACK OF THIS SURVEY OR ATTACH ADDITIONAL SHEETS OF PAPER.
THANK YOU VERY MUCH FOR YOUR ASSISTANCE.

1.   Have you been made aware of any records retention/
disposition schedules which have been established in your state
which would pertain to the retention and disposition of public
library records? (Public library records include circulation and
registration records, correspondence, papers, and documents
prepared or received by the library relating to the conduct of
its public business.)

Yes _____   No _____

a.   If you answered Yes to Question Number 1,
please attach copies of such schedules or identify
the source of such schedules.

b.   If you answered No to Question Number 1,
please indicate to the best of your knowledge
whether public librarians in your state know when
they can dispose of library records.

2.   Have you been made aware of any instances in your state in
which public librarians were asked to reveal to a third party
either circulation or registration records of library users?

Yes _____   No _____

If your answer to Question Number 2 is Yes, please state
your knowledge of such instances or identify the libraries
involved so that more information might be obtained.

3.   Have you been made aware of any local ordinances in your
state which govern the retention or disposition of public library
records or which govern the confidentiality of public library
records? (Local ordinances are laws enacted by cities, towns,
villages, or other municipalities, but do not include state
laws.)

Yes _____   No _____

If your answer to Question Number 3 is Yes, please attach
copies of such ordinances or provide identifying information
about such ordinances so that copies might be obtained.

Appendix C (continued)

4.   Please add any comments or questions you have concerning records retention schedules and confidentiality issues as they relate to public libraries in your state.

Name, address, phone number, and title of person answering this Survey:

_____
Name

_____
Address

_____
Telephone number (including area code)

_____
Title

Thank you for your time!

Appendix D
Library Record Confidentiality Laws

STATE AND CODE #	EXCEPTIONS TO CONFI'Y (See Key)	TYPE OF LIBRARY (See Key)	RECORDS PROTECTED (See Key)	MANDATORY/ DISCRET'Y
ALABAMA 41-8-10	A,G,DD,II	A	B	M
ALABAMA 36-12-40	DD	A	B	M

Alabama has two confidentiality statutes. The first listed is in the library statute; the second is an exemption from the open records act.

STATE AND CODE #	EXCEPTIONS TO CONFI'Y (See Key)	TYPE OF LIBRARY (See Key)	RECORDS PROTECTED (See Key)	MANDATORY/ DISCRET'Y
ALASKA 9.25.140	R,FF	H	B	M
ARIZONA 41-1354	B,K,S	I	B	M
ARKANSAS 13-2-701 to 13-2-706	D,L,O,U,II	J	B	M
CALIFORNIA GOV'T 6254, 6267	C,E,K,R,II	B	A	M
COLORADO 24-90-119 24-72-204	B,K,T	B	B	M

Colorado has two confidentiality statutes. The first listed is in the library statute; the second is an exemption from the open records act.

STATE AND CODE #	EXCEPTIONS TO CONFI'Y (See Key)	TYPE OF LIBRARY (See Key)	RECORDS PROTECTED (See Key)	MANDATORY/ DISCRET'Y
CONNECTICUT 11-25	--	V	A*	M

*"personally identifiable information contained in the circulation records . . . ."

STATE AND CODE #	EXCEPTIONS TO CONFI'Y (See Key)	TYPE OF LIBRARY (See Key)	RECORDS PROTECTED (See Key)	MANDATORY/ DISCRET'Y
DELAWARE Tit. 29, sec.10002	--	V	B	D*

*"Any records . . . which contain the identity of a user . . . shall not be deemed public" for purposes of the open records act.

STATE AND CODE #	EXCEPTIONS TO CONFI'Y (See Key)	TYPE OF LIBRARY (See Key)	RECORDS PROTECTED (See Key)	MANDATORY/ DISCRET'Y
DISTRICT OF COLUMBIA 37-106.2	B,K,R,JJ	V	B	M

Appendix D (continued)

STATE AND CODE #	EXCEPTIONS TO CONFI'Y (See Key)	TYPE OF LIBRARY (See Key)	RECORDS PROTECTED (See Key)	MANDATORY/ DISCRET'Y
FLORIDA 257.261	II	V	A*	M

*Circulation record: "all information which identifies the patrons borrowing particular books and other materials"

STATE AND CODE #	EXCEPTIONS TO CONFI'Y	TYPE OF LIBRARY	RECORDS PROTECTED	MANDATORY/ DISCRET'Y
GEORGIA 24-9-46	F,K,W,EE,KK E		B	M

HAWAII: NO CONFIDENTIALITY STATUTE, but section 92F-13 exempts from open records act "records which, if disclosed, would constitute a clearly unwarranted invasion of personal privacy."

STATE AND CODE #	EXCEPTIONS TO CONFI'Y	TYPE OF LIBRARY	RECORDS PROTECTED	MANDATORY/ DISCRET'Y
IDAHO 9-340	--	E	B	D*

*Library records are exempt from open records act.

STATE AND CODE #	EXCEPTIONS TO CONFI'Y	TYPE OF LIBRARY	RECORDS PROTECTED	MANDATORY/ DISCRET'Y
ILLINOIS chap.81 para.1201, 1202	R,II	D	A*	M

*Circulation record: "all information identifying the individual borrowing particular books or materials"

STATE AND CODE #	EXCEPTIONS TO CONFI'Y	TYPE OF LIBRARY	RECORDS PROTECTED	MANDATORY/ DISCRET'Y
ILLINOIS chap. 116 para.207	--	E	B*	D**

*Illinois has two confidentiality statutes. The first is a library statute; the second is an exemption from the open records act. The latter protects records which identify library users with specific materials. **When applied with the library statute, this statute becomes mandatory.

STATE AND CODE #	EXCEPTIONS TO CONFI'Y	TYPE OF LIBRARY	RECORDS PROTECTED	MANDATORY/ DISCRET'Y
INDIANA 5-14-3-4	--	E	B	D*

*Library records are exempt from the open records act "at the discretion" of the library.

STATE AND CODE #	EXCEPTIONS TO CONFI'Y	TYPE OF LIBRARY	RECORDS PROTECTED	MANDATORY/ DISCRET'Y
IOWA 22.7	R	E	B	D*

Appendix D (continued)

STATE AND CODE #	EXCEPTIONS TO CONFI'Y (See Key)	TYPE OF LIBRARY (See Key)	RECORDS PROTECTED (See Key)	MANDATORY/ DISCRET'Y
	*Library records "shall be kept confidential, unless otherwise ordered . . . by the lawful custodian of the records . . . ." But records can be released to a criminal justice agency only under specified conditions.			
KANSAS 45-221	S	E	B*	D**
	*"Library patron and circulation records which pertain to identifiable individuals" **"not required to be open" under open records act			
KENTUCKY	NO CONFIDENTIALITY STATUTE, but section 61.878 exempts from open records act "records containing information of a personal nature where the public disclosure thereof would constitute a clearly unwarranted invasion of personal privacy." Interpreted by Attorney General Opinions 81-159 & 82-149 to include records of all tax supported libraries and all private libraries which receive as much as 25% of their funds from state or local authority. Discretionary only.			
LOUISIANA Tit.44, sec. 13	E,K,R,EE	F	B	M
MAINE Tit.27, sec.121	K,R	L	B	M
MARYLAND State govt.10- 616;Educ. 23-107	H	M	B	M
	Maryland has two confidentiality statutes. The first is a library statute; the second is an exemption from the open records act.			
MASS. ch.78, sec.7	I	V	B*	D**

Appendix D (continued)

STATE AND CODE #	EXCEPTIONS TO CONFI'Y (See Key)	TYPE OF LIBRARY (See Key)	RECORDS PROTECTED (See Key)	MANDATORY/ DISCRET'Y
	*Protects "[t]hat part of the records . . . which reveals the identity and intellectual pursuits of a person using such library." **Library records "shall not be a public record," hence must not be disclosed pursuant to the open records act.			
MICHIGAN 397.603	K,R,II	N	B*	M
	*"a document, record, or other method of storing information . . . that identifies a person as having requested or obtained specific materials"			
445.1711- 445.1715	K,C,R,V	E	B	M
	Michigan has two confidentiality statutes. The first is a library statute; the second is a statute governing the "Purchase, Rental, or Borrowing of Books, or Sound or Video Recordings." It prohibits "a person, or an employee or agent of the person, engaged in the business of . . . renting, or lending books or other written materials, sound recordings, or video recordings" from disclosing "to any person . . . a record or information concerning the . . . rental, or borrowing of those materials by a customer that indicates the identity of the customer." Exceptions include action "[p]ursuant to a search warrant issued by a state or federal court or grand jury subpoena."			
MINNESOTA 13.40, 13.02(12)	M,R	O	B*	M
	*"That portion of data . . . which links a . . . patron's name with materials requested or borrowed . . . or with a specific subject about which the patron has requested information or materials"			
MISSISSIPPI 39-3-365	C,K,R,II	B	B*	M

Appendix D (continued)

STATE AND CODE #	EXCEPTIONS TO CONFI'Y (See Key)	TYPE OF LIBRARY (See Key)	RECORDS PROTECTED (See Key)	MANDATORY/ DISCRET'Y
	*"information relating to the identity of a library user, relative to the user's use of books or other materials at the library"			
MISSOURI 182.815, 182.817	K,X,II	N	B	D*
	*"no library . . . shall be required to release or disclose" library records.			
MONTANA 22-1-1101 to -1111	D,K,Y,II	N	B	M
NEBRASKA 84-712.05	--	Q	B	D*
	*records "may be withheld"			
NEVADA 239.013	X	E	B*	M
	*"records . . . which contain the identity of a user and the books, documents, films, recordings or other property of the library which he used"			
NEW HAMPSHIRE 91-A:5; 201-D:11	B,N,T,II	E	B	M
	New Hampshire has two confidentiality statutes. The first is an exemption from the open records act; the second is a library statute.			
NEW JERSEY 18A: 73-43.1 to -43.2	B,O,W	R	B	M
NEW MEXICO 18-9-2 to 18-9-6	C,K,R,GG	S	B	M
NEW YORK Civ.Prac. Law & Rules 4509	B,N,T	K	B	M

214

Appendix D (continued)

STATE AND CODE #	EXCEPTIONS TO CONFI'Y (See Key)	TYPE OF LIBRARY (See Key)	RECORDS PROTECTED (See Key)	MANDATORY/ DISCRET'Y
NORTH CAROLINA 125-19	B,K,T,II	N	B	M
NORTH DAKOTA 40-38-12	W	B	B*	D

*"record . . . which provides a library patron's name or information sufficient to identify a patron together with the subject about which the patron requested information"

OHIO	NO CONFIDENTIALITY STATUTE			
OKLAHOMA tit.65, sec.1-105	E,K,R	F	B*	M

*"records indicating which of its documents or other materials . . . have been loaned to or used by an identifiable individual or group"

OREGON 192.501	--	V	A*	D**

*"circulation records . . . showing use of specific library materials by named persons."
**Exempt from open records act "unless the public interest requires disclosure in the particular instance"

PENNSYL-VANIA tit.24, sec.4428	AA	G	A*	M

*"Records related to the circulation of library materials which contain the names or other personally identifying details regarding the users"

RHODE ISLAND 38-2-2	--	E	B	D*

*These records "shall not be deemed public."

215

STATE AND CODE #	EXCEPTIONS TO CONFI'Y (See Key)	TYPE OF LIBRARY (See Key)	RECORDS PROTECTED (See Key)	MANDATORY/ DISCRET'Y
SOUTH CAROLINA 30-4-20, 60-4-10	E,P,Z,II	T	B	M

South Carolina has two confidentiality statutes. The first is an exemption from the open records act; the second is a library statute.

STATE AND CODE #	EXCEPTIONS TO CONFI'Y	TYPE OF LIBRARY	RECORDS PROTECTED	MANDATORY/DISCRET'Y
SOUTH DAKOTA 14-2-51	R,J,EE	W	B	M
TENNESSEE 10-8-101, 10-8-102	D,K,R,II	P	B	M

TEXAS   NO CONFIDENTIALITY STATUTE, but Attorney General Open Records Decision No. 100 (July 10, 1975) protects library circulation records and the identity of library patrons in connection "with the object of his or her attention," under the First Amendment. However, "the fact that a person has used the library, owes or has paid a fine" is not protected.

STATE AND CODE #	EXCEPTIONS TO CONFI'Y	TYPE OF LIBRARY	RECORDS PROTECTED	MANDATORY/DISCRET'Y
UTAH 63-2-202, 63-2-302	O,Q,BB,EE	Q	B	D*

*Library records are private, but "[n]othing . . . prohibits a governmental entity from disclosing a record . . . if the governmental entity determines that disclosure is in the public interest."

STATE AND CODE #	EXCEPTIONS TO CONFI'Y	TYPE OF LIBRARY	RECORDS PROTECTED	MANDATORY/DISCRET'Y
VERMONT Tit.1, sec.317	--	E	B	D*

*Library records are not public records; therefore, the public has no right to them. However, no language prohibits library employees from disclosing them.

STATE AND CODE #	EXCEPTIONS TO CONFI'Y	TYPE OF LIBRARY	RECORDS PROTECTED	MANDATORY/DISCRET'Y
VIRGINIA 2.1-342	--	E	A*	D

Appendix D (continued)

STATE AND CODE #	EXCEPTIONS TO CONFI'Y (See Key)	TYPE OF LIBRARY (See Key)	RECORDS PROTECTED (See Key)	MANDATORY/ DISCRET'Y
	*Records "which can be used to identify both (i) any library patron who has borrowed material from a library and (ii) the material such patron borrowed" are exempt from the state open records law.			
WASHINGTON 42.17.310	CC,II	E	B	D*
	*Library records are exempt from disclosure; therefore, the public has no <u>right</u> to them. However, no language prohibits library employees from disclosing them.			
WEST VIRGINIA 10-1-22	F,K,EE,W	U	B*	M
	*"Circulation and similar records . . . which identify the user of library materials" are protected from disclosure.			
WISCONSIN 43.30	E,I,R,P	C	B	M
WYOMING 16-4-203	E,S,EE	E	A	M

Appendix D (continued)

THE LIBRARY'S USE

A -   The library itself

B -   The library itself if necessary for the reasonable operation of the library

C -   Records of fines or overdue notices

D -   Library or any business operating jointly with a library for the purpose of collecting overdue materials or fines on overdue materials (Montana law does not include "any business operating jointly with a library," but neither is the law restricted to library employees only.)

E -   Persons acting within the scope of their duties within the administration of library

F -   To members of the library staff in the ordinary course of business

G -   State education department or state public library service for a library under its jurisdiction when necessary to assure the proper operation of such library

H -   In connection with the library's ordinary business and only for the purposes for which the record was created

I -   For the purposes of inter-library cooperation and coordination (Wisconsin: then only under specific circumstances)

J -   Acts by library officers or employees in maintaining a check out system

CONSENT

K -   Written consent of the user

L -   To the patron or any person with informed, written consent of patron

M -   Informed consent, defined as a statement in plain language, dated, specific in designating the person or agency authorized to disclose and the person or agency to whom the data shall be disclosed, specific as to the purpose of disclosure and as to the expiration date, ordinarily less than one year

N -   Upon request by or consent of the user

O -   Requested by the user

P -   Persons authorized by the patron to inspect his records

Q -   To individual who has a power of attorney from the record's subject or submits a notarized release from the subject or

218

Appendix D (continued)

his legal representative dated no more than 30 days before
the date of the request

<u>COURT ORDER</u>

R – Court order

S – Court order or if required by law (Wyoming: only if
required by law)

T – Subpoena, court order, or where otherwise required by law

U – To law enforcement agency or civil court, pursuant to
search warrant

V – Proper judicial order

W – Court order or subpoena

X – Court order upon a finding that the disclosure of such
record is necessary to protect the public safety or to
prosecute a crime

Y – Court order upon a finding that the disclosure of such
record is necessary because the merits of public disclosure
clearly exceed the demand for individual privacy

Z – Court order upon a finding that disclosure is necessary to
protect public safety, to prosecute a crime, or upon
showing of good cause before the presiding judge in a civil
matter

AA– Court order in a criminal proceeding

BB– Court order signed by a judge from a state or federal court
(but not a justice of the peace) to the extent that the
record deals with a matter in controversy over which the
court has jurisdiction after the court has considered the
merits of the record request

CC– If the superior court in the county in which record is
maintained finds, after a hearing with notice thereof to
every person in interest and the agency, that the exemption
of such records is clearly unnecessary to protect any
individual's right of privacy or any vital governmental
function

<u>RECORDS OF A MINOR OR INCAPACITATED PERSON</u>

DD– Any parent of a minor child has the right to inspect the
records of any school or public library that pertain to his
or her child

EE– Parent or custodian of a minor child (Utah: and to legal
guardian of legally incapacitated individual)

FF– Records of a public elementary or secondary school library
identifying a minor child to a parent or guardian of that
child

Appendix D (continued)

GG– Records of school libraries to the legal guardian of unemancipated minors or legally incapacitated persons

HH– Upon written consent of the user's parents or guardian if the user is a minor or ward

MISCELLANEOUS EXCEPTIONS

II– Statistical compilations which do not identify individuals

JJ– Library may disclose relevant information on a patron to the Corporation Counsel of the District of Columbia or legal counsel retained to represent the public library in a civil action

KK– Used for research purposes by qualified researchers, who must agree to keep the records confidential.

Appendix D (continued)

A -   Public, public school or college and university libraries

B -   Any library which is in whole or in part supported by public funds

C -   Any library which is in whole or in part supported by public funds, including the records of a public library system

D -   Any public library or library of an educational, historical or eleemosynary institution, organization or society

E -   Any library

F -   Any library, which is in whole or in part supported by public funds, including the records of public, academic, school, and special libraries and the state library (Oklahoma: no language which includes state library)

G -   State library or any local library which is established or maintained under any law of the state or the library of any university, college or educational institution chartered by the state or the library of any public school or branch reading room, deposit station or agency operated in connection therewith

H -   Library which makes materials available to the public including libraries operated by the state, a municipality, or a public school, including the state university

I -   Library or library system supported by public monies

J -   Public, school, academic, and special libraries and library systems supported in whole or in part by public funds

K -   Public, free association, school, college and university libraries and library systems of the state

L -   Any public municipal library, including the state library

M -   Public library; free association, school, college or university library

N -   Library which is established by the state; a county, city, township, village, school district, or other local unit of government or authority or combination of local units of governments and authorities; a community college district; a college or university; or any private library open to the public

O -   Library or historical records repository (but not the state archives) operated by any state agency, political subdivision or statewide system

P -   Library that is open to the public and established or operated by: the state, a county, city, town, school district or any other political subdivision of the state; or a combination of governmental units or authorities; a

221

Appendix D (continued)

university or community college; or any private library that is open to the public

Q - Publicly funded library

R - Library maintained by any state or local governmental agency, school, college or industrial, commercial or other special group, association or agency, whether public or private

S - Any library receiving public funds, any library that is a state agency and any library established by the state, an instrumentality of the state, a local government, district or authority, whether or not that library is regularly open to the public

T - Public, private, school, college, technical college, university, and state institutional libraries and library systems, supported in whole or in part by public funds or expending public funds

U - Library maintained wholly or in part by any governing authority from funds derived by taxation and the services of which are free to the public, but does not include special libraries, such as law, medical or other professional libraries, or school libraries which are maintained primarily for school purposes

V - All public libraries

W - Any library that serves free of charge all residents of a local governmental unit and receives its financial support in whole or in part from public funds made available by the governing body of that unit

KEY - RECORDS PROTECTED

A - Registration and/or circulation records

B - Records containing personally identifying information; any information which would identify a patron or a patron's library use

Appendix E
Respondents—State Public Records Officers, Public Librarians, and ALA State Chapter Executives

State and Name	Title	Address
ALABAMA Richard Y. Wang	Appraisal Archivist	Records Management Division Alabama Dept. of Archives and History 624 Washington Ave. Montgomery, AL 36130
ALASKA George V. Smith	Acting Director	Division of Libraries Archives & Museums, DOE P.O. Box 6 Juneau AK 99811
ARIZONA Martin Richelsoph	CRM, Division Director	Department of Library Archives & Public Records Records Management Division 1919 W. Jefferson Phoenix, AZ 85009
ARKANSAS John L. Ferguson	State Historian	Arkansas History Commission One Capitol Mall Little Rock, AR 72201
ARKANSAS Sherry Walker	Executive Director	Arkansas Library Association 1100 North University, Suite 109 Little Rock, AR 72207
ARKANSAS Linda Bly	Assistant Director	Central Arkansas Library System 700 Louisiana Street Little Rock, AR 72201-4698
CALIFORNIA Nancy Zimmelman	Archivist II	California State Archives 1020 "O" Street, Room 130 Sacramento, CA 95814
CALIFORNIA Cy Silver	Consultant	California State Library Library Development Services 1001 - 6th Street, Suite 300 Sacramento, CA 95814
COLORADO Terry Ketelsen	State Archivist	Division of State Archives and Public Records Centennial Building, 1313 Sherman Street Denver, CO 80203

Appendix E (continued)

State and Name	Title	Address
CONNECTICUT		Public Records Administration Connecticut State Library 231 Capitol Ave., Hartford, CT 06106
DELAWARE Penelope A. Rainey	Coordinator of Records Services	Delaware State Archives Hall of Records P.O. Box 1401 Dover, DE 19903
DELAWARE Charlesa Lowell	Deputy State Librarian	Delaware Division of Libraries 43 S. DuPont Highway Dover, DE. 19901
D.C. Roxanna L. Deane	Chief, Washingtoniana Division	Martin Luther King Memorial Library 901 G. Street, N.W., Room 307 Washington, DC 20001
FLORIDA Barratt Wilkins	Director	State Library of Florida R.A. Gray Building Tallahassee, FL 32399-0250
GEORGIA Peter E. Schinkel	Head, Schedule Section	Georgia Dept. Archives & History 330 Capitol Avenue, S.E. Atlanta, GA 30334
GEORGIA Joe Forsee	Director, Public Library Services	Division of Public Library Services 156 Trinity Ave., S.W. Atlanta, GA 30303
IDAHO William E. Tydeman	State Archivist	Idaho State Historical Society 450 N. 4th St. Boise, ID 83702
IDAHO Marilyn Poertner	Assistant Director	Boise Public Library 715 S. Capitol Blvd. Boise, ID 83702
IDAHO Karen Strege	Public Library Consultant	Idaho State Library Northern Field Office P.O. Box 8949 Moscow, ID 83843-1449

224

ILLINOIS
Marlene Devel

Deputy Director

Illinois State Library
Centennial Bldg., Room 275
Springfield, IL 62756

ILLINOIS
Barbara Cunningham

Executive Director

Illinois Library Association
33 West Grand, Suite 301
Chicago, IL 60610

INDIANA
Stephen E. Towne

Assistant Archivist,
Program Director for
Local Government Records
Program

Indiana State Archives
140 North Senate Ave.
Indianapolis, IN 46204

INDIANA
Jeffrey R. Krull

Director

Allen Co. Public Library
Box 2270
Fort Wayne, IN 46801

INDIANA
Sandi Thompson

Public Library Consultant

Indiana State Library
140 North Senate Avenue
Indianapolis, IN 46204

KANSAS
Dan Fitzgerald

Local Records Archivist

Kansas State Historical Society
120 West Tenth
Topeka, KS 66612-1291

KENTUCKY
Dalarna T. Breetz

Branch Manager

Kentucky Department for Libraries &
Archives
300 Coffee Tree Road
P.O. Box 537
Frankfort, KY 40602-0537

KENTUCKY
Diana Moses

Manager, State Records
Branch, Public Records
Division

Kentucky Dept. for Libraries & Archives
300 Coffee Tree Road
P.O. Box 537
Frankfort, KY 40602-0537

LOUISIANA
Gary O. Rolstad

Associate State Librarian

State Library of Louisiana
P.O. Box 131
Baton Rouge, LA 70821-0131

MAINE
Benjamin F. Keating

Division Director

Maine State Library
LMA Building
State House Station 64
Augusta, ME 04333

225

Appendix E (continued)

State and Name	Title	Address
MARYLAND Kevin Swanson	Director, State and Local Records Program	Maryland State Archives 350 Rowe Blvd. Annapolis, MD 21401
MARYLAND J. Maurice Travillian	Assistant State Superintendent	Maryland State Dept. of Education 200 W. Baltimore Street Baltimore, MD 21201
MASSACHUSETTS Kathryn Hammond Baker	Asst. Archivist for Records Management and Acquisitions	Massachusetts Archives at Columbia Point 220 Morrissey Blvd. Boston, MA 02125
MASSACHUSETTS Brian Donoghue	Librarian	Massachusetts Board of Library Commissioners 648 Beacon Street Boston, MA 02215
MICHIGAN David J. Johnson	State Archivist	State Archives, Department of State 717 West Allegan Lansing, MI 48918-1837
MICHIGAN Florence R. Tucker	Associate Director for Support Services	Detroit Public Library 5201 Woodward Ave. Detroit, MI 48202
MICHIGAN Marianne Gessner	Executive Director	Michigan Library Association 1000 Long Blvd. Suite 1 Lansing, MI 48911
MINNESOTA Deborah Struzyk	Administrative Assistant	Minneapolis Public Library 300 Nicollet Mall Minneapolis, MN 55401
MINNESOTA William G. Asp	Director	Office of Library Development and Services 440 Capitol Square 550 Cedar Street St. Paul, MN 55101
MINNESOTA Duane P. Swanson	Deputy State Archivist Division of Library and Archives	Minnesota Historical Society Research Center 1500 Mississippi Street St. Paul, MN 55101

MISSISSIPPI
H.T. Holmes

Director

Archives & Library Division
Mississippi Dept. of Archives and History
P.O. Box 571
Jackson, MS 39205-0571

MISSISSIPPI
Thomas H. Ballard

Director

Jackson - Hinds Library System
300 North State Street
Jackson, MS 39201

MISSOURI
Monteria Hightower

Associate Commissioner
for Libraries, State
Librarian

Coordinating Board for Higher Education
Missouri State Library & Wolfner Library
P.O. Box 387
Jefferson City, MO 65102-0387

NEBRASKA
Steven R. Wolz

Public Records Officer

Nebraska State Historical Society
1500 R Street, Box 82554
Lincoln, NE 68501

NEBRASKA
Rod Wagner

Director

Nebraska Library Commission
1420 P Street
Lincoln, NE 68508

NEBRASKA
Michael Phipps

Director

Omaha Public Library
215 South 15th Street
Omaha, NE 68102

NEVADA
Robert H. Van Straten

State Records Manager

Nevada State Library and Archives
Division of Archives and Records
Capital Complex
3579 Highway 50 East
Carson City, NV 89710

NEVADA
Carol Madsen

Nevada Library
Association Secretary

Nevada State Library and Archives
Capitol Complex
Carson City, NV 89710

NEVADA
Lew Rogers

Controller

Las Vegas - Clark County Library District
833 Las Vegas Boulevard North
Las Vegas, NV 89101

NEW HAMPSHIRE
Kendall Wiggin

State Librarian

New Hampshire State Library
20 Park St.
Concord, NH 03301

227

Appendix E (continued)

State and Name	Title	Address
NEW JERSEY Joseph L. Falca	Records Analyst 1	Division of Archives & Records Management Department of State 2300 Stuyvesant Ave. Trenton, NJ 08625
NEW JERSEY Bruce E. Ford	Assistant Director for Technical Services	Newark Public Library P.O. Box 630 Newark, NJ 07101
NEW JERSEY Robert Fortenbaugh	Assistant Coordinator, Library Programs	State of New Jersey Department of Education, State Library CN 520 Trenton, NJ 08625
NEW MEXICO Karen Watkins	State Librarian	New Mexico State Library 325 Don Gaspar Santa Fe, NM 87503
NEW YORK Warren F. Broderick	Public Records Analyst	New York State Education Department 10A63, CEC Albany, NY 12230
NEW YORK Thomas D. Norris	Principal Publics Records Analyst, Bureau of Records Analysis and Disposition	The State Education Department The University of the State of New York Albany, NY 12230
NORTH CAROLINA John Welch	Assistant State Librarian	North Carolina Division of State Library 109 E. Jones Street Raleigh, NC 27601-2807
NORTH CAROLINA David J. Olson	State Archives and Records Administrator	North Carolina Dept. of Cultural Resources 109 East Jones Street Raleigh, NC 27611
NORTH DAKOTA Delores Vyzralek	Chief Librarian	State Historical Society of North Dakota North Dakota Heritage Center Bismarck, ND 58505

OHIO
Mona Connolly — Assistant to the State Librarian — The State Library of Ohio, 65 South Front Street, Columbus, OH 43266-0334

OHIO
John Stewart — Assistant State Archivist — Ohio Historical Society, Archives/Library Division, 1982 Velma Ave., Columbus, OH 43211-2497

OKLAHOMA
Jimmy Welch — Director of System Operations — Metropolitan Library System, 334 S.W. 26, Oklahoma City, OK 73109

OKLAHOMA
Robert Clark — Director — The Oklahoma Department of Libraries, 200 Northeast 18th Street, Oklahoma City, OK 73105-3298

OREGON
Layne Sawyer — Deputy State Archivist — Archives Division, 1005 Broadway N.E., Salem, Oregon 97310

OREGON
Mary Ginnane — Acting Library Development Administrator — Oregon State Library, State Library Building, Salem, OR 97310

PENNSYLVANIA
Sara Parker — Commissioner of Libraries — State Library of Pennsylvania, Box 1601, Harrisburg, PA 17105

PENNSYLVANIA
Diane Smith Wallace — Head, Local Government & Public Services Section Division of Archival and Records Management Services — Commonwealth of Pennsylvania, Pennsylvania Historical and Museum Commission, Third and North Streets, Box 1026, Harrisburg, PA 17108-1026

PENNSYLVANIA
Margaret S. Bauer — CAE, Executive Director — Pennsylvania Library Association, 3107 N. Front Street, Harrisburg, PA 17110

RHODE ISLAND
Beth Perry — Chief, Regional Library for the Blind — State of Rhode Island & Providence Plantations, Rhode Island Dept. of Library Services, 300 Richmond Street, Providence, RI 02903-4222

229

Appendix E (continued)

State and Name	Title	Address
RHODE ISLAND Judith A. Paster	President, Rhode Island Library Association	Rhode Island Library Association 52 Seaview Ave. Cranston, RI 02905
RHODE ISLAND Peter E. Bennett	Chief of Support Services	Providence Public Library 225 Washington St. Providence, RI 02903
SOUTH CAROLINA John D. Mackintosh	Records Analyst II, Local Records Analysis Program	South Carolina Dept. of Archives & History 1430 Senate Street P.O. Box 11,669 Columbia, South Carolina 29211
SOUTH CAROLINA Charles M. Smith	State Records Program Supervisor	State Records Center 1919 Blanding Street Columbia, SC 29209
SOUTH CAROLINA Charles Grubbs	Coordinator of Main Library Services	The Greenville County Library 300 College Street Greenville, SC 29601
SOUTH DAKOTA Jane Kolbe	State Librarian	South Dakota State Library 800 Governors Drive Pierre, SD 57501-2294
SOUTH DAKOTA Jim Dertien	City Librarian	Sioux Falls Public Library 201 N. Main Avenue Sioux Falls, SD 57102
TENNESSEE Betty Nance	Executive Secretary	Tennessee Library Association P.O. Box 158417 Nashville, TN 37215-8417
TEXAS Marilyn von Kohl	Director, Local Records Division	Texas State Library P.O. Box 12927 Austin, TX 78711-2927
TEXAS Patricia Smith	Executive Director, Texas Library Association	Texas Library Association 3355 Bee Cave Road, Suite 603 Austin, TX 78711
UTAH Jeffery O. Johnson	Director	State of Utah Division of Archives and Records Service State Capitol Archives Building Salt Lake City, UT 84114

230

UTAH
Eileen B. Longsworth

Director

Salt Lake County Library System
2197 East 7000 South
Salt Lake City, UT 84121-3188

VIRGINIA
Louis H. Manarin

State Archivist

Commonwealth of Virginia
Virginia State Library and Archives
11th Street at Capitol Square
Richmond, VA 23219-3491

WASHINGTON
Mary Y. Moore

Chief, Library Planning &
Development

Washington State Library
Library Planning & Development
P.O. Box 42472
Olympia, WA 95804-2460

WASHINGTON
Barbara Tolliver

President, Washington
Library Association

King County Library System
300 Eighth Avenue North
Seattle, WA 98109-5191

WEST VIRGINIA
Shirley A. Smith

Field Services Director

West Virginia Library Commission
Cultural Center
Charleston, WV 25305-0620

WISCONSIN
Leslyn M. Shires

Assistant Superintendent
Division for Library
Services

State of Wisconsin
Department of Public Instruction
P.O. Box 7841
Madison, WI 53707

WYOMING
Jerry Krois

Deputy State Librarian

Wyoming State Library
Supreme Court & State Library Bldg.
Cheyenne, WY 82002

WYOMING
Tony Adams

Records Manager

State of Wyoming
Department of Commerce
State Archives & Records Management
   Section
Parks & Cultural Resources Division
2301 Central Avenue
Cheyenne, Wy 82002

231

Selected Bibliography

PRIMARY SOURCES

Armstrong v. Executive Office of the President, 61 U.S.L.W. 2427 (D.C. D.C. Jan. 26, 1993).

Baldridge v. Shapiro, 455 U.S. 345 (1982).

Brown v. Johnston, 328 N.W. 2d 510 (Iowa 1983).

Chambers v. Birmingham News Co., 552 So. 2d 854 (Ala. 1989).

City of Fayetteville v. Rose, 743 S.W.2d 817 (Ark. 1988).

The Decatur Public Library v. The District Attorney's Office of Wise County, No. 90–05–192 (Tex. 271st Judicial District Court, May 9, 1990).

Federal Rules of Civil Procedure 45.

Federal Rules of Evidence 501.

Fuentes v. Shevin, 407 U.S. 67 (1972).

Gibson v. Florida Legislative Investigation Committee, 372 U.S. 539 (1963).

International Tel. & Tel. Co. v. United Tel. Co. of Fla., 60 F.R.D. 177 (D.C. Fla. 1973).

Luey v. Sterling Drug, Inc., 240 F. Supp. 632 (D.C. Mich. 1965).

Martin v. City of Struthers, 319 U.S. 141 (1943).

Mullane v. Central Hanover Bank & Trust Co., 339 U.S. 306 (1950).

Municipality of Anchorage v. Anchorage Daily News, 794 P.2d 584 (Alaska 1990).

NAACP v. Alabama, 357 U.S. 449 (1958).

Rosenblatt v. Northwest Airlines, Inc., 54 F.R.D. 21 (D.C.N.Y. 1921).

Seigle v. Barry, 422 So. 2d 63 (Fla. Dist. Ct. App. 1982).

Stone v. Consolidated Publishing Co., 404 So. 2d 678 (Ala. 1981).

Stanley v. Georgia, 394 U.S. 557 (1969).

Thomas v. Collins, 323 U.S. 516 (1945).

U.S. Constitution, amend. I.

Walsh v. Barnes, 541 So. 2d 33 (Ala. 1989).

Note: Federal and state statutes and state attorney general opinions are cited throughout and comprise the basis for most of the research for this work. They are not included in the bibliography.

SECONDARY SOURCES

Additional Overdue Books Listed by Public Library, Lebanon Reporter, Mar. 5, 1986.

Advisory Statement to U.S. Libraries from the American Library Association, 19 Newsl. on Intell. Freedom 65 (1970).

American Library Association Office for Intellectual Freedom, Intellectual Freedom Manual (3d ed. 1989).

American Library Association, Policy Manual (1991–92).

Black's Law Dictionary (6th ed. 1990).

Brown, Gary E., *The Right to Inspect Public Records in Ohio*, 37 Ohio State L.J. 518 (1976).

Crooks, Joyce, *Civil Liberties, Libraries, and Computers*, Libr. J. 482 (Feb. 1, 1976).

Cummings, Bruce, *Judge Quashes Subpoena of Decatur Library Records*, Wise County Messenger, May 13, 1990, at 1.

Dearstyne, Bruce W., The Management of Local Government Records: A Guide for Local Officials (American Association for State and Local History, Nashville, 1988).

FBI Asks Librarians to Help in the Search for Spies, Philadelphia Inquirer, Feb. 23, 1988, at 17A.

Fedders, John M. & Lauryn H. Guttenplan, *Document Retention and Destruction: Practical, Legal and Ethical Considerations*, The Notre Dame Lawyer 5 (Oct. 1980).

Foerstel, Herbert N., Surveillance in the Stacks: The FBI's Library Awareness Program (1991).

Fontaine, Sue, *Dismissal With Prejudice*, Libr. J. 1273 (June 15, 1981).

Geller, Evelyn, Forbidden Books in American Public Libraries, 1876–1939: A Study in Cultural Change (1984).

Harter, Stephen & Charles Busha, *Libraries and Privacy Legislation*, 1976 Libr. J. 475.

Hinz, Carolyn, Comment, *Brown v. Johnston: The Unexamined Issue of Privacy in Public Library Circulation Records in Iowa*, 69 Iowa L. Rev. 535 (Jan. 1984).

Johnson, Bruce S., *"A More Cooperative Clerk": The Confidentiality of Library Records*, 81 L. Libr. J. 769 (1989).

Jones, H. G., Local Government Records: An Introduction to Their Management, Preservation, and Use (American Association for State and Local History, Nashville, 1980).

Kennedy, Bruce M., *Confidentiality of Library Records: A Survey of Problems, Policies, and Laws*, 81 L. Libr. J. 733 (1989).

Knott, William A., *Confidentiality of Records*, 106 Libr. J. 2162 (1981).

Krug, Judith F. & James A. Harvey, *ALA and Intellectual Freedom: A Historical Overview*, American Library Association Office for Intellectual Freedom, Intellectual Freedom Manual xiii–xiv (3d ed. 1989).

Lee, Janis M., *Confidentiality: From the Stacks to the Witness Stand*, Am. Libr. 444 (June 1988).

Library Director Warns of Invasion of Privacy, The Capital Times, Dec. 27, 1990, at 3D.

Library Naming Names to Shut Book on Late Items, The Indianapolis Star, Mar. 8, 1986, at 13.

MacNeil, Heather, Without Consent: The Ethics of Disclosing Personal Information in Public Archives (1992).

Million, Angela C. & Kim N. Fisher, *Library Records: A Review of Confidentiality Laws and Policies*, 11 J. Acad. Librarianship 346 (1986).

National Archives & Records Administration, Guide to Record Retention Requirements in the Code of Federal Regulations (1986).

National Archives & Records Administration, NARA Files Maintenance and Records Disposition Manual (Sept. 28, 1990).

An Open Book? Library Privacy Guarded, 72 A.B.A.J. 21 (March 1, 1986).

Patrons Urged to Return Overdue Books to Lebanon Public Library, Lebanon Reporter, Mar. 1, 1986.

Police Are Forced to Play by Book to Check Out Clue, But Find Only a Blank Page, Minneapolis Star and Tribune, Oct. 1, 1985, at 3B.

Quarles, Dennis P., Comment, *Informational Privacy Under the Open Records Act*, 32 Mercer L. Rev. 393 (Fall 1980).

Ranlett, Louis F., *The Librarians Have a Word for It: Ethics*, 64 Libr. J. 738 (1939).

Skupsky, Donald, Legal Requirements for Business Records: Guide to Records Retention and Recordkeeping Requirements: Federal Requirements (1990).

Skupsky, Donald, Legal Requirements for Business Records: Guide to Records Retention and Recordkeeping Requirements: State Requirements (1989 & Supp. 1990).

Skupsky, Donald, Recordkeeping Requirements (The First Practical Guide to Help You Control Your Records . . . What You Need to Keep and What You Can Safely Destroy!) (2d ed. 1989).

Susman, Thomas M., *The Privacy Act and the Freedom of Information Act: Conflict and Resolution*, 21 J. Marshall L. Rev. 703 (1988).

Swan, John C., *Public Records & Library Privacy*, Libr. J. 1645 (Sept. 1, 1983).

Wigmore on Evidence (1961).

Wilson, Mark K., Comment, *Surveillance of Individual Reading Habits: Constitutional Limitations on Disclosure of Library Borrower Lists*, 30 Amer. U. L. Rev. 275 (1980).

Witch-Hunting in High School, Harper's Magazine, Dec. 1990, at 20.

Index

Page numbers in **bold** refer to each state's law.

About the Author

SHIRLEY A. WIEGAND is Professor of Law at the University of Oklahoma. A specialist in civil procedure, public records law, and discrimination, she has published in the *Oregon Law Review*, the *Kentucky Law Journal*, and the *Oklahoma Bar Journal*.